JENSEN'S VOCABULARY

First printing: January 2017
Second printing: July 2018

Master Books®, P.O. Box 726, Green Forest, AR 72638

Master Books® is a division of the New Leaf Publishing Group, Inc.

ISBN: 978-0-89051-995-0
ISBN: 978-1-61458-564-0 (digital)

Printed in the United States of America

Please visit our website for other great titles:
www.masterbooks.com

For information regarding author interviews,
please contact the publicity department at (870) 438-5288.

"I'm loving this whole line so much. It's changed our homeschool for the better!
—Amy ★★★★★

"Your reputation as a publisher is stellar. It is a blessing knowing anything I purchase from you is going to be worth every penny!
—Cheri ★★★★★

"Last year we found Master Books and it has made a HUGE difference.
—Melanie ★★★★★

"We love Master Books and the way it's set up for easy planning!
—Melissa ★★★★★

"You have done a great job. MASTER BOOKS ROCKS!
—Stephanie ★★★★★

"Physically high-quality, Biblically faithful, and well-written.
—Danika ★★★★★

"Best books ever. Their illustrations are captivating and content amazing!
—Kathy ★★★★★

Affordable
Flexible
Faith Building

MASTERBOOKS
—CURRICULUM—

Table of Contents

Dedication

Dedicated to my friends, Ralph and Joan English, former missionaries to Suriname, and to the students in the Christian school there who helped proofread this text in its pre-publication format.

— Frode Jensen

Using This Workbook

Features: The suggested weekly schedule enclosed has easy-to-manage lessons that guide the reading, worksheets, and all assessments. The pages of this guide are perforated and three-hole punched so materials are easy to tear out, hand out, grade, and store. Teachers are encouraged to adjust the schedule and materials needed in order to best work within their unique educational program.

Lesson Scheduling: Students are instructed to read the pages in their book and then complete the corresponding section provided by the teacher. Assessments that may include worksheets, activities, quizzes, and tests are given at regular intervals with space to record each grade. Space is provided on the weekly schedule for assignment dates, and flexibility in scheduling is encouraged. Teachers may adapt the scheduled days per each unique student situation. As the student completes each assignment, this can be marked with an "X" in the box.

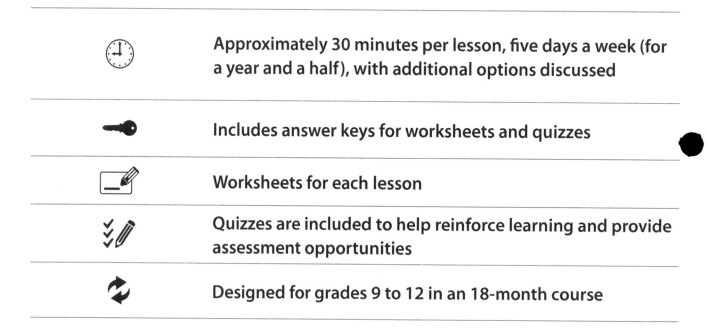

Approximately 30 minutes per lesson, five days a week (for a year and a half), with additional options discussed

Includes answer keys for worksheets and quizzes

Worksheets for each lesson

Quizzes are included to help reinforce learning and provide assessment opportunities

Designed for grades 9 to 12 in an 18-month course

Course Description

Jensen's Vocabulary allows constant repetition for long-term retention by students, as well as a simple format to follow with great results. The course provides a systematic approach to learning vocabulary, with over 1,000 valuable words from basic roots. With either schedule 1 or schedule 2, students are given weekly reinforcement so that Greek and Latin-based words become easy with four types of exercises for each set of words. When a student finishes the course, he or she will have increased ability to intelligently guess new words, enhancing his or her reading and writing skills in any situation.

Hints and Tips

Be sure to read this section before beginning this curriculum. It is necessary to understand the philosophy and methodology of the book.

Vocabulary Course Options

Option A (one year): In this option, a student can focus either on Latin I and Latin II, or focus on Latin I and Greek for a single year vocabulary study. This can easily be done by simply following the Suggested Daily Schedule and choosing the selected semesters you desire.

Option B (18 months): This unique course was originally written to cover 18 months of vocabulary learning, and the original intention of the author has been maintained in the schedule provided in this workbook. Simply follow this schedule as outlined for you.

Option C (two years): With the addition of Intro to Biblical Greek by Master Books (a video-based learning program that is a basic introduction to biblical or Koine Greek), the course can easily become a full two-year vocabulary study. One simply follows the current schedule in this workbook, with Latin I and Latin II as the first year, Greek as the first semester of the second year, and then transitions to Intro to Biblical Greek as the second semester.

Option D (self-paced): Because the course work included with this current workbook generally takes less than a half hour per day, one might desire to simply complete two days of work each day, or at least a few times a week, thus completing the full course in considerably less time.

As you begin the course

The student should keep the roots and affixes sheets available for immediate access at all times during the exercises. This avoids flipping back and forth constantly.

Know that it is fine to use a dictionary. Also, use the roots and affixes sheets provided in the appendix. Attempt to figure out the words and their parts. It will be a little tougher at first to do it this way, but you will learn more and get a feel for the book faster by doing so. You can also make use of the Word Parts Lists in the appendix section. Learning to recognize the parts will help you with many other words, not just the ones with which you might currently be working.

Using the answers and lists

All the basic answers to the exercises are found in the answer section. The A lesson answer list gives the number of the definition that fits the word to its immediate right. The B lesson answer list gives only the root in a single form. You are left to determine what segment of the vocabulary word should be circled. The C and D lesson answer lists simply list the words by the number that they should accompany.

The word parts list will be of help with the B lessons. It would be nice if all the words had very definite breaks with no spelling variations or obscure derivations (sigh!). The English language is not quite so cooperative, however. In order to make life in this manual somewhat consistent, certain practices were adopted.

Let's look at the roots first. You will note that a root may occur in various spellings: CEDE, CEED, or even CESS. For consistency this manual will only use the first spelling. The decision to handle the information in this manner was arbitrary and simply served to provide some logic or pattern to the items. The upshot is that you and the students will have to recognize that TAIN is also TEN and TIN or that SED is also SESS and SID; of course these are only a few of the possible examples.

Second let's look at the vocabulary words themselves. A word such as VERDICT is composed of two roots in combination, and both roots are from the basic list in Latin I. Such words are very mannerly and straightforward. The word MALADY, on the other hand, comes from Latin via Old French to Middle English to Modern English. The MAL part is quite identifiable, but the HABITUS of Latin is indistinguishable.

Another variation on this theme is played with a word such as VOLUME; the root is obvious, but the ending is dubious. The references used for this undertaking either hedged or made no comment whatsoever; the result is a best guess. All this is just to say that the ability to trace every letter or syllable in each word in English is beyond the ken of this author. Spelling variations seem to occur as pronunciation aids; letters are added or dropped to make the word flow in speech. For the most part the material given is basic and accurate; whatever etymological errors occur will be minor and the responsibility of the author. You are encouraged to utilize other source materials yourself in order to fully appreciate the history and origin of the various words.

The alphabetical word lists are for ready reference for whatever reasons you might like to use them, perhaps in gaining insights into the root families themselves. They are included for your convenience.

Exercises and tests

The lessons are designed so that the student should not use a dictionary except as a last resort and then only on the A lessons. The entire philosophy of the course is based on spaced repetition. The student should be encouraged to use all prior exercises, as well as the sheets containing roots and affixes found in the appendices.

For each of the lessons, a grade can be given, but that is strictly at each teacher's discretion There are a variety of methods for correcting the papers as well. The answers can be given orally or discussed by the instructor and students.

The time spent on the individual lessons varies. The A lessons are probably the most time consuming and important since they are the basis for the rest of the week. A general estimate of from 20 to 30 minutes per A lesson is about right. The other lessons are shorter and should be completed in no more than

15 minutes apiece. The lessons could be done independently or in a group setting; again, the option is that of the teacher. The lessons should all be corrected but need not be graded and recorded. The quarterly tests can take from 15 minutes to an hour, depending on the preparedness of the students.

Initially there is a steep learning curve with these books. The students are not familiar with the system and do not know the roots and affixes well, if at all. After about two or three weeks into the system, most students get the hang of the program and are able to proceed on their own with little or no instruction from the teacher. They will have to be helped the first few times, however.

The students should work through the lesson using the roots and affixes sheets. After a determined amount of time, make sure that each student has the correct definitions for the words. An uncaught mistake on the A lesson will cause grief throughout the week. For the A lesson, the most effective strategy is to have the student write out the words with the correct definitions following them on a separate sheet of paper. Making such a list for themselves provides them with a personal study sheet, as well as an additional writing experience with the words. Copying the list is a learning experience. When doing the A exercise, the student would be wise to follow the process of elimination and do the easier and more obvious items first.

The B lesson follows on the next day. This lesson should be fairly simple. Some explanation may be needed on certain words. It is the prerogative of the teacher to decide how to grade such an exercise and what answers would be correct. The students need to know if the variant forms of the roots are acceptable as answers, for instance.

The C lesson comes on the third day. It is quite easy to grade since there is only one right answer per blank. Again, this lesson should go rather quickly. A good student will realize that the B and C lessons are quite closely tied together. The whole idea is to get the students familiar with the parts of the words for both spelling and meaning purposes.

The D lesson comes on the fourth day. It is also a one right answer situation and is easily corrected. Spelling should count since the students can copy the words from their list. It is best to give the students some time on the D lesson without their word lists first and then allow them some time with the lists to finish the exercise. This technique will help them remember the words and will force them to depend on their memory a bit more.

The lesson for the fifth day in the schedule is for review, extra study time, or quarterly tests. If an open study day, use this time

- for review,
- to create flashcards,
- writing out sentences with the words,
- writing a story using the words,
- teacher generated weekly tests
- or to test yourself with the flash cards.

After the first week, review words should always be studied. A good technique is to find two or three words from the previous lesson and then add two or three others from lessons farther back. It is valuable to the students to pick those words that are more common but still difficult. It is even fun sometimes for them to suggest the review words.

Using the words each day of the week is an immense help for the students. The spaced repetition helps them to recognize the words on the tests and elsewhere. Spelling bees or vocabulary bees, puzzles, writing exercises, and various other creative exercises could also be used to integrate the use of the words into their speech and writing patterns. Simple software can provide extra practice with a matching situation or a definition that requires the word to be typed in. Vocabulary is important for clear communication.

Various tests, experiments, and experiences have shown some remarkable findings regarding vocabulary. A good vocabulary means better communication. A limited vocabulary often equates to limited success in many non-English areas of life. One study involving one hundred young men studying to be business executives showed that five years after a vocabulary test had been given, every man who had scored in the top 10 percent of that test had an executive position, but that not one man who had scored in the lower 25 percent of the vocabulary test had attained an executive station on the job.

Over time the single characteristic identified for outstandingly successful people has been an extensive knowledge of the exact meaning of English words. That means vocabulary is the one and only common identifiable characteristic of those who have made notable achievement in the business world or the arts.

A good vocabulary does not guarantee success, but it certainly makes the success more attainable.

The methodology for studying vocabulary is equally important. Wide reading is a great help. Exposure to new words and an understanding of how they are put together generates an interest in them. A systematic plan of acquiring new words through study is of great benefit to anyone, especially the young and those who read but little.

This workbook seeks to follow the spaced repetition method of learning. Isaiah 28:10 talks about line upon line and precept upon precept. An old proverb says that practice makes perfect. Both refer to a systematic program based on some incremental approach. The words here are presented in such a manner that they are to be worked with each day of the week. The basic roots appear in lesson after lesson so that they become quite familiar. Knowing part of a word enables an educated guess at its meaning.

LATIN I
WORKSHEETS

DIRECTIONS: Use your LATIN roots and affixes sheets; try to match the definitions with the words; look at the roots, prefixes, and suffixes for clues. Do NOT use a dictionary except as a last resort.

___ ADDICT

___ ANIMATE

___ ANNUITY

___ BIPED

___ CIRCUMSCRIBE

___ CLOISTER

___ CONDUCIVE

___ CONVOLUTED

___ CURIOUS

___ DECEIVE

___ DISSECT

___ FACILE

___ GRADIENT

___ JUSTIFY

___ MALADY

___ PRINCIPAL

___ PROCEED

___ REJECT

___ SUBSIDY

___ TENURE

1. n) an investment yielding fixed payments, esp. yearly

2. n) a monastery or convent

3. a) chief; head; first in rank or importance

4. v) to make habitual
   n) one devoted to habit

5. n) the holding or length of holding property or office

6. v) delude; mislead; to make one believe what is not true

7. a) eager to know and learn; unusual or odd

8. v) to give life or motion to; to inspire
   a) living

9. v) to encircle; encompass; trace a line around; to limit

10. a) twisted; coiled; spiraled

11. a) helpful; contributive; leading or tending to

12. v) to refuse to take; decline; discard; throw out

13. a) easy; not hard to do; fluent; moves or works quickly and easily

14. n) a grant of money from the government as aid

15. v) to show to be right or correct; to free from blame; absolve; to give good reasons for

16. n) any two-footed animal

17. n) the degree of slope; a slope

18. v) to advance or go on, esp. after stopping

19. v) to cut apart piece by piece; examine closely

20. n) sickness; disease; an ailment

DIRECTIONS: Use your LATIN roots and affixes sheets; try to find the root in each vocabulary word. Write the root and its meaning; also circle the root in the vocabulary word.

vocabulary word	root	meaning
ADDICT	_____	_____
ANIMATE	_____	_____
ANNUITY	_____	_____
BIPED	_____	_____
CIRCUMSCRIBE	_____	_____
CLOISTER	_____	_____
CONDUCIVE	_____	_____
CONVOLUTED	_____	_____
CURIOUS	_____	_____
DECEIVE	_____	_____
DISSECT	_____	_____
FACILE	_____	_____
GRADIENT	_____	_____
JUSTIFY	_____	_____
MALADY	_____	_____
PRINCIPAL	_____	_____
PROCEED	_____	_____
REJECT	_____	_____
SUBSIDY	_____	_____
TENURE	_____	_____

DIRECTIONS: Use your LATIN roots and affixes sheets; try to find the word that is represented by the meanings of the roots and affixes. Write the word in the blank.

1. _____ around + to write

2. _____ apart, not + to cut

3. _____ with, together + to roll + past action

4. _____ shut, close + that which

5. _____ with, together + to lead + having the power of

6. _____ two + foot

7. _____ to step + like, related to, that which

8. _____ bad + French/Latin derivative

9. _____ care + having the quality of

10. _____ year + state, quality, act

11. _____ back, again + to throw

12. _____ to hold + that which

13. _____ to make, do + like, related to

14. _____ to, at + to speak

15. _____ for, forward + go, yield

16. _____ law, right + to make, do

17. _____ spirit + to make, do

18. _____ first + to take + like, related to

19. _____ under + to sit + quality, condition

20. _____ down, away + to take

DIRECTIONS: For each blank write one vocabulary word. All words will be used only once. Look for context clues in the sentence.

_____ 1. In Biology 1B it is customary to --- a frog.

_____ 2. Prudent men establish a(n) --- for retirement.

_____ 3. A cat is reputed to be a(n) --- creature.

_____ 4. Someone enslaved by habit is often termed a(n) ---.

_____ 5. His normal --- as president was cut short by extenuating circumstances.

_____ 6. A(n) --- over 7 percent is considered rather steep.

_____ 7. Satan attempts to --- men into thinking evil is harmless or even good.

_____ 8. The --- person in charge usually holds the highest rank.

_____ 9. A business that accepts a(n) --- is not practicing free enterprise.

_____ 10. A million-dollar inheritance was --- to his early retirement.

_____ 11. The track of a(n) --- reveals only one set of prints.

_____ 12. Smallpox is a(n) --- that is almost defeated.

_____ 13. The snail shell has a(n) --- pattern to it.

_____ 14. A cartoonist will often --- his figures with gestures or facial expressions.

_____ 15. It is often difficult to --- on a hike after a relaxing noon rest.

_____ 16. It is best to --- a specific area when playing marbles or hide and seek.

_____ 17. The best action is to --- an offer of a ride from a stranger.

_____ 18. People who live in a(n) --- are not often seen by those living on the outside.

_____ 19. The musician had a(n) --- hand, which made his expertness appear easy.

_____ 20. A criminal usually tries to --- his action with some excuse.

DIRECTIONS: Use your LATIN roots and affixes sheets; try to match the definitions with the words; look at the roots, prefixes, and suffixes for clues. Do NOT use a dictionary except as a last resort.

___ BENEDICTION

___ CENTENNIAL

___ CLOSET

___ CONDUIT

___ CONSCRIPT

___ CURATOR

___ DEVOLVE

___ FACILITY

___ GRADUAL

___ IMPEDE

___ INSECT

___ JUROR

___ MALIGNANT

___ PERCEPTION

___ PRECEDE

___ PUSILLANIMOUS

___ RECEPTOR

___ SESSILE

___ SUBJACENT

___ TENET

1. n) that which takes in; (phys.) sense organ or nerve ending

2. a) underlying; situated beneath

3. n) the mental grasp of something; insight or intuition

4. a) attached directly by its base; fixed; immobile

5. a) having an evil influence; very harmful; likely to cause death

6. n) pipe or channel for conveying fluid; a tube for electrical wires

7. v) to hinder the progress of; obstruct

8. n) small room for clothes or supplies;
   v) to shut up in a room for a private talk

9. n) skill; dexterity; absence of difficulty; building which aids an activity

10. n) a 100th anniversary or its celebration

11. a) timid; cowardly

12. n) a principle, doctrine or belief held as truth

13. n) any of a large class of small, usually winged, invertebrates having three pairs of legs

14. v) to pass on (duties, tasks) to another

15. a) little by little; taking place by degrees

16. n) a blessing; a giving of thanks

17. n) one sworn to oath on a jury

18. v) to be, come, or go before in rank, time or place

19. n) a draftee;
    v) to force into gov't service

20. n) person in charge of a museum, library, etc.

DIRECTIONS: Use your LATIN roots and affixes sheets; try to find the root in each vocabulary word. Write the root and its meaning; also circle the root in the vocabulary word.

vocabulary word	root	meaning
BENEDICTION	_____	_____
CENTENNIAL	_____	_____
CLOSET	_____	_____
CONDUIT	_____	_____
CONSCRIPT	_____	_____
CURATOR	_____	_____
DEVOLVE	_____	_____
FACILITY	_____	_____
GRADUAL	_____	_____
IMPEDE	_____	_____
INSECT	_____	_____
JUROR	_____	_____
MALIGNANT	_____	_____
PERCEPTION	_____	_____
PRECEDE	_____	_____
PUSILLANIMOUS	_____	_____
RECEPTOR	_____	_____
SESSILE	_____	_____
SUBJACENT	_____	_____
TENET	_____	_____

DIRECTIONS: Use your LATIN roots and affixes sheets; try to find the word that is represented by the meanings of the roots and affixes. Write the word in the blank.

1. _____ care + one who

2. _____ with, together + to write

3. _____ not + foot

4. _____ to hold

5. _____ down, away + to roll

6. _____ in, not + to cut

7. _____ to step + like, related to

8. _____ bad, evil, ill + birth, race + like, related to

9. _____ back, again + to take + one who, that which

10. _____ tiny + spirit + having the quality of

11. _____ with, together + to lead

12. _____ hundred + year + like, related to

13. _____ under + to throw + like, related to

14. _____ law, right + one who

15. _____ before + go, yield

16. _____ shut, close + small

17. _____ good + to speak + state, quality, act

18. _____ to sit + like, related to

19. _____ through + to take + state, quality, act

20. _____ to make, do + like, related to + state, quality

DIRECTIONS: For each blank write one vocabulary word. All words will be used only once. Look for context clues in the sentence.

_____ 1. The job of writing a letter will --- to the secretary of the club.

_____ 2. Death is the usual result of a(n) --- disease.

_____ 3. The gymnast performed his routine with ---.

_____ 4. It is customary to close a church service with a(n) ---.

_____ 5. One --- of Christianity is the sovereignty of God

_____ 6. The road flooded when the --- overflowed.

_____ 7. A leaf growing directly from the stem is said to be ---.

_____ 8. An armed guard will --- the dictator in the annual revolutionary parade.

_____ 9. The demonstrator vowed to --- the flow of traffic into the parking lot.

_____ 10. David's attitude was not --- when he faced Goliath.

_____ 11. Very few people attend the --- of their own birth.

_____ 12. The decision of one --- kept the verdict from being unanimously guilty.

_____ 13. The new --- changed the hours at the museum.

_____ 14. A single --- pushed forth from the alien plant.

_____ 15. A dream house will usually feature a walk-in --- with full-length mirrors.

_____ 16. The chair was positioned --- to the table.

_____ 17. Warm, swampy areas usually have a large --- population.

_____ 18. The homeland defense corps had a ratio of five volunteers for every ---.

_____ 19. The --- of an issue is often determined by the personal experience and presuppositions of the viewer.

_____ 20. The --- change that occurred was not easily noticeable on a daily basis.

DIRECTIONS: Use your LATIN roots and affixes sheets; try to match the definitions with the words; look at the roots, prefixes, and suffixes for clues. Do NOT use a dictionary except as a last resort.

___ AMANUENSIS

1. n) one who has completed a course of study; v) to give a degree or diploma at completion

___ CLOTURE

2. n) a statement in words that gives a picture or account of something

___ CONDITION

3. n) bridge made of a series of arches to carry a road or track over a span

___ DESCRIPTION

4. n) one who takes calls, receives visitors, makes appointments, gives information

___ EVOLUTION

5. a) situated above or over another item

___ EXPEDITE

6. n) a dwelling house; building, offices, apartments held by another

___ FACSIMILE

7. n) a requirement, provision, or stipulation; a state of being

___ GRADUATE

8. n) manner or method of doing something; the established course of action

___ INTERSECTION

9. n) place where two roads, lines, etc., meet or cross

___ JUDICIAL

10. n) matter that settles to the bottom of liquid

___ MAGNANIMOUS

11. n) an unfolding; process of change

___ MALODOROUS

12. n) an exact reproduction or copy

___ MILLENNIUM

13. a) of law courts; unbiased; carefully considering

___ PARTICIPATE

14. n) secretary; one who takes dictation or copies something already written

___ PROCEDURE

15. v) to speed up the progress; to do quickly

___ RECEPTIONIST

16. n) ending of a legal debate by voting immediately

___ SEDIMENT

17. a) noble in mind; generous in overlooking insult

___ SUPERJACENT

18. a) stinking; having a bad odor

___ TENEMENT

19. n) a period of 1000 years; any period of peace, happiness, and prosperity

___ VIADUCT

20. v) to take part in; partake; share.

DIRECTIONS: Use your LATIN roots and affixes sheets; try to find the root in each vocabulary word.

Write the root and its meaning; also circle the root in the vocabulary word.

vocabulary word	root	meaning
AMANUENSIS	_____	_____
CLOTURE	_____	_____
CONDITION	_____	_____
DESCRIPTION	_____	_____
EVOLUTION	_____	_____
EXPEDITE	_____	_____
FACSIMILE	_____	_____
GRADUATE	_____	_____
INTERSECTION	_____	_____
JUDICIAL	_____	_____
MAGNANIMOUS	_____	_____
MALODOROUS	_____	_____
MILLENNIUM	_____	_____
PARTICIPATE	_____	_____
PROCEDURE	_____	_____
RECEPTIONIST	_____	_____
SEDIMENT	_____	_____
SUPERJACENT	_____	_____
TENEMENT	_____	_____
VIADUCT	_____	_____

DIRECTIONS: Use your LATIN roots and affixes sheets; try to find the word that is represented by the meanings of the roots and affixes. Write the word in the blank.

1. _____ bad, evil, ill + odor, smell + having the quality

2. _____ to hold + state, quality, that which

3. _____ thousand + year + Latin ending

4. _____ over, above + to throw + like, related to

5. _____ to make, do + like

6. _____ with, together + to speak + state, quality, act

7. _____ great + spirit + having the quality of

8. _____ back, again + to take + state, quality + one who

9. _____ way, road + to lead

10. _____ to sit + that which, state, quality

11. _____ out, away + foot + like, related to

12. _____ shut, close + that which

13. _____ part + to take + to make, do

14. _____ law, right + to speak + like, related to

15. _____ out, away + to roll + state, quality, act

16. _____ to step + to make, do

17. _____ from + hand + like, relating to

18. _____ for, forward + go, yield + state, quality, act

19. _____ between + to cut + state, quality, act

20. _____ down, away + to write + state, quality, act

DIRECTIONS: For each blank write one vocabulary word. All words will be used only once. Look for context clues in the sentence.

_____ 1. It is wrong to --- in actions that harm innocent people.

_____ 2. Using a lubricant will often --- a process.

_____ 3. Many firms will only hire a(n) --- with a degree.

_____ 4. The initiation of officers follows a standard ---.

_____ 5. The --- at Pont du Garde is three rows of arches.

_____ 6. The prince was --- as he pardoned the rebel dukes.

_____ 7. A dictaphone has replaced the --- in some offices.

_____ 8. A nice smile, neatness, and organizational talents are qualities found in a good ---.

_____ 9. Discussion of the bill ended with a vote for ---.

_____ 10. A hat is usually placed --- to the head.

_____ 11. An identical twin is thought of as a(n) ---.

_____ 12. The rotting salmon along the river were ---.

_____ 13. The police usually ask for a(n) --- of the suspect.

_____ 14. Only one --- was placed on the conquered army.

_____ 15. Many poor people in ghetto areas live in a(n) ---.

_____ 16. Metamorphosis is a good example of ---.

_____ 17. At times a(n) --- opinion or ruling is necessary to resolve a problem.

_____ 18. There was a layer of --- at the bottom of his coffee pot.

_____ 19. There are differences of opinion among believers as to when the --- begins.

_____ 20. Five highways met at the major --- in Beltsville.

DIRECTIONS: Use your LATIN roots and affixes sheets; try to match the definitions with the words; look at the roots, prefixes, and suffixes for clues. Do NOT use a dictionary except as a last resort.

___ ACCURATE

___ ANNALS

___ CONCLAVE

___ CONTRADICT

___ DISCIPLE

___ FACTION

___ GRADE

___ INANIMATE

___ INJUSTICE

___ INSCRIPTION

___ INTERCESSION

___ INVOLVE

___ MALIGN

___ OCTOPUS

___ RECEIPT

___ REDUCE

___ SEDENTARY

___ SUBJECT

___ TENANT

___ VIVISECTION

1. v) to lessen in any way; diminish; decrease; lose weight

2. n) written acknowledgment that something (goods, money) has been received

3. n) a pupil, follower, or adherent of any teacher or school of learning

4. n) renter; occupant; one who dwells or occupies

5. a) accustomed to sit much of the time

6. n) surgery performed on a living animal

7. a) under authority of; contingent upon
   n) topic; main idea; course
   v) cause to undergo

8. n) clique; group within a body having common interests usually in opposition to the majority

9. v) deny; to assert the opposite

10. a) dead; dull; spiritless; having no life

11. n) written account of events year by year; historical records

12. n) a private meeting

13. a) careful and exact; free from errors

14. n) step; degree; stage; amount of slope
    v) to rate by quality or rank; move ground

15. n) words or symbols engraved on a surface

16. n) wrong; an act that violates rights

17. n) mediation, prayer, or pleading on behalf of others

18. v) include; envelop or enfold; complicate or entangle

19. v) to defame; slander; speak evil of
    a) evil; baleful; sinister

20. n) mollusk with eight legs covered with suckers

DIRECTIONS: Use your LATIN roots and affixes sheets; try to find the root in each vocabulary word.

Write the root and its meaning; also circle the root in the vocabulary word.

vocabulary word	root	meaning
ACCURATE	_____	_____
ANNALS	_____	_____
CONCLAVE	_____	_____
CONTRADICT	_____	_____
DISCIPLE	_____	_____
FACTION	_____	_____
GRADE	_____	_____
INANIMATE	_____	_____
INJUSTICE	_____	_____
INSCRIPTION	_____	_____
INTERCESSION	_____	_____
INVOLVE	_____	_____
MALIGN	_____	_____
OCTOPUS	_____	_____
RECEIPT	_____	_____
REDUCE	_____	_____
SEDENTARY	_____	_____
SUBJECT	_____	_____
TENANT	_____	_____
VIVISECTION	_____	_____

DIRECTIONS: Use your LATIN roots and affixes sheets; try to find the word that is represented by the meanings of the roots and affixes. Write the word in the blank.

1. _____ in, not + to roll

2. _____ to make, do + state, quality, act

3. _____ in, not + law, right + act of

4. _____ to hold + one who

5. _____ bad, evil, ill + birth, race, kind

6. _____ to step

7. _____ under + to throw

8. _____ apart, not + to take + one who

9. _____ eight + foot

10. _____ year + like, related to + plural

11. _____ in, not + spirit + to make, do

12. _____ to sit + that which + like related to

13. _____ against + to speak

14. _____ back, again + to take

15. _____ between + go, yield + state, quality, act

16. _____ to, at + care + having the quality of

17. _____ in, not + to write + state, quality, act

18. _____ to live + to cut + state, quality, act

19. _____ with, together + shut, close

20. _____ back, again + to lead

DIRECTIONS: For each blank write one vocabulary word. All words will be used only once. Look for context clues in the sentence.

_____ 1. The --- from Marineland climbed over the glass wall using its suction grippers.

_____ 2. The --- on the ring said "Love Forever."

_____ 3. Computer operators have a(n) --- job.

_____ 4. A gossip will --- you behind your back.

_____ 5. The --- of West Point make interesting reading.

_____ 6. The salesman handed us the --- with a smile.

_____ 7. The cardinals held a(n) --- to select the new Pope.

_____ 8. That micrometer is --- to a thousandth of an inch.

_____ 9. The pro-gold --- made two demands of the caucus.

_____ 10. A loyal --- doffs his hat before his king.

_____ 11. It takes practice to correctly --- lumber.

_____ 12. It is not always easy to --- the bills we pay each month.

_____ 13. The former --- said he liked the apartment.

_____ 14. A cold snake seems --- until it warms up.

_____ 15. A good organizer will --- many people in a project.

_____ 16. Peter was a(n) --- of Jesus Christ.

_____ 17. Christ makes --- for His people to God.

_____ 18. It is best not to --- a man who has the facts.

_____ 19. Theft is a(n) ---, and so is murder.

_____ 20. The researchers performed a(n) --- on a pig.

DIRECTIONS: Use your LATIN roots and affixes sheets; try to match the definitions with the words; look at the roots, prefixes, and suffixes for clues. Do NOT use a dictionary except as a last resort.

___ AGGRESSION

___ BIENNIAL

___ CONCLUDE

___ DEDICATE

___ EXCEPTION

___ FACTOR

___ INJURY

___ INVOLUTE

___ MALNUTRITION

___ MANUSCRIPT

___ MILLEPEDE*

___ NECESSARY

___ PEDICURE

___ RECEPTION

___ RESIDUE

___ SECANT

___ SEDUCE

___ TENACITY

___ TRAJECTORY

___ UNANIMOUS

1. n) remainder; what is left after part is removed

2. n) wormlike arthropod with two pairs of legs on each of most of its segments

3. v) to set apart for a deity or special purpose; consecrate; devote

4. a) perseverance; firmness of hold; persistence

5. v) lure; lead astray; persuade to do something disloyal or disobedient

6. n) the curved path of something hurtling through space

7. n) social function for receiving guests; reproductive quality of incoming signals

8. n) one who does business for another; agent; any of the conditions that bring about a result

9. v) to end; finish; decide; deduce; determine

10. n) an unprovoked attack or warlike act

11. n) any straight line intersecting a curve at two or more points

12. a) agreeing completely; united in opinion

13. n) original, first copy (written by hand)

14. n) person or thing different from others of its class; case in which the rule does not apply

15. n) physical or legal harm or damage to person or property

16. a) essential; required; indispensable; inevitable

17. n) undernourishment from insufficient food or improper diet

18. a) happening every two years

19. a) intricate; involved; rolled up or curled in a spiral; rolled inward at the edges

20. n) a trimming, cleaning, etc., of the toenails

* also spelled milleped, millipede, & milliped

DIRECTIONS: Use your LATIN roots and affixes sheets; try to find the root in each vocabulary word. Write the root and its meaning; also circle the root in the vocabulary word.

vocabulary word	root	meaning
AGGRESSION	_____	_____
BIENNIAL	_____	_____
CONCLUDE	_____	_____
DEDICATE	_____	_____
EXCEPTION	_____	_____
FACTOR	_____	_____
INJURY	_____	_____
INVOLUTE	_____	_____
MALNUTRITION	_____	_____
MANUSCRIPT	_____	_____
MILLEPEDE	_____	_____
NECESSARY	_____	_____
PEDICURE	_____	_____
RECEPTION	_____	_____
RESIDUE	_____	_____
SECANT	_____	_____
SEDUCE	_____	_____
TENACITY	_____	_____
TRAJECTORY	_____	_____
UNANIMOUS	_____	_____

DIRECTIONS: Use your LATIN roots and affixes sheets; try to find the word that is represented by the meanings of the roots and affixes. Write the word in the blank.

1. _____ to hold + having the quality of + state, quality

2. _____ bad, evil, ill + nourish + state, quality, act

3. _____ across + to throw + like, related to

4. _____ thousand + foot

5. _____ back, again + to take + state, quality, act

6. _____ in, not + law, right + quality, condition

7. _____ apart + to lead

8. _____ hand + to write

9. _____ back, again + to sit

10. _____ two + year + like, related to

11. _____ down, away + to speak + to make, do

12. _____ to make, do + one who, that which

13. _____ to cut + like, related to

14. _____ in, not + to roll

15. _____ foot + care

16. _____ to, at + to step + state, quality, act

17. _____ with, together + shut, close

18. _____ out, away + to take + state, quality, act

19. _____ one + spirit + having the quality of

20. _____ not + go, yield + like, related to

DIRECTIONS: For each blank write one vocabulary word. All words will be used only once. Look for context clues in the sentence.

_____ 1. Authors will often --- a book to a friend.

_____ 2. The appearance of the leaf was ---.

_____ 3. It is time to --- the matter and go on.

_____ 4. There was a thick --- at the bottom of the sink.

_____ 5. The villain tried to --- the heroine but failed.

_____ 6. The --- walked up the wall with ease.

_____ 7. For once the legislature made a(n) --- decision.

_____ 8. Low oil prices were only one --- in causing a failing economy.

_____ 9. The --- will bloom only once every two years.

_____ 10. A serious --- can cause death in some cases.

_____ 11. Normally it is --- to eat in order to live.

_____ 12. Not eating correctly can cause ---.

_____ 13. The --- is a common function in trigonometry.

_____ 14. A varmint rifle has a flat --- for better accuracy.

_____ 15. Barefooted folks could benefit from a(n) ---.

_____ 16. Shelling the fort was an act of ---.

_____ 17. A bulldog is known for its ---.

_____ 18. Almost every spelling rule has a(n) ---.

_____ 19. The wedding --- was held in the garden.

_____ 20. The author's --- was lost in the mail.

DIRECTIONS: Use your LATIN roots and affixes sheets; try to match the definitions with the words; look at the roots, prefixes, and suffixes for clues. Do NOT use a dictionary except as a last resort.

___ ABJURE

1. n) spite; active ill will; desire to harm others

___ ABSTAIN

2. n) one who lives in a place (not a visitor)

___ ANIMOSITY

3. n) the foot or bottom support of a column, pillar, vase, lamp, etc.

___ ANNUAL

4. v) to give up rights on oath; renounce; recant

___ CONCEIVE

5. n) wall built into the water to restrain currents to protect a harbor, pier, etc.

___ CONGRESS

6. a) having overlapping margins (said of leaves or petals)

___ DICTATOR

7. n) a coming together; an assembly or conference; a legislature

___ DISCLOSE

8. a) continual; not stopping; never ceasing; constant

___ FACTUAL

9. a) lacking in distinctive features or qualities; hard to classify

___ INCESSANT

10. n) strong hatred; ill will; open or active hostility; enmity

___ JETTY

11. v) to bring forth; yield; bring to view
    n) farm products

___ MALICE

12. n) container; vessel; used to hold something else

___ NONDESCRIPT

13. v) to reveal; make known; uncover; bring out

___ OBVOLUTE

14. n) section; division; part; any part which is separable from the others

___ PEDESTAL

15. v) to become pregnant with; imagine; apprehend; understand; think of

___ PROCTOR

16. v) to keep oneself back; refrain; voluntarily do without

___ PRODUCE

17. a) yearly; comes once a year; alive for only one year or season
    n) yearbook

___ RECEPTACLE

18. a) real; actual; of or containing real things

___ RESIDENT

19. n) one who rules with power and authority; one who speaks words for others to write

___ SEGMENT

20. n) agent; one who manages affairs for others; official who supervises an examination

DIRECTIONS: Use your LATIN roots and affixes sheets; try to find the root in each vocabulary word. Write the root and its meaning; also circle the root in the vocabulary word.

vocabulary word	root	meaning
ABJURE	_____	_____
ABSTAIN	_____	_____
ANIMOSITY	_____	_____
ANNUAL	_____	_____
CONCEIVE	_____	_____
CONGRESS	_____	_____
DICTATOR	_____	_____
DISCLOSE	_____	_____
FACTUAL	_____	_____
INCESSANT	_____	_____
JETTY	_____	_____
MALICE	_____	_____
NONDESCRIPT	_____	_____
OBVOLUTE	_____	_____
PEDESTAL	_____	_____
PROCTOR	_____	_____
PRODUCE	_____	_____
RECEPTACLE	_____	_____
RESIDENT	_____	_____
SEGMENT	_____	_____

DIRECTIONS: Use your LATIN roots and affixes sheets; try to find the word that is represented by the meanings of the roots and affixes. Write the word in the blank.

1. _____ to cut + that which, quality, state

2. _____ to throw

3. _____ back, again + to sit + one who

4. _____ apart, not + shut, close

5. _____ year + like, related to

6. _____ to make, do + like, related to

7. _____ to, against + to roll

8. _____ foot + place, a rest

9. _____ to speak + to make, do + one who

10. _____ away, from + law, right

11. _____ in, not + go, yield + like, related to

12. _____ not + down, away + to write

13. _____ back, again + to take + small

14. _____ with, together + to take

15. _____ away, from + to hold

16. _____ bad, evil, ill + quality of

17. _____ for, forward + to lead

18. _____ spirit + state, quality, act

19. _____ with, together + to step

20. _____ for, forward + care + one who

DIRECTIONS: For each blank write one vocabulary word. All words will be used only once. Look for context clues in the sentence.

_____ 1. The bust of Caesar sat on a high ---.

_____ 2. A shrewish woman is often a(n) --- talker.

_____ 3. One --- of the worm remained on the shovel.

_____ 4. The --- company picnic usually comes near the Fourth of July.

_____ 5. Hitler was an example of a modern ---.

_____ 6. The south --- was piled with logs from the storm.

_____ 7. Only a local --- could find the fishing hole.

_____ 8. The job of the --- is to make laws.

_____ 9. It is difficult for most people to --- from eating chocolate.

_____ 10. The front page of a newspaper is a good place to --- a story to the general public.

_____ 11. The dog was a(n) --- cur of limited value.

_____ 12. Much trash does not get put into its proper ---.

_____ 13. The --- picked up the exam right on time.

_____ 14. A non-fiction story is --- in content.

_____ 15. Dogs seem to have a natural --- for cats.

_____ 16. Most people will --- something under pressure.

_____ 17. Bob's --- was evident when he tried to hurt Joe.

_____ 18. The defendant will --- his right to counsel.

_____ 19. It is best to --- a plan before acting.

_____ 20. The petals of the flower were --- in design.

DIRECTIONS: Use your LATIN roots and affixes sheets; try to match the definitions with the words; look at the roots, prefixes, and suffixes for clues. Do NOT use a dictionary except as a last resort.

___ ABSTENTION

___ ADJUDICATE

___ ANIMISM

___ ARTIFACT

___ CONCEPT

___ DEGRADE

___ DICTION

___ ENCLAVE

___ INTERCEDE

___ JOIST

___ MALICIOUS

___ PEDAL

___ POSTSCRIPT

___ PRESIDENT

___ PROCURE

___ PRODUCTIVE

___ RECEPTIVE

___ REVOLVE

___ SECTOR

___ SUPERFICIAL

1. v) to obtain; to get

2. n) a foot lever as on a bicycle, organ, etc.

3. v) to demote; to lower in quality, character, or dignity; debase; dishonor

4. n) the highest office of a company, club, country

5. a) of or being on the surface; quick and cursory; concerned with and understanding only the obvious

6. v) to rotate; to recur at intervals; to move in a circle or orbit

7. a) able or ready to accept suggestions, new ideas, etc.

8. a) fertile; marked by abundant bringing forth or manufacturing of goods

9. n) a false belief that natural objects as rocks, trees, the wind, etc., are alive and have spirits

10. n) any object made by human work; esp. a primitive tool

11. n) part of a circle bounded by 2 radii and the included arc; an area, division, or portion

12. n) beam that holds up floor panels

13. v) to mediate; to plead in behalf of another

14. a) spiteful; intentionally harmful

15. n) an idea; general notion

16. v) to act as judge; to hear and decide; to give judgment

17. n) a territory surrounded by another country's territory

18. n) the act or condition of refraining

19. n) enunciation; wording; manner of expression in words

20. n) a note or paragraph added to the main work as an afterthought

DIRECTIONS: Use your LATIN roots and affixes sheets; try to find the root in each vocabulary word. Write the root and its meaning; also circle the root in the vocabulary word.

vocabulary word	root	meaning
ABSTENTION	_____	_____
ADJUDICATE	_____	_____
ANIMISM	_____	_____
ARTIFACT	_____	_____
CONCEPT	_____	_____
DEGRADE	_____	_____
DICTION	_____	_____
ENCLAVE	_____	_____
INTERCEDE	_____	_____
JOIST	_____	_____
MALICIOUS	_____	_____
PEDAL	_____	_____
POSTSCRIPT	_____	_____
PRESIDENT	_____	_____
PROCURE	_____	_____
PRODUCTIVE	_____	_____
RECEPTIVE	_____	_____
REVOLVE	_____	_____
SECTOR	_____	_____
SUPERFICIAL	_____	_____

DIRECTIONS: Use your LATIN roots and affixes sheets; try to find the word that is represented by the meanings of the roots and affixes. Write the word in the blank.

1. _____ bad, evil, ill + quality of + having the quality

2. _____ in, into + shut, close

3. _____ to cut + that which

4. _____ with, together + to take

5. _____ to, at + law, right + to speak + to make, do

6. _____ before + to sit + one who

7. _____ back, again + to roll

8. _____ foot + like, related to

9. _____ over, above + to make, do + like, related to

10. _____ to speak + state, quality, act

11. _____ away, from + to hold + state, quality, act

12. _____ after + to write

13. _____ to throw

14. _____ back, again + to take + having the power of

15. _____ spirit + belief

16. _____ for, forward + care

17. _____ between + go, yield

18. _____ down, away + to step

19. _____ for, forward + to lead + having the power of

20. _____ skill + to make, do

DIRECTIONS: For each blank write one vocabulary word. All words will be used only once. Look for context clues in the sentence.

_____ 1. George Washington was our first ---.

_____ 2. If a(n) --- breaks, the floor will sag.

_____ 3. The sun does not --- around the earth.

_____ 4. Good --- is necessary when speaking in public.

_____ 5. Using a(n) --- may propel certain vehicles.

_____ 6. One --- of the town was secured by the army.

_____ 7. It is poor manners to --- a person in public.

_____ 8. The diggers found a(n) --- in the ruins.

_____ 9. Wise men used to be called upon to --- disputes.

_____ 10. The usual place for a(n) --- is at the bottom of a letter.

_____ 11. --- from something desirable shows self-control.

_____ 12. An abstract --- is not easily grasped by some.

_____ 13. The new owner was quite --- to ideas from those who had worked there before his time.

_____ 14. The patriots had a small --- in the mountains held by the insurgents.

_____ 15. The man escaped the wreck with only --- wounds.

_____ 16. It is best to --- supplies when they are cheap.

_____ 17. Imps are --- in their behavior.

_____ 18. The tree by the spring is very --- each year.

_____ 19. A close friend may --- on behalf of the accused.

_____ 20. Many primitive people once believe in ---.

DIRECTIONS: Use your LATIN roots and affixes sheets; try to match the definitions with the words; look at the roots, prefixes, and suffixes for clues. Do NOT use a dictionary except as a last resort.

___ ABSTINENCE   1. v) to write beforehand; order, direct or advise

___ ARTIFICE   2. v) to be enough or adequate

___ BENEFACTOR   3. n) a formal statement of opinion; a saying or adage

___ CAPTION   4. v) to die

___ CORPULENT   5. n) a small platform (as for a lecturer)

___ DECEASE   6. v) to place formally in an office or group; to enroll in the armed forces

___ DEGREE   7. n) a refraining from some or all food, drink, or other pleasures

___ DICTUM   8. n) wrongdoing or misconduct, esp. in handling of public affairs

___ ENCLOSE   9. v) to throw in between; interrupt with

___ INDUCT   10. a) free from fear, care, danger, etc.; safe; firm (as a knot)
     v) to protect; to obtain; to make certain; to make firm or fast

___ INTERJECT   11. n) a tool with a crescent-shaped blade on a short handle used to cut tall grass or weeds

___ MALFEASANCE   12. a) easily influenced or affected by

___ PODIUM   13. n) a patron; one who gives help or financial aid

___ PRESCRIBE   14. n) trickery; skill or ingenuity

___ PRESIDE   15. n) a heading or title (found on illustrations)

___ SECURE   16. n) a device that regulates flow by means of a membrane, flap, lid, etc.

___ SICKLE   17. v) to serve as chairman; to have authority or control over

___ SUFFICE   18. a) fat; obese; stout

___ SUSCEPTIBLE   19. v) to shut in all around; surround; put within an envelope

___ VALVE   20. n) any of successive steps in a process; social or official rank; unit of measurement for angles and arcs

DIRECTIONS: Use your LATIN roots and affixes sheets; try to find the root in each vocabulary word. Write the root and its meaning; also circle the root in the vocabulary word.

vocabulary word	root	meaning
ABSTINENCE	_____	_____
ARTIFICE	_____	_____
BENEFACTOR	_____	_____
CAPTION	_____	_____
CORPULENT	_____	_____
DECEASE	_____	_____
DEGREE	_____	_____
DICTUM	_____	_____
ENCLOSE	_____	_____
INDUCT	_____	_____
INTERJECT	_____	_____
MALFEASANCE	_____	_____
PODIUM	_____	_____
PRESCRIBE	_____	_____
PRESIDE	_____	_____
SECURE	_____	_____
SICKLE	_____	_____
SUFFICE	_____	_____
SUSCEPTIBLE	_____	_____
VALVE	_____	_____

DIRECTIONS: Use your LATIN roots and affixes sheets; try to find the word that is represented by the meanings of the roots and affixes. Write the word in the blank.

1. _____ foot + Latin ending

2. _____ apart + care

3. _____ away, from + to hold + state, quality, act

4. _____ in, not + to lead

5. _____ to speak + Latin ending

6. _____ bad, evil, ill + to make, do + state, quality, act

7. _____ between + to throw

8. _____ before + to sit

9. _____ under + to make, do

10. _____ to roll

11. _____ good + to make, do + one who

12. _____ in, into + shut, close

13. _____ body + like, related to

14. _____ down, away + to step

15. _____ to take + state, quality, act

16. _____ under + to take + able to be

17. _____ to cut + a thing used

18. _____ down, away + go, yield

19. _____ skill + to make, do

20. _____ before + to write

DIRECTIONS: For each blank write one vocabulary word. All words will be used only once. Look for context clues in the sentence.

_____ 1. The doctor will often --- medicine for a patient.

_____ 2. The gun was elevated to a 30 --- angle.

_____ 3. A safety deposit box is --- from most dangers.

_____ 4. One meal a day could --- for most of us.

_____ 5. When sending away for information, --- a stamped, self-addressed envelope (SASE) for quick response.

_____ 6. Rude people --- comments into the discussions of others.

_____ 7. Eglon was so --- that Ehud's sword disappeared within his body. (Judges 3:22)

_____ 8. Kings often make a(n) --- about important items.

_____ 9. A person in poor health is --- to pneumonia.

_____ 10. The group leader will often --- at its meetings.

_____ 11. Boss Tweed of Tammany Hall was guilty of ---.

_____ 12. History shows that every man will --- some day.

_____ 13. The --- is not as fast as a mower when cutting an entire acre of grass.

_____ 14. Total --- is often easier than partially limiting one's consumption.

_____ 15. A(n) --- may be made of various materials depending upon its use.

_____ 16. Pip's unknown --- supplied many needs for him.

_____ 17. The lodge will --- ten new members next meeting.

_____ 18. Without the --- some cartoons would make no sense.

_____ 19. The magician used every --- he knew to impress us.

_____ 20. Good speakers don't lean on the ---.

DIRECTIONS: Use your LATIN roots and affixes sheets; try to match the definitions with the words; look at the roots, prefixes, and suffixes for clues. Do NOT use a dictionary except as a last resort.

___ APPERTAIN

___ BENEFICIAL

___ CAPTOR

___ CONFECTION

___ DIGRESSION

___ EDICT

___ ENCLOSURE

___ EXCESS

___ INCORPORATE

___ INTRODUCE

___ MALFORMED

___ OBJECT

___ PEDIGREE

___ RECIPE

___ RESIDE

___ SCRIBE

___ SINECURE

___ SURFACE

___ TRANSECT

___ VAULT

1. n) one who takes prisoners

2. v) to cut across; divide by cutting

3. v) to combine; include; embody; merge; to unite into one group or body

4. n) list of ancestors; descent; lineage

5. a) misshapen; abnormally shaped

6. n) an arched chamber or space; a room for storage or safekeeping
   v) to leap or jump

7. v) to belong to; be connected or associated

8. n) thing which may be seen or touched; a goal or purpose
   v) express disapproval or opposition

9. n) a position that brings profit with little work

10. n) exterior of an object; the face of a solid
    a) external   v) to come to the top; to cover

11. n) writer, author, professional penman; instrument for marking a line on wood or stone

12. v) to put in; insert; to make acquainted; to start; begin; to bring in

13. a) advantageous; favorable; productive of good

14. n) a decree; an official proclamation

15. n) a candy, ice cream, preserves, etc.

16. n) something contained in an envelope; a walled-in area

17. n) a turning aside from the main subject in writing or speaking

18. v) to dwell for a long time; to be inherent

19. n) list of materials and directions for preparing a dish or drink

20. n/a) surplus; extra; goes beyond normal limits

DIRECTIONS: Use your LATIN roots and affixes sheets; try to find the root in each vocabulary word. Write the root and its meaning; also circle the root in the vocabulary word.

vocabulary word	root	meaning
APPERTAIN	_____	_____
BENEFICIAL	_____	_____
CAPTOR	_____	_____
CONFECTION	_____	_____
DIGRESSION	_____	_____
EDICT	_____	_____
ENCLOSURE	_____	_____
EXCESS	_____	_____
INCORPORATE	_____	_____
INTRODUCE	_____	_____
MALFORMED	_____	_____
OBJECT	_____	_____
PEDIGREE	_____	_____
RECIPE	_____	_____
RESIDE	_____	_____
SCRIBE	_____	_____
SINECURE	_____	_____
SURFACE	_____	_____
TRANSECT	_____	_____
VAULT	_____	_____

DIRECTIONS: Use your LATIN roots and affixes sheets; try to find the word that is represented by the meanings of the roots and affixes. Write the word in the blank.

1. _____ with, together + to make, do + state, quality, act

2. _____ without + care

3. _____ in, into + shut, close + that which

4. _____ good + to make, do + like, related to

5. _____ foot + to step

6. _____ bad, evil, ill + form, shape + past action

7. _____ apart, not + to step + state, quality, act

8. _____ to roll

9. _____ in, not + body + to make, do

10. _____ out, away + to speak

11. _____ away, from + through + to hold

12. _____ back, again + to take

13. _____ under + face

14. _____ out, away + go, yield

15. _____ to, against + to throw

16. _____ to write

17. _____ to take + one who

18. _____ across + to cut

19. _____ back, again + to sit

20. _____ inside + to lead

DIRECTIONS: For each blank write one vocabulary word. All words will be used only once. Look for context clues in the sentence.

_____ 1. The M.C. will --- the head table at the banquet.

_____ 2. The --- for slumgullion was very simple.

_____ 3. The king's --- determined policy about the matter.

_____ 4. A balanced meal would be --- for most of us.

_____ 5. The --- food at some houses goes to the chickens.

_____ 6. The new highway will --- our lower pasture.

_____ 7. Figuring the --- area of some shapes is tricky.

_____ 8. A(n) --- usually detracts from the argument.

_____ 9. The dwarf was --- in his back and shoulders.

_____ 10. The job of dog catcher is usually a(n) ---.

_____ 11. The --- placed iron collars on his prisoners.

_____ 12. Many folks would like to --- in a nice climate.

_____ 13. The show horse had a long --- to prove his blood lines were pure.

_____ 14. The sun porch was a nice --- on the house.

_____ 15. The point did not --- to the man on trial.

_____ 16. All good patriots --- to a loss of freedom.

_____ 17. The bank stores its money in the ---.

_____ 18. The --- provides others with writings to read.

_____ 19. We will --- some humor into future exercises.

_____ 20. A good --- is usually quite sweet.

DIRECTIONS: Use your LATIN roots and affixes sheets; try to match the definitions with the words; look at the roots, prefixes, and suffixes for clues. Do NOT use a dictionary except as a last resort.

___ BENEFICIARY

___ CAPSTAN

___ CONCEDE

___ CONTINENT

___ DEFACED

___ EDUCATE

___ EGRESS

___ EJECT

___ EXCLUDE

___ FUGUE

___ INDICT

___ MALEFICENT

___ MANDATE

___ OCCUPATION

___ POSSESS

___ PROFICIENT

___ SCRIPT

___ TRIPOD

___ TRISECT

___ VERACIOUS

1. n) exit; a way out

2. a) marred; spoiled in looks

3. n) musical work in which a theme is successively taken up and developed by parts in counterpoint

4. a) highly competent; skilled

5. v) to admit as true, valid or certain; to grant as a right

6. n) a three-legged cauldron, stool, support, etc.

7. a) harmful; hurtful; evil

8. a) habitually truthful; honest

9. n) one who receives good things, esp. inheritance

10. v) to cut or divide into three equal parts

11. v) teach; to develop the knowledge, skill, or character of, esp. by formal schooling

12. n) work; profession; the holding of a territory or position

13. n) upright drum around which cables are wound

14. v) accuse; to bring criminal charges against

15. n) any of the main large land areas of the earth

16. n) written part of a play, radio drama, or film; handwriting, style of writing

17. n) an order or command; the will of constituents expressed to their representatives

18. v) to refuse to admit or consider; reject

19. v) to have as belonging to one; own; to have as an attribute or quality

20. v) expel; discharge; to throw out or force out

DIRECTIONS: Use your LATIN roots and affixes sheets; try to find the root in each vocabulary word. Write the root and its meaning; also circle the root in the vocabulary word.

vocabulary word	root	meaning
BENEFICIARY	_____	_____
CAPSTAN	_____	_____
CONCEDE	_____	_____
CONTINENT	_____	_____
DEFACED	_____	_____
EDUCATE	_____	_____
EGRESS	_____	_____
EJECT	_____	_____
EXCLUDE	_____	_____
FUGUE	_____	_____
INDICT	_____	_____
MALEFICENT	_____	_____
MANDATE	_____	_____
OCCUPATION	_____	_____
POSSESS	_____	_____
PROFICIENT	_____	_____
SCRIPT	_____	_____
TRIPOD	_____	_____
TRISECT	_____	_____
VERACIOUS	_____	_____

DIRECTIONS: Use your LATIN roots and affixes sheets; try to find the word that is represented by the meanings of the roots and affixes. Write the word in the blank.

1. _____ to, against + to take + state, quality, act

2. _____ to take

3. _____ good + to make, do + like, related to

4. _____ with, together + go, yield

5. _____ bad, evil, ill + to make, do + like, related to

6. _____ to flee

7. _____ out, away + to lead + to make, do

8. _____ three + to cut

9. _____ in, into + to speak

10. _____ hand + to give

11. _____ with, together + to hold + that which, like

12. _____ out, away + to step

13. _____ down, away + face + past action

14. _____ three + foot

15. _____ for, forward + to make, do + like, related to

16. _____ to write

17. _____ out, away + to throw

18. _____ true + having the quality of

19. _____ out, away + shut, close

20. _____ after + to sit

DIRECTIONS: For each blank write one vocabulary word. All words will be used only once. Look for context clues in the sentence.

_____ 1. The pilot will --- from a plane in dire straits.

_____ 2. The --- of the average American changes three times in his lifetime.

_____ 3. A professional cameraman often uses a ---.

_____ 4. The ogre and troll are considered --- characters.

_____ 5. The anchor rope was snubbed securely around the --- on the prow.

_____ 6. It is wise to --- certain foods from one's diet.

_____ 7. The actors followed the --- exactly.

_____ 8. The primary --- in a will is often the marriage partner or a close relative.

_____ 9. An election with a majority over 65% is considered a(n) --- by most political commentators.

_____ 10. Africa was once known as the dark ---.

_____ 11. A(n) --- man soon gains credibility among the people with whom he associates regularly.

_____ 12. To --- an angle accurately by estimation takes a good eye and a sense of proportion.

_____ 13. Many victims were denied --- by falling rocks and timbers, which blocked forward progress.

_____ 14. The wall was --- by spray paint and graffitti.

_____ 15. The grand jury will --- suspects for some crimes.

_____ 16. Faith, hope, and love are nice qualities to ---.

_____ 17. Reading widely will --- one in many disciplines.

_____ 18. The --- was a popular music form in Bach's time.

_____ 19. A master of a craft is --- in what he does.

_____ 20. It is dangerous to --- a point early in a debate.

DIRECTIONS: Use your LATIN roots and affixes sheets; try to match the definitions with the words; look at the roots, prefixes, and suffixes for clues. Do NOT use a dictionary except as a last resort.

___ BENEFIT

___ CAPSULE

___ CONCESSION

___ COUNTENANCE

___ DEFECT

___ EDUCE

___ FORECLOSE

___ INGREDIENT

___ INJECT

___ INTERDICT

___ MALEVOLENT

___ MANUFACTURE

___ MUNICIPAL

___ OBSESSION

___ PEDESTRIAN

___ REFUGE

___ SUBSCRIBER

___ SUFFICIENT

___ VENESECTION

___ VERIFY

1. n) shelter; place of safety from danger

2. v) to force into a cavity; to throw in a remark

3. n) the act of an evil spirit possessing someone; being ruled by an idea or desire

4. v) to draw out or elicit

5. n) phlebotomy; bloodletting for therapy

6. n) advantage; anything contributing to an advantage; a favor; a payment
   v) to help or aid

7. a) as much as needed; enough; meets requirements

8. n) one who signs a document agreeing to support its conditions

9. n) a privilege given; something admitted as true

10. n) a component part; element; any of the parts of which a mixture is made

11. n) walker; one who goes on foot
    a) dull; prosaic; lacking interest or imagination

12. v) to forbid or restrain an action or use

13. n) imperfection; fault
    v) to forsake a cause

14. v) to shut out; exclude; to deny the right to redeem (a mortgage)

15. a) having ill will; wishing evil on others

16. v) confirm; substantiate; to prove to be true by testimony, evidence, or demonstration

17. n) a soluble gelatin container holding a dose of medicine
    a) in concise form

18. a) of a city, town, or its local government

19. v) to make by hand or machinery, usually on a large scale; make; fabricate; invent

20. n) the face; visage; facial expression; approval

DIRECTIONS: Use your LATIN roots and affixes sheets; try to find the root in each vocabulary word. Write the root and its meaning; also circle the root in the vocabulary word.

vocabulary word	root	meaning
BENEFIT	_____	_____
CAPSULE	_____	_____
CONCESSION	_____	_____
COUNTENANCE	_____	_____
DEFECT	_____	_____
EDUCE	_____	_____
FORECLOSE	_____	_____
INGREDIENT	_____	_____
INJECT	_____	_____
INTERDICT	_____	_____
MALEVOLENT	_____	_____
MANUFACTURE	_____	_____
MUNICIPAL	_____	_____
OBSESSION	_____	_____
PEDESTRIAN	_____	_____
REFUGE	_____	_____
SUBSCRIBER	_____	_____
SUFFICIENT	_____	_____
VENESECTION	_____	_____
VERIFY	_____	_____

DIRECTIONS: Use your LATIN roots and affixes sheets; try to find the word that is represented by the meanings of the roots and affixes. Write the word in the blank.

1. _____ with, together + go, yield + state, quality, act

2. _____ bad, evil, ill + will, wish + like, related to

3. _____ back, again + to flee

4. _____ out, away + to lead

5. _____ true + to make, do

6. _____ under + to write + one who

7. _____ good + to make, do

8. _____ in, not + to step + that which, like, related to

9. _____ gift, service + to take + like, related to

10. _____ vein + to cut + state, quality, act

11. _____ down, away + to make, do

12. _____ to take + small

13. _____ in, not + to throw

14. _____ before + shut, close

15. _____ under + to make, do + like, related to

16. _____ between + to speak

17. _____ to, against + to sit + state, quality, act

18. _____ with, together + to hold + state, quality, act

19. _____ hand + to make, do + that which

20. _____ foot + one who

DIRECTIONS: For each blank write one vocabulary word. All words will be used only once. Look for context clues in the sentence.

_____ 1. The --- government was located in city hall.

_____ 2. In the 1930s a bank would often --- on a farm to collect its money.

_____ 3. A game --- usually allows no shooting.

_____ 4. A minor --- may lower the price of the product.

_____ 5. It is difficult to --- some pieces of evidence.

_____ 6. The court will --- two companies from merging under certain circumstances.

_____ 7. A man should --- from his own work.

_____ 8. The --- left only a small scar on the patient.

_____ 9. A good lawyer will try to --- information from a witness on the stand.

_____ 10. Flour is a major --- in many recipes.

_____ 11. A loyal --- pays his newspaper bill on time.

_____ 12. $5.00 is no longer --- to fill a gas tank.

_____ 13. Satan is a very --- creature.

_____ 14. A cold --- may have timed release components.

_____ 15. The --- should cross the street in a crosswalk.

_____ 16. Henry Ford used mass production techniques to --- the Model T.

_____ 17. The nurse will --- the medication into the patient.

_____ 18. The --- stand sold only root beer and hot dogs.

_____ 19. The young man's --- was to earn one million dollars.

_____ 20. Cain's --- was downcast when God confronted him.

DIRECTIONS: Use your LATIN roots and affixes sheets; try to match the definitions with the words; look at the roots, prefixes, and suffixes for clues. Do NOT use a dictionary except as a last resort.

___ ANTECEDENT

___ APPURTENANCE

___ BENEVOLENT

___ CAPACIOUS

___ CORPUSCLE

___ DEDUCE

___ DEFICIENT

___ DEJECTION

___ DETAIN

___ DICTAPHONE

___ FRAGILE

___ INCLUDE

___ INGRESS

___ INSIDIOUS

___ JUDICIOUS

___ MALCONTENT

___ MANIPULATE

___ PERFECT

___ SUBSCRIPT

___ VERISIMILITUDE

1. v) to infer or decide by reasoning

2. a) characterized by treachery or slyness

3. a) complete; flawless; completely accurate
   v) to complete or finish in all aspects

4. n) lowness of spirits; depression; discouragement

5. n) machine for recording and reproducing words spoken into its mouthpiece

6. n) something added to a more important thing; apparatus or equipment

7. a) dissatisfied; rebellious
   n) a rebel

8. n) a number, letter, or symbol written underneath

9. a) roomy; spacious

10. a) wise and careful; having, applying, or showing sound judgment

11. a) prior; previous
    n) anything prior to another; that which comes before

12. a) lacking in some essential; incomplete; inadequate

13. v) to enclose; contain; comprise; to have as part of a whole

14. v) confine; keep in custody; keep from going on

15. a) kind; kindly; charitable; inclined to do good

16. n) the appearance of being true or real

17. n) entrance

18. v) to handle skillfully; to alter (figures, etc.) for one's own purposes

19. a) easily broken or damaged; delicate

20. n) a very small particle; any of the blood cells

DIRECTIONS: Use your LATIN roots and affixes sheets; try to find the root in each vocabulary word. Write the root and its meaning; also circle the root in the vocabulary word.

vocabulary word	root	meaning
ANTECEDENT	_____	_____
APPURTENANCE	_____	_____
BENEVOLENT	_____	_____
CAPACIOUS	_____	_____
CORPUSCLE	_____	_____
DEDUCE	_____	_____
DEFICIENT	_____	_____
DEJECTION	_____	_____
DETAIN	_____	_____
DICTAPHONE	_____	_____
FRAGILE	_____	_____
INCLUDE	_____	_____
INGRESS	_____	_____
INSIDIOUS	_____	_____
JUDICIOUS	_____	_____
MALCONTENT	_____	_____
MANIPULATE	_____	_____
PERFECT	_____	_____
SUBSCRIPT	_____	_____
VERISIMILITUDE	_____	_____

DIRECTIONS: Use your LATIN roots and affixes sheets; try to find the word that is represented by the meanings of the roots and affixes. Write the word in the blank.

1. _____ body + small

2. _____ in, not + to step

3. _____ under + to write

4. _____ down, away + to lead

5. _____ to break + like, related to

6. _____ hand + to fill + to make, do

7. _____ down, away + to hold

8. _____ to speak + sound

9. _____ good + will, wish + like, related to

10. _____ bad, evil, ill + with, together + to hold

11. _____ before + go, yield + one who, that which

12. _____ law, right + to speak + having the quality of

13. _____ in, not + to sit + having the quality of

14. _____ down, away + to make, do + like, related to

15. _____ to, at + through + to hold + state, quality

16. _____ true + like + state, quality

17. _____ through + to make, do

18. _____ in, not + shut, close

19. _____ to take + having the quality of

20. _____ down, away + to throw + state, quality, act

DIRECTIONS: For each blank write one vocabulary word. All words will be used only once. Look for context clues in the sentence.

_____ 1. Many private clubs are established to do --- acts.

_____ 2. The --- caused much trouble for his family.

_____ 3. The --- laugh came from the villain in hiding.

_____ 4. The police may --- a suspect for questioning.

_____ 5. His story expressed --- but left one doubt.

_____ 6. The --- of a pronoun always precedes it.

_____ 7. Practice makes ---.

_____ 8. The referee made a(n) --- choice in the matter.

_____ 9. In some plots one can --- the outcome very early.

_____ 10. The inside of the van was surprisingly ---.

_____ 11. The communists --- others in their quest for world domination.

_____ 12. The loss of his dog put the boy into deep ---.

_____ 13. The chemical symbol for water contains a(n) ---.

_____ 14. It is proper to --- prayer in devotion time.

_____ 15. Each type of blood --- has its own function.

_____ 16. While commuting, the executive recorded his letters on the --- to save time at the office.

_____ 17. Glass is quite --- to ship by mail.

_____ 18. --- was allowed only by an air lock at the bay section of the rocket plane.

_____ 19. The soldier had one obvious --- on his gun.

_____ 20. His output was ---, so he did not get a raise.

DIRECTIONS: Use your LATIN roots and affixes sheets; try to match the definitions with the words; look at the roots, prefixes, and suffixes for clues. Do NOT use a dictionary except as a last resort.

___ BENIGN

___ CAPACITY

___ CESSATION

___ DEDUCT

___ DEFICIT

___ DETENTION

___ DISCIPLINE

___ DISSIDENT

___ EJACULATE

___ ENTERTAIN

___ FRAGMENT

___ JURISDICTION

___ MALEFACTOR

___ MANICURE

___ OCCLUSION

___ PREFECT

___ PROGRESSION

___ SECTION

___ SUPERSCRIPT

___ VOLUBLE

1. n) an evildoer; a criminal

2. a) talkative; described by a great flow of words

3. n) a trimming, polishing, etc., of the fingernails

4. n) the ability to contain, absorb, or receive; volume; ability; position; maximum output

5. v) to eject abruptly; to utter suddenly; exclaim

6. n) a cutting apart; a part cut off; portion; any distinct part

7. n) any of various administrators

8. a) good natured; favorable; med. doing little or no harm

9. n) a ceasing or stopping

10. n) training that develops self-control and obedience; a system of rules for conduct

11. n) a number, letter, or symbol written above and to the side of another

12. n) a moving forward; a succession of something; math a series of numbers increasing or decreasing by a given factor

13. n) a part broken away from the whole
v) to break up

14. n) kept in custody; pretrial confinement time

15. v) to take away or subtract

16. v) to amuse; divert; to have as a guest; to have in mind; consider

17. n) one who disagrees

18. n) that which blocks; met. when a cold front blocks a warm front; dent. the fit of teeth when brought together

19. n) the amount by which a sum of money is less than the required amount

20. n) range of authority; power or authority to do something

DIRECTIONS: Use your LATIN roots and affixes sheets; try to find the root in each vocabulary word. Write the root and its meaning; also circle the root in the vocabulary word.

vocabulary word	root	meaning
BENIGN	_____	_____
CAPACITY	_____	_____
CESSATION	_____	_____
DEDUCT	_____	_____
DEFICIT	_____	_____
DETENTION	_____	_____
DISCIPLINE	_____	_____
DISSIDENT	_____	_____
EJACULATE	_____	_____
ENTERTAIN	_____	_____
FRAGMENT	_____	_____
JURISDICTION	_____	_____
MALEFACTOR	_____	_____
MANICURE	_____	_____
OCCLUSION	_____	_____
PREFECT	_____	_____
PROGRESSION	_____	_____
SECTION	_____	_____
SUPERSCRIPT	_____	_____
VOLUBLE	_____	_____

DIRECTIONS: Use your LATIN roots and affixes sheets; try to find the word that is represented by the meanings of the roots and affixes. Write the word in the blank.

1. _____ down, away + to lead

2. _____ between + to hold

3. _____ hand + care

4. _____ to roll + able to be

5. _____ good + birth, race, kind

6. _____ law, right + to speak + state, quality, act

7. _____ down, away + to make, do

8. _____ before + to make, do

9. _____ over, above + to write

10. _____ to take + state, quality, act

11. _____ out, away + to throw + to make, do

12. _____ down, away + to hold + state, quality, act

13. _____ go, yield + state, quality, act

14. _____ for, forward + to step + state, quality, act

15. _____ to, against + shut, close + state, quality, act

16. _____ to cut + state, quality, act

17. _____ bad, evil, ill + to make, do + one who

18. _____ apart, not + to take + having the nature of

19. _____ to break + state, quality, that which

20. _____ apart, not + to sit + one who

DIRECTIONS: For each blank write one vocabulary word. All words will be used only once. Look for context clues in the sentence.

_____ 1. The dentist says improper --- makes a poor bite.

_____ 2. Good --- requires consistency to be effective.

_____ 3. The western --- of the farm was a hay field.

_____ 4. The --- of fighting was a relief to everyone.

_____ 5. A footnote is marked by a(n) ---.

_____ 6. If is often unwise to --- an oath in conversation.

_____ 7. The crime was committed by a known ---.

_____ 8. The car's tank has a(n) --- of 11.4 gallons.

_____ 9. N, N+2, N+4, N+6 is a simple arithmetic ---.

_____ 10. A total --- leaves one's hands looking nice.

_____ 11. A tumor is usually --- or malignant.

_____ 12. It is fun to --- one's friends.

_____ 13. A lone --- voted against the proposal.

_____ 14. The current --- spending practices of the government may eventually bankrupt us all.

_____ 15. The politician made a particularly --- speech.

_____ 16. The court's --- did not extend to the next county.

_____ 17. The bad boys were given --- time after school.

_____ 18. The Roman governor was known as a(n) ---.

_____ 19. To figure profits one must --- expenses from income.

_____ 20. Only one small --- of the cart remained after the explosion.

DIRECTIONS: Use your LATIN roots and affixes sheets; try to match the definitions with the words; look at the roots, prefixes, and suffixes for clues. Do NOT use a dictionary except as a last resort.

___ ABSCESS

___ APPERCEIVE

___ AQUEDUCT

___ ASSESS

___ BONUS

___ CENTRIFUGAL

___ CIRCUMJACENT

___ CORPORATION

___ EFFACE

___ FRACTION

___ IMPERCEPTIBLE

___ IMPERTINENT

___ MALEDICTION

___ MANACLE

___ MUNIFICENCE

___ PRECLUDE

___ REGRESS

___ RETINUE

___ SUCCEED

___ TRANSCRIBE

1. v) to rub out; erase; to make inconspicuous

2. n) a gift of something over what is customary

3. n) a curse or slander; a calling down of evil

4. v) to interpret (new ideas, etc) by the help of past experience

5. a) situated around the sides; surrounding

6. n) a small part, amount, etc.; math a number less than a whole number

7. n) generosity in giving; lavishness

8. v) to make a written copy of notes; to adapt music for a different voice or instrument

9. v) to go back

10. n) a large pipe or conduit for bringing water from a distant source

11. v) to follow, as in office; to come after; to gain a favorable result

12. n) a group of persons attending an individual of rank or importance

13. v) to set an estimated value for taxation; to levy a tax or fine; to judge the value of

14. a) impudent; insolent; not relevant to the matter

15. n) an inflamed area in body tissues and containing pus

16. n) a group of people organized under a charter granting them as a body some of the legal rights of an individual

17. v) prevent; to make impossible (esp. in advance)

18. a) not easily perceived by the senses or the mind; very slight or subtle

19. n) a handcuff
    v) put handcuffs on; restrain

20. a) moving or tending to move away from the center

DIRECTIONS: Use your LATIN roots and affixes sheets; try to find the root in each vocabulary word. Write the root and its meaning; also circle the root in the vocabulary word.

vocabulary word	root	meaning
ABSCESS	_____	_____
APPERCEIVE	_____	_____
AQUEDUCT	_____	_____
ASSESS	_____	_____
BONUS	_____	_____
CENTRIFUGAL	_____	_____
CIRCUMJACENT	_____	_____
CORPORATION	_____	_____
EFFACE	_____	_____
FRACTION	_____	_____
IMPERCEPTIBLE	_____	_____
IMPERTINENT	_____	_____
MALEDICTION	_____	_____
MANACLE	_____	_____
MUNIFICENCE	_____	_____
PRECLUDE	_____	_____
REGRESS	_____	_____
RETINUE	_____	_____
SUCCEED	_____	_____
TRANSCRIBE	_____	_____

DIRECTIONS: Use your LATIN roots and affixes sheets; try to find the word that is represented by the meanings of the roots and affixes. Write the word in the blank.

1. _____ before + shut, close

2. _____ water + to lead

3. _____ back, again + to hold

4. _____ out, away + face

5. _____ good

6. _____ away, from + go, yield

7. _____ hand + small

8. _____ gift, service + to make, do + state, quality, act

9. _____ under + go, yield

10. _____ not + through + to hold + like, related to

11. _____ center + to flee + like, related to

12. _____ back, again + to step

13. _____ not + through + to take + able to be

14. _____ around + to throw + like, related to

15. _____ to break + state, quality, act

16. _____ to, at + to sit

17. _____ to, at + through + to take

18. _____ body + to make, do + state, quality, act

19. _____ across + to write

20. _____ bad, evil, ill + to speak + state, quality, act

DIRECTIONS: For each blank write one vocabulary word. All words will be used only once. Look for context clues in the sentence.

_____ 1. The witch issued a(n) --- against the king.

_____ 2. The duke's --- was composed of Swiss knights.

_____ 3. A wise man will --- his mistakes.

_____ 4. The chief showed his --- with a gift of silver.

_____ 5. The patient's condition will continue to --- if he loses more blood.

_____ 6. Normally that --- pays a quarterly dividend.

_____ 7. Few musicians can easily --- a piece of music.

_____ 8. The bailiff will rarely --- his prisoner in court.

_____ 9. The county likes to --- a property tax every year.

_____ 10. Much travel and experience aid one who must --- new situations on a regular basis.

_____ 11. The dog had a large, red --- on his neck.

_____ 12. The Romans built the ---, which brought water to the town of Nice in France.

_____ 13. In the effort to ---, some lose sight of reality.

_____ 14. The suburbs were --- to the old inner city.

_____ 15. Only the guide saw the --- movement in the brush.

_____ 16. The --- remark had no business in the discussion.

_____ 17. A generous boss may give a(n) --- at Christmas.

_____ 18. Lack of men and materiel did not --- their chance of victory.

_____ 19. Only a small --- of crop was destroyed by frost.

_____ 20. The --- force of the earth is balanced by the attraction of the sun.

DIRECTIONS: Use your LATIN roots and affixes sheets; try to match the definitions with the words; look at the roots, prefixes, and suffixes for clues. Do NOT use a dictionary except as a last resort.

___ ACCEDE   1. a) having ability; skilled; competent

___ ASSIZE   2. n) a steward or buyer of provisions (for an institution)

___ BOON   3. v) to foretell; to make known beforehand

___ CAPABLE   4. n) a body, esp. a dead one; a body of laws or writings

___ CONDUCT   5. v) to assent; agree to; enter upon the duties of

___ CONJECTURE   6. n) behavior; management
    v) to lead; escort; manage; direct; convey

___ CORPUS   7. n) origin; commencement; start; a beginning

___ EFFICACIOUS   8. v) support; to keep supplied; provide for; carry the burden of; endure; encourage

___ FRACTURE   9. n) a written or typewritten copy of proceedings

___ INCEPTION   10. n) court session held periodically in each county in England

___ MAINTAIN   11. a/v) a moving backward; retreating; going back to a previous condition; declining

___ MALCONDUCT   12. n) guesswork; a guess; predicting based on incomplete or uncertain evidence
    v) to guess

___ MANCIPLE   13. v) to keep up; carry on; continue on with; keep in existence; preserve; defend; support; affirm

___ ORIFICE   14. n/v) break; crack; split

___ PREDICT   15. v) to withdraw formal membership from a group

___ RECLUSE   16. n) an opening; mouth or outlet of a tube or cavity; vent

___ RETROGRADE   17. n) hermit; one who lives a solitary, secluded life

___ SECEDE   18. a) effective; having the intended result

___ SUSTAIN   19. n) improper behavior

___ TRANSCRIPT   20. n) a favor or request; blessing or welcome benefit

DIRECTIONS: Use your LATIN roots and affixes sheets; try to find the root in each vocabulary word. Write the root and its meaning; also circle the root in the vocabulary word.

vocabulary word	root	meaning
ACCEDE	_____	_____
ASSIZE	_____	_____
BOON	_____	_____
CAPABLE	_____	_____
CONDUCT	_____	_____
CONJECTURE	_____	_____
CORPUS	_____	_____
EFFICACIOUS	_____	_____
FRACTURE	_____	_____
INCEPTION	_____	_____
MAINTAIN	_____	_____
MALCONDUCT	_____	_____
MANCIPLE	_____	_____
ORIFICE	_____	_____
PREDICT	_____	_____
RECLUSE	_____	_____
RETROGRADE	_____	_____
SECEDE	_____	_____
SUSTAIN	_____	_____
TRANSCRIPT	_____	_____

DIRECTIONS: Use your LATIN roots and affixes sheets; try to find the word that is represented by the meanings of the roots and affixes. Write the word in the blank.

1. _____ good

2. _____ before + to speak

3. _____ in, into + to take + state, quality, act

4. _____ body + Latin ending

5. _____ to break + that which, state, quality, act

6. _____ to, at + go, yield

7. _____ mouth + to make, do

8. _____ to take + able to be

9. _____ bad, evil, ill + with, together + to lead

10. _____ out, away + to make, do + having the quality of

11. _____ backwards + to step

12. _____ under + to hold

13. _____ across + to write

14. _____ hand + to take + one who

15. _____ hand + to hold

16. _____ to, at + to sit + having the quality of

17. _____ apart + go, yield

18. _____ with, together + to throw + that which, state, quality

19. _____ back, again + shut, close

20. _____ with, together + to lead

DIRECTIONS: For each blank write one vocabulary word. All words will be used only once. Look for context clues in the sentence.

_____ 1. The strong man was --- of lifting all the weights.

_____ 2. The campaign was --- in changing the law.

_____ 3. The gardener was told to --- the lawn in good condition.

_____ 4. His --- behavior was evidenced by his increased consumption of alcohol and drugs.

_____ 5. The man suffered a bad --- from his fall.

_____ 6. The Confederacy did --- from the Union in the middle of the 19th century.

_____ 7. The fortune teller claimed to --- the future.

_____ 8. My uncle's help was a real --- to the family.

_____ 9. The university secured a(n) --- to manage all of its supply purchases and allocations.

_____ 10. A guide was hired to --- the party down the river.

_____ 11. A(n) --- of the seminar was available for $15.00.

_____ 12. At the --- of the group, the bylaws were formed.

_____ 13. Five criminals appeared at the quarterly ---.

_____ 14. An old --- lived in a cave above the river.

_____ 15. Harry's conclusion was pure ---.

_____ 16. Food and water are necessary to --- life.

_____ 17. The boy's --- earned him a bad reputation.

_____ 18. The enemy will --- to our terms after they lose to us in battle.

_____ 19. A small covering concealed the --- of the shaft.

_____ 20. Brad collected a large --- of his favorite author's works.

DIRECTIONS: Use your LATIN roots and affixes sheets; try to match the definitions with the words; look at the roots, prefixes, and suffixes for clues. Do NOT use a dictionary except as a last resort.

___ ABDUCT   1. n) a breaking of a law or pact; violation; infringement

___ ABJECT   2. v) procure; to get possession of

___ ACCEPT   3. n) Holy Writ; the Bible

___ ANCESTOR   4. n) a fraud or imposture; an illusion; a trick meant to mislead

___ ASSIDUOUS   5. a) relevant; to the point; related to the matter

___ CORPS   6. v) to move backward; decline; degenerate

___ DECEPTION   7. v) to contaminate with something producing disease; to corrupt; to affect with one's feelings or beliefs

___ DISMAL   8. n) device or artifice; plan to evade something disagreeable or unpleasant; a deception

___ EFFICIENT   9. v) to receive; approve; agree to; believe in

___ INFECT   10. a) solitude; retirement; isolation; privacy

___ INFRACTION   11. n) a roll of parchment; a scroll; one book of a set; amount of space occupied in three dimensions; bulk or quantity; loudness of sound

___ OBTAIN   12. a) busy; diligent; persevering; done with constant and careful attention

___ PERTINENT   13. a) effective; producing the desired effect with minimal effort, expense, or waste; working well

___ RETROCEDE   14. a) miserable; wretched; degraded

___ RETROGRESS   15. n) a farewell; something said in parting

___ SCRIPTURE   16. a) bleak; dreary; depressing; gloomy

___ SECLUSION   17. n) forebear; a person from whom one is descended

___ SUBTERFUGE   18. n) body of people united under common direction

___ VALEDICTION   19. v) to kidnap

___ VOLUME   20. v) to go back; recede

DIRECTIONS: Use your LATIN roots and affixes sheets; try to find the root in each vocabulary word. Write the root and its meaning; also circle the root in the vocabulary word.

vocabulary word	root	meaning
ABDUCT	_____	_____
ABJECT	_____	_____
ACCEPT	_____	_____
ANCESTOR	_____	_____
ASSIDUOUS	_____	_____
CORPS	_____	_____
DECEPTION	_____	_____
DISMAL	_____	_____
EFFICIENT	_____	_____
INFECT	_____	_____
INFRACTION	_____	_____
OBTAIN	_____	_____
PERTINENT	_____	_____
RETROCEDE	_____	_____
RETROGRESS	_____	_____
SCRIPTURE	_____	_____
SECLUSION	_____	_____
SUBTERFUGE	_____	_____
VALEDICTION	_____	_____
VOLUME	_____	_____

DIRECTIONS: Use your LATIN roots and affixes sheets: try to find the word that is represented by the meanings of the roots and affixes. Write the word in the blank.

1. _____ in, not + to make, do

2. _____ to write + that which, state, quality, act

3. _____ to, at + to take

4. _____ to roll + Latin ending?

5. _____ in, not + to break + state, quality, act

6. _____ through + to hold + like, related to

7. _____ before + go, yield

8. _____ down, away + to take + state, quality, act

9. _____ farewell + to speak + state, quality, act

10. _____ to, against + to hold

11. _____ backward + to step

12. _____ under + to flee

13. _____ away, from + to lead

14. _____ away, negative + bad, ill, evil

15. _____ apart + shut, close + state, quality, act

16. _____ away, from + to throw

17. _____ backward + go, yield

18. _____ out, away + to make, do + like, related to

19. _____ body

20. _____ to, at + to sit + having the quality of

DIRECTIONS: For each blank write one vocabulary word. All words will be used only once. Look for context clues in the sentence.

_____ 1. The weather report indicated a(n) --- weekend.

_____ 2. Infallible truth can be found anywhere in the ---.

_____ 3. The evolutionist believes he has a monkey for his ---.

_____ 4. The rancher wanted to --- water rights for irrigation purposes.

_____ 5. Individuals often seek --- upon retiring from public life.

_____ 6. The --- of a pyramid is computed with a formula.

_____ 7. The downcast look on his face evidenced his --- condition of mind.

_____ 8. The best scholar gave his --- at graduation.

_____ 9. Most of the points made were --- to the main discussion.

_____ 10. The boys fell for the --- and spent their money.

_____ 11. The newlyweds were happy to --- the gifts.

_____ 12. The condition of the property will --- without proper care and maintenance.

_____ 13. The most --- method usually is the cheapest.

_____ 14. His --- successfully got him out of the distasteful job situation.

_____ 15. The terrorists planned to --- the diplomat.

_____ 16. Eight boys were guilty of a major --- of school regulations.

_____ 17. The paratroopers formed an elite --- within the division.

_____ 18. The tide will --- for the next few hours.

_____ 19. Her --- nature made her an excellent worker.

_____ 20. The germ can --- anyone with blood types A or O.

DIRECTIONS: Use your LATIN roots and affixes sheets; try to match the definitions with the words; look at the roots, prefixes, and suffixes for clues. Do NOT use a dictionary except as a last resort.

___ ADDUCE

___ ADJACENT

___ ANTICIPATE

___ CLOSURE

___ CORPSE

___ FACET

___ FORCEPS

___ MAGNIFICENCE

___ MALADJUSTED

___ PERTAIN

___ PROCESSION

___ RECEDE

___ REFRACTORY

___ REFUGEE

___ RETENTION

___ SCRIBBLE

___ SEDATE

___ TRANSGRESS

___ VERDICT

___ VOLUMINOUS

1. n) a dead body, usually of a person

2. v) to belong; be connected with

3. v) to sin; to break a law or command; to go beyond a limit

4. n) a holding back; capacity for being held or kept

5. v) to give as a reason or proof

6. v) to move, go, or slope backward; diminish

7. a) calm or composed; serious and unemotional;
   v) to calm by giving drugs or medicine

8. a) hard to manage; obstinate

9. v) to look forward to; take care of in advance

10. v) to write carelessly or illegibly

11. n) small tongs or pincers for grasping, compressing, and pulling

12. n) one who flees his home or country to seek safety elsewhere

13. n) a phase; any of the surfaces of a cut gem; a side or aspect (of a personality or problem)

14. a) large; bulky; full

15. a) near or close; adjoining

16. n) a number of persons or things moving forward, as in a parade

17. n) a decision or judgment; the findings of a jury

18. n) richness and splendor; grandeur; stately or imposing beauty

19. n) a finish; end; conclusion; that which closes

20. a) not doing well in the situation; poorly adapted

DIRECTIONS: Use your LATIN roots and affixes sheets; try to find the root in each vocabulary word. Write the root and its meaning; also circle the root in the vocabulary word.

vocabulary word	root	meaning
ADDUCE	_____	_____
ADJACENT	_____	_____
ANTICIPATE	_____	_____
CLOSURE	_____	_____
CORPSE	_____	_____
FACET	_____	_____
FORCEPS	_____	_____
MAGNIFICENCE	_____	_____
MALADJUSTED	_____	_____
PERTAIN	_____	_____
PROCESSION	_____	_____
RECEDE	_____	_____
REFRACTORY	_____	_____
REFUGEE	_____	_____
RETENTION	_____	_____
SCRIBBLE	_____	_____
SEDATE	_____	_____
TRANSGRESS	_____	_____
VERDICT	_____	_____
VOLUMINOUS	_____	_____

DIRECTIONS: Use your LATIN roots and affixes sheets; try to find the word that is represented by the meanings of the roots and affixes. Write the word in the blank.

1. _____ back, again + to hold + state, quality, act

2. _____ across + to step

3. _____ back, again + to flee + one who

4. _____ before + to take + like, related to

5. _____ back, again + to break + like, related to

6. _____ true + to speak

7. _____ back, again + go, yield

8. _____ hot + to take + plural

9. _____ for, forward + go, yield + state, quality, act

10. _____ to write + small?

11. _____ body

12. _____ to roll + Latin ending? + having the quality of

13. _____ to, at + to lead

14. _____ bad, evil, ill + to, at + law, right + past action

15. _____ face + small

16. _____ through + to hold

17. _____ shut, close + that which

18. _____ to sit + to make, do

19. _____ to, at + to throw + like, related to

20. _____ great + to make, do + state, quality, act

DIRECTIONS: For each blank write one vocabulary word. All words will be used only once. Look for context clues in the sentence.

_____ 1. A misfit is one who may be ---.

_____ 2. Little children and careless students --- on their assignments.

_____ 3. They always --- their ancestors as proof of their nobility.

_____ 4. The --- was guilt by association.

_____ 5. The --- of the king's wardrobe was unbelievable.

_____ 6. The trees apparently --- in the distance.

_____ 7. Only one --- in the wall was breached by the enemy in the first assault.

_____ 8. A photographic memory has excellent ---.

_____ 9. The duke's retinue made a(n) --- in the hall.

_____ 10. The harvest brought a(n) --- quantity of zucchini.

_____ 11. Young people --- their birthdays more than adults.

_____ 12. If a people willfully --- the law, it is a sign their culture is in decay.

_____ 13. One --- of business is keeping the accounts.

_____ 14. About half the meeting will --- to the current building project.

_____ 15. The --- was very happy to cross the border.

_____ 16. A(n) --- property sits just across the fence.

_____ 17. The doctor used a(n) --- to pinch off the artery.

_____ 18. His --- expression belies his anger within.

_____ 19. One --- dog in the team caused many problems.

_____ 20. According to the coroner, the --- had been undiscovered for days.

LATIN II WORKSHEETS

DIRECTIONS: Use your LATIN roots and affixes sheets; try to match the definitions with the words; look at the roots, prefixes, and suffixes for clues. Do NOT use a dictionary except as a last resort.

_____ ACCIDENT

1. a) tenfold; ten times as large
   v) multiply by ten

_____ AMPHORA

2. n) system of signaling by lights, flags, & arms

_____ ASPECT

3. n) an element; a part; ingredient

_____ AUTOMOBILE

4. v) to sell oneself for unworthy purposes;
   n) a harlot

_____ COMPONENT

5. a) about to happen

_____ CONSECUTIVE

6. n) an unforeseen happening, often unfortunate in outcome

_____ CONTORT

7. v) to convey or send from one person or place to another; to allow passage of

_____ CONTROVERSY

8. v) to scatter; drive away; cause to vanish; disperse

_____ DECUPLE

9. v) to answer in words; echo; to respond by action

_____ DEVISE

10. a) a following in order; without interruption

_____ DISPEL

11. n) the way one appears; looks; view; exposure; phase

_____ IMPENDING

12. a) negligent; heedless; inattentive; unintentional

_____ INADVERTENT

13. n) a tall jar with narrow neck and two handles near the top

_____ METONYMY

14. v) to draw back in; to withdraw; recant

_____ PROSTITUTE

15. n) argument; debate; quarrel; dispute

_____ REPLY

16. n) device for regulating temperature, esp. heat

_____ RETRACT

17. n) a car, usually with four wheels and motor

_____ SEMAPHORE

18. n) use of the name of one thing for that of another associated with it

_____ THERMOSTAT

19. v) to think out; plan; invent; contrive

_____ TRANSMIT

20. v) deform; force out of shape by bending, twisting, etc.

DIRECTIONS: Use your LATIN roots and affixes sheets; try to find the root in each vocabulary word. Write the root and its meaning; also circle the root in the vocabulary word.

vocabulary word	root	meaning
ACCIDENT	_____	_____
AMPHORA	_____	_____
ASPECT	_____	_____
AUTOMOBILE	_____	_____
COMPONENT	_____	_____
CONSECUTIVE	_____	_____
CONTORT	_____	_____
CONTROVERSY	_____	_____
DECUPLE	_____	_____
DEVISE	_____	_____
DISPEL	_____	_____
IMPENDING	_____	_____
INADVERTENT	_____	_____
METONYMY	_____	_____
PROSTITUTE	_____	_____
REPLY	_____	_____
RETRACT	_____	_____
SEMAPHORE	_____	_____
THERMOSTAT	_____	_____
TRANSMIT	_____	_____

DIRECTIONS: Use your LATIN roots and affixes sheets; try to find the word that is represented by the meanings of the roots and affixes. Write the word in the blank.

1. _____ with, together + to place, put + that which

2. _____ across + to send

3. _____ heat + to stand, set

4. _____ to, toward + to fall, happen + like, related to

5. _____ down, away, negative + to see

6. _____ forth, before + to stand, set

7. _____ a sign + to carry, bear

8. _____ both + to carry, bear

9. _____ with, together + to twist

10. _____ not + to, toward + to turn + like, related to

11. _____ to, toward + to look

12. _____ back, again + to draw, drag

13. _____ in, into + to hang, weigh, pay + ppt ending

14. _____ self + to move + able to (be)

15. _____ ten + to fold

16. _____ away, negative + to push

17. _____ against, opposite + to turn + state, condition

18. _____ back, again + to fold

19. _____ with, together + to follow + that which

20. _____ change + name + state, condition

DIRECTIONS: For each blank write one vocabulary word. All words will be used only once. Look for context clues in the sentence.

_____ 1. The --- developed into a full-blown fistfight.

_____ 2. A(n) --- set for 70 degrees pleases most people.

_____ 3. The warrior's --- was to draw his sword and attack.

_____ 4. The salad lacked one vital --- to make it tasty.

_____ 5. The horse and carriage was replaced by the ---.

_____ 6. The turtle may --- its head and feet when in danger.

_____ 7. Rahab the --- hid the spies that Joshua had sent to Jericho.

_____ 8. The army sometimes uses --- to communicate.

_____ 9. Our long-term goal was to --- our production.

_____ 10. For an engaged couple, marriage is a(n) --- event.

_____ 11. A horrible --- happened at the bridge yesterday.

_____ 12. The numbers three, four, and five are ---.

_____ 13. A sword standing for war is an example of ---.

_____ 14. The engineer was able to --- our fears about the bridge.

_____ 15. The Greeks and Romans used the --- to store and carry many items.

_____ 16. Forgetting his book at home was a(n) --- mistake.

_____ 17. The station will --- signals every three hours.

_____ 18. The hero's physical --- was quite awesome.

_____ 19. It is wise to --- a plan ahead of time rather than just plunge ahead blindly.

_____ 20. A 180 degree turn of most things will --- them.

DIRECTIONS: Use your LATIN roots and affixes sheets; try to match the definitions with the words; look at the roots, prefixes, and suffixes for clues. Do NOT use a dictionary except as a last resort.

_____ AUSPICE

_____ AVERT

_____ CADAVER

_____ CIRCUMFERENCE

_____ COMMOTION

_____ COMPOSE

_____ COMPULSORY

_____ CONSEQUENCE

_____ DEPLOY

_____ DISTORT

_____ ENVISAGE

_____ INDEPENDENT

_____ INTROVERT

_____ MISNOMER

_____ PROSTATE

_____ SEXTUPLE

_____ SUBTRACT

_____ SURMISE

_____ SYSTEMIC

_____ TRANSFER

1. n) violent motion; turmoil; agitation; confusion; disturbance

2. v) to see in the mind; form a mental image

3. n) result; effect; logical conclusion; importance as a cause

4. n) a bad sign or prophecy

5. v) to take away or deduct

6. v) to bend inward
   n) person who dwells on himself

7. a) of or affecting the entire organism

8. v) to make up; to put together; to create; to calm; to adjust

9. v) to turn away; ward off; prevent

10. a) refers to a muscular gland at the base of a male's bladder

11. n) the distance around a circle

12. v) to move or send from one person, place, or position to another

13. a) required; obligatory; coercive; forced

14. v) to twist out of shape; misrepresent; misstate; pervert

15. n) a guess; a conjecture; idea formed from inconclusive evidence

16. a) free from influence or control of others; self-governing

17. n) act of applying the wrong name to a person or thing

18. n) a dead body; a corpse

19. v) to multiply by six
    a) six fold

20. v) to spread out to form a wider front of narrow depth

DIRECTIONS: Use your LATIN roots and affixes sheets; try to find the root in each vocabulary word. Write the root and its meaning; also circle the root in the vocabulary word.

vocabulary word	root	meaning
AUSPICE	_____	_____
AVERT	_____	_____
CADAVER	_____	_____
CIRCUMFERENCE	_____	_____
COMMOTION	_____	_____
COMPOSE	_____	_____
COMPULSORY	_____	_____
CONSEQUENCE	_____	_____
DEPLOY	_____	_____
DISTORT	_____	_____
ENVISAGE	_____	_____
INDEPENDENT	_____	_____
INTROVERT	_____	_____
MISNOMER	_____	_____
PROSTATE	_____	_____
SEXTUPLE	_____	_____
SUBTRACT	_____	_____
SURMISE	_____	_____
SYSTEMIC	_____	_____
TRANSFER	_____	_____

DIRECTIONS: Use your LATIN roots and affixes sheets; try to find the word that is represented by the meanings of the roots and affixes. Write the word in the blank.

1. _____ away + to twist

2. _____ with + to follow + state or quality

3. _____ bad + name + that which

4. _____ around + to carry, bear + state or quality

5. _____ under + to draw, drag

6. _____ not + down + to hang, weigh, pay + like

7. _____ bird + to look

8. _____ with + to push + like, related to

9. _____ above + to send

10. _____ six + to fold

11. _____ in + to see + state, quality, act

12. _____ with + to move + state, quality, act

13. _____ across + to carry, bear

14. _____ inward + to turn

15. _____ down + to fold

16. _____ to fall, happen

17. _____ for, forward + to stand, set

18. _____ from + to turn

19. _____ with + to stand, set + like, related to

20. _____ with + to place, put

DIRECTIONS: For each blank write one vocabulary word. All words will be used only once. Look for context clues in the sentence.

_____ 1. A(n) --- usually tries to avoid social contacts.

_____ 2. Well-behaved children are often the --- of loving and prompt discipline by parents.

_____ 3. Our --- about the outcome proved to be false.

_____ 4. The constant 3.14 is used to figure ---.

_____ 5. The --- increase in orders surprised everyone.

_____ 6. Some considered the vulture circling overhead as a poor --- for the upcoming battle.

_____ 7. People in the armed services often get --- orders.

_____ 8. A biased reporter will --- a news story.

_____ 9. The --- in the hall was a diversion for the escape.

_____ 10. The duchy hoped to remain --- of its large neighbor.

_____ 11. A good shield will --- most blows.

_____ 12. Greenland was a --- purposely applied to fool people.

_____ 13. It takes creativity to --- a work of art.

_____ 14. The suitor could --- his lover awaiting his call.

_____ 15. The --- poison worked its way into the whole tree.

_____ 16. A good field officer will know when to --- his troops under certain conditions.

_____ 17. The --- was examined by the county coroner to help determine the cause of death.

_____ 18. Even a tyro in math can --- simple numbers.

_____ 19. --- school attendance does not set well with some.

_____ 20. Older men often suffer from --- problems.

DIRECTIONS: Use your LATIN roots and affixes sheets; try to match the definitions with the words; look at the roots, prefixes, and suffixes for clues. Do NOT use a dictionary except as a last resort.

_____ CADENCE

_____ CATAPULT

_____ CIRCUMSPECT

_____ COMPOST

_____ CONFER

_____ DEMOTE

_____ DISPLAY

_____ ENVY

_____ EXECUTE

_____ EXTORT

_____ EXTROVERT

_____ INVERSE

_____ NOMENCLATURE

_____ PENCHANT

_____ PERSIST

_____ SUBMISSIVE

_____ SUPERSTITION

_____ SUSPECT

_____ TRACE

_____ TRIPLEX

1. v) bestow; discuss; converse; exchange ideas

2. n) person thought to have done a crime, etc.;
   v) to distrust; believe someone guilty with little or no evidence

3. v) to follow out or carry out; do; perform; administer; kill

4. n) a path or trail; a visible mark left by something; a barely observable quantity

5. a) reversed in order; directly opposite

6. n) flow of rhythm; beat; measured movement in dancing, etc.

7. v) to continue; refuse to quit; endure

8. a) threefold; triple
   n) house or building split into three separate living units

9. v) lower in rank; reduce to a lower grade

10. a) careful; cautious; attentive to all factors

11. n) a strong liking or fondness; inclination; taste

12. n) false belief in charms, omens, etc.; an attitude inconsistent with known laws of science

13. n) person who is active and expressive; one more interested in others than himself

14. v) to feel ill will at another for his advantages

15. n) a mixture of decaying vegetable refuse, manure, etc.

16. v) to get money by violence, threats, etc.

17. n) system of names used in a branch of learning

18. a) docile; yielding; giving in without resistance

19. v) to unfold; spread out; exhibit to advantage
    n) exhibition; show

20. v) to launch or leap
    n) ancient military device for throwing large objects

DIRECTIONS: Use your LATIN roots and affixes sheets; try to find the root in each vocabulary word. Write the root and its meaning; also circle the root in the vocabulary word.

vocabulary word	root	meaning
CADENCE	_____	_____
CATAPULT	_____	_____
CIRCUMSPECT	_____	_____
COMPOST	_____	_____
CONFER	_____	_____
DEMOTE	_____	_____
DISPLAY	_____	_____
ENVY	_____	_____
EXECUTE	_____	_____
EXTORT	_____	_____
EXTROVERT	_____	_____
INVERSE	_____	_____
NOMENCLATURE	_____	_____
PENCHANT	_____	_____
PERSIST	_____	_____
SUBMISSIVE	_____	_____
SUPERSTITION	_____	_____
SUSPECT	_____	_____
TRACE	_____	_____
TRIPLEX	_____	_____

DIRECTIONS: Use your LATIN roots and affixes sheets; try to find the word that is represented by the meanings of the roots and affixes. Write the word in the blank.

1. _____ out + to twist

2. _____ in + to turn

3. _____ down + to push

4. _____ under + to send + that which

5. _____ out + to follow

6. _____ to fall, to happen + state, quality, act

7. _____ three + to fold

8. _____ with + to place, to put

9. _____ to hang, to weigh, to pay + that which

10. _____ to draw, to drag

11. _____ away + to fold

12. _____ under + to look

13. _____ around + to look

14. _____ through + to stand, to set

15. _____ outside + to turn

16. _____ down + to move

17. _____ name + to call + that which

18. _____ in + to see

19. _____ above + to stand, to set + state, quality

20. _____ with + to carry, to bear

DIRECTIONS: For each blank write one vocabulary word. All words will be used only once. Look for context clues in the sentence.

_____ 1. A comedian or actor is usually a(n) ---.

_____ 2. The police dog found just a(n) --- of a smell.

_____ 3. The Bible says that a good wife is --- to her spouse.

_____ 4. The step beyond jealousy is ---.

_____ 5. The connoisseur had a(n) --- for fine wines.

_____ 6. The jury will --- about the case in private.

_____ 7. The --- of a fraction is its reciprocal.

_____ 8. The besiegers used their --- to throw fire over the walls into the castle.

_____ 9. The --- of macrobiotics is strange to most people.

_____ 10. A mixture of --- and vermiculite is excellent for use as potting soil.

_____ 11. The drummers keep the --- while the band marches.

_____ 12. The new store set up a big --- in their front window.

_____ 13. It is pure --- to think that breaking a mirror brings bad luck.

_____ 14. The criminal's aim was to --- one million dollars.

_____ 15. The glassblower was quite --- about his work.

_____ 16. Three generations lived together in the ---.

_____ 17. It was difficult to --- the faithful captain due to his age and infirmity.

_____ 18. The shifty-eyed character in black was the prime ---.

_____ 19. The officer could be counted on to properly --- his commands no matter how tough they were.

_____ 20. A strong salesman will --- until he gets the sale.

DIRECTIONS: Use your LATIN roots and affixes sheets; try to match the definitions with the words; look at the roots, prefixes, and suffixes for clues. Do NOT use a dictionary except as a last resort.

_____ APPEAL

_____ CADENZA

_____ COMPOUND

_____ CONSPICUOUS

_____ DEFERENCE

_____ DIVERTICULUM

_____ DUPLEX

_____ EVIDENCE

_____ EXTRACT

_____ EXTRINSIC

_____ MOBILE

_____ NOMINAL

_____ OBSTINATE

_____ OBVERSE

_____ PENDULOUS

_____ REMISS

_____ SUBSTITUTE

_____ SUSPICIOUS

_____ TRACTABLE

_____ TRIPLICATE

1. n) a thing formed by two or more elements
   v) to mix or combine; compute interest at intervals

2. n) a pouch or sac opening out of a tubular organ or main cavity

3. a) swinging; hanging freely (no rigid connection)

4. a) arousing feelings of caution or mistrust

5. v) to draw out by effort; pull out; obtain by pressing, drilling, boiling, etc.
   n) a concentrated form; an excerpt

6. a) movable; can be moved

7. a) easily managed, taught, or controlled; docile; obedient

8. v) to make urgent request; to be attractive
   n) a call or request

9. a) stubborn; resisting remedy; not yielding to reason or plea

10. a) double; two fold
    n) a house or apartment with two units in it

11. n) honor; courteous regard; yielding in opinion, wishes, etc.

12. a) turned to the observer
    n) side of a coin with the main image on it

13. a) extraneous; not inherent; belongs outside

14. v) to put in place of another
    n) one put in place of another

15. n) an elaborate musical solo played in a concerto, usually near the end of the first movement

16. n) made in three identical copies

17. n) proof; indication; sign; ground for belief

18. a) irresponsible; lax in performance of duty

19. a) in name but not in fact; very small or slight in comparison to expectations

20. a) noticeable; easy to see; obvious; remarkable

DIRECTIONS: Use your LATIN roots and affixes sheets; try to find the root in each vocabulary word. Write the root and its meaning; also circle the root in the vocabulary word.

vocabulary word	root	meaning
APPEAL	_____	_____
CADENZA	_____	_____
COMPOUND	_____	_____
CONSPICUOUS	_____	_____
DEFERENCE	_____	_____
DIVERTICULUM	_____	_____
DUPLEX	_____	_____
EVIDENCE	_____	_____
EXTRACT	_____	_____
EXTRINSIC	_____	_____
MOBILE	_____	_____
NOMINAL	_____	_____
OBSTINATE	_____	_____
OBVERSE	_____	_____
PENDULOUS	_____	_____
REMISS	_____	_____
SUBSTITUTE	_____	_____
SUSPICIOUS	_____	_____
TRACTABLE	_____	_____
TRIPLICATE	_____	_____

DIRECTIONS: Use your LATIN roots and affixes sheets; try to find the word that is represented by the meanings of the roots and affixes. Write the word in the blank.

1. _____ away + to turn + Latin ending

2. _____ out + to draw, to drag

3. _____ name + like, related to

4. _____ to move + like

5. _____ under + to stand, set + ??

6. _____ with + to place, to put

7. _____ with + to look + having the quality of

8. _____ to, toward + to stand, set + having quality of

9. _____ three + to fold + having the quality of

10. _____ out + to see + state, quality

11. _____ outside + to follow

12. _____ to, at, against + to push

13. _____ down + to send

14. _____ under + to look + quality of

15. _____ back, again + to send

16. _____ to, toward + to turn

17. _____ to fall

18. _____ to draw, drag + able to

19. _____ two + to fold

20. _____ to hang, weigh, pay + having the quality of

DIRECTIONS: For each blank write one vocabulary word. All words will be used only once. Look for context clues in the sentence.

_____ 1. The --- is a common housing unit in some areas.

_____ 2. A chemical --- may be dangerous or harmless.

_____ 3. The collector studied the --- of the coin carefully.

_____ 4. There was ample --- that the dog had ruined the paper.

_____ 5. His master had been --- of such behavior before.

_____ 6. The soloist's --- moved everyone in the hall to tears.

_____ 7. A cow is usually considered a(n) --- animal.

_____ 8. If it's not nailed down, it's probably ---.

_____ 9. His --- to the king was obvious to all.

_____ 10. Many business forms come in ---.

_____ 11. The man's ulcer was located at a(n) ---.

_____ 12. The old man was more --- than his mule.

_____ 13. The green marble was very --- among all the yellow marbles.

_____ 14. Most people receive at least one --- for money each month from some organization.

_____ 15. Money is no --- for happiness.

_____ 16. The firemen used special tools to --- the man from his mangled car.

_____ 17. The sentry was --- for sleeping at his post.

_____ 18. A fee of five dollars was only a(n) --- sum.

_____ 19. Life forms that breathe chlorine are --- to earth.

_____ 20. The clapper in a bell is described as ---.

DIRECTIONS: Use your LATIN roots and affixes sheets; try to match the definitions with the words; look at the roots, prefixes, and suffixes for clues. Do NOT use a dictionary except as a last resort.

_____ ACCOMPLICE

_____ ARMISTICE

_____ CASCADE

_____ DEPOSIT

_____ DESPICABLE

_____ DIFFERENTIATE

_____ DIVERT

_____ DUPLICATE

_____ IMPROVISE

_____ INTRINSIC

_____ MOTIVATE

_____ NOMINATE

_____ OBSTACLE

_____ PENSION

_____ PERVERSION

_____ PROMISE

_____ REPULSIVE

_____ SUBSTANTIATE

_____ TART

_____ TRACTION

1. n) truce or temporary stopping of warfare by mutual agreement

2. v) to compose or perform on the spot without preparation

3. n) regular payment made after retirement

4. a) inherent; essential; belonging to

5. a) disgusting; offensive; causing strong dislike

6. n) a pulling over a surface; adhesive friction

7. n) small, steep waterfall; a shower
   v) to fall in ripples or showers

8. a) sharp in taste; sour; acid; sharp in answering
   n) small pastry shell filled with jam, jelly, etc.

9. v) amuse; entertain; deflect; turn aside

10. a) contemptible; that which is scorned

11. v) to give evidence of; confirm; prove

12. n) a partner in crime

13. a) corresponding exactly
    n) exact copy
    v) to do again; reproduce exactly

14. v) to make unlike; tell apart; distinguish

15. n) an abnormal form; something wicked or contrary

16. n) anything that hinders; obstruction

17. v) incite; to provide with motives

18. v) to place for safekeeping; to leave lying
    n) money in the bank; a pledge of payment; something left lying

19. v) to pledge or give a basis for expectation
    n) a vow; agreement to do or not do something

20. v) to name a person as a candidate for election or appointment

DIRECTIONS: Use your LATIN roots and affixes sheets; try to find the root in each vocabulary word. Write the root and its meaning; also circle the root in the vocabulary word.

vocabulary word	root	meaning
ACCOMPLICE	_____	_____
ARMISTICE	_____	_____
CASCADE	_____	_____
DEPOSIT	_____	_____
DESPICABLE	_____	_____
DIFFERENTIATE	_____	_____
DIVERT	_____	_____
DUPLICATE	_____	_____
IMPROVISE	_____	_____
INTRINSIC	_____	_____
MOTIVATE	_____	_____
NOMINATE	_____	_____
OBSTACLE	_____	_____
PENSION	_____	_____
PERVERSION	_____	_____
PROMISE	_____	_____
REPULSIVE	_____	_____
SUBSTANTIATE	_____	_____
TART	_____	_____
TRACTION	_____	_____

DIRECTIONS: Use your LATIN roots and affixes sheets; try to find the word that is represented by the meanings of the roots and affixes. Write the word in the blank.

1. _____ to twist

2. _____ away + to turn

3. _____ to hang, weigh, pay + state, quality, act

4. _____ down, away + to look + able to be

5. _____ name + to do

6. _____ two + to fold + to do

7. _____ to draw, to drag + state, quality, act

8. _____ apart + to carry, bear + like + to do

9. _____ arms + to stand, set

10. _____ to, toward, against + to stand, set + small

11. _____ under + to stand, set + that which + to do

12. _____ to fall

13. _____ to move + that which + to do

14. _____ in, into, not + before + to see

15. _____ back, again + to push + that which

16. _____ to, at + with + to fold

17. _____ through + to turn + state, quality, act

18. _____ inward + to follow

19. _____ down, away + to place, put

20. _____ for, forward + to send

DIRECTIONS: For each blank write one vocabulary word. All words will be used only once. Look for context clues in the sentence.

_____   1. A good actor can --- at a moment's notice.

_____   2. The lemon has a(n) --- taste to it.

_____   3. Lying is a(n) --- of moral behavior.

_____   4. It may be an honor to --- a person for a position.

_____   5. A large purchase often requires a(n) --- of some size.

_____   6. Some people will --- anything just to get their way.

_____   7. His --- in the theft was a trained monkey.

_____   8. The moat was a(n) --- for the attacking knights.

_____   9. The sparks fell in a(n) --- from the welding table.

_____   10. Sandbags are often used to --- flooding waters.

_____   11. Icy roads afford little --- at even low speeds.

_____   12. A good show judge can --- between two closely matched contestants.

_____   13. Gold coins have a(n) --- value.

_____   14. The villain was quite a(n) --- character.

_____   15. The veteran received his --- once each month.

_____   16. A snail in your soup is a(n) --- sight.

_____   17. A copy machine can --- many different documents.

_____   18. The --- lasted only 13 hours before an attack came.

_____   19. A rich reward will often --- a strong performance.

_____   20. The witness will --- the defendant's claims.

DIRECTIONS: Use your LATIN roots and affixes sheets; try to match the definitions with the words; look at the roots, prefixes, and suffixes for clues. Do NOT use a dictionary except as a last resort.

_____ APPLICANT

_____ ASSIST

_____ CASUALTY

_____ DESPITE

_____ DISPOSE

_____ DIVERSIFY

_____ DUPLICITY

_____ FERRY

_____ INTERVIEW

_____ METASTASIS

_____ MOTIVE

_____ NOMINATIVE

_____ OBSEQUIOUS

_____ PENSIVE

_____ PREMISE

_____ REPEL

_____ RETORT

_____ RETROVERSION

_____ SUBSIST

_____ TRACTILE

1. v) to take across a river or narrow water body
   n) a boat which does the above

2. v) to turn an insult or deed back on a person
   n) a sharp, witty reply

3. v) to vary; give variety to; to make different

4. a) ductile; tensile; can be drawn out in length

5. n) one who requests employment, help, aid, etc.

6. v) to continue to exist; remain barely alive

7. v) to drive back; force back; ward off; cause a dislike or distaste in; spurn or refuse

8. a) named or appointed as opposed to elected; in grammar the subjective case

9. a) thinking deeply or seriously; thoughtful or reflective, often with sadness

10. n) anyone hurt or killed in an accident or war; a bad accident, especially a fatal one

11. n) a turning or tilting backward

12. n) a meeting of people face to face to confer

13. n) contemptuous act; injury; insult
    prep) notwithstanding; in spite of

14. a) servile; overly submissive; overly willing to do service

15. n) hypocritical cunning or deception; double-dealing

16. n) a shift of disease from one part of the body to another

17. v) to help or aid
    n) act of helping

18. n) a previous statement serving as the basis for an argument

19. n) inner drive that causes one to do something; incentive; goal

20. v) to put in order; arrange or settle matters; throw away; sell; bestow; get rid of

DIRECTIONS: Use your LATIN roots and affixes sheets; try to find the root in each vocabulary word. Write the root and its meaning; also circle the root in the vocabulary word.

vocabulary word	root	meaning
APPLICANT	_____	_____
ASSIST	_____	_____
CASUALTY	_____	_____
DESPITE	_____	_____
DISPOSE	_____	_____
DIVERSIFY	_____	_____
DUPLICITY	_____	_____
FERRY	_____	_____
INTERVIEW	_____	_____
METASTASIS	_____	_____
MOTIVE	_____	_____
NOMINATIVE	_____	_____
OBSEQUIOUS	_____	_____
PENSIVE	_____	_____
PREMISE	_____	_____
REPEL	_____	_____
RETORT	_____	_____
RETROVERSION	_____	_____
SUBSIST	_____	_____
TRACTILE	_____	_____

DIRECTIONS: Use your LATIN roots and affixes sheets; try to find the word that is represented by the meanings of the roots and affixes. Write the word in the blank.

1. _____ change + to stand (standing)

2. _____ under + to stand, set

3. _____ back + to twist

4. _____ away + to place, put

5. _____ back + to push

6. _____ two + to fold + state, quality

7. _____ before + to send

8. _____ away + to turn + to do

9. _____ between + to see

10. _____ to hang, weigh, pay + having the quality of

11. _____ down, away + to look

12. _____ to, at + to stand, set

13. _____ backward + to turn + state, quality, act

14. _____ to, toward + to follow + having the quality of

15. _____ to fall, happen + related to + state, quality

16. _____ to drag, draw + like, able to be

17. _____ to, at + to fold + one who

18. _____ name + to do + that which

19. _____ to carry, bear + quality

20. _____ to move + that which

DIRECTIONS: For each blank write one vocabulary word. All words will be used only once. Look for context clues in the sentence.

_____   1. His quick --- to the heckler pleased the crowd.

_____   2. A dog was the only --- in the accident.

_____   3. The crime had no apparent --- at first.

_____   4. The silver wire had a(n) --- quality to it.

_____   5. We took the --- over to Long Island.

_____   6. The boy seemed --- after hearing the news.

_____   7. She was the one --- accepted out of all those who tried.

_____   8. The cancer went into --- and spread rapidly.

_____   9. The home guard was able to --- the invaders.

_____   10. The defenders fought well --- their lack of numbers.

_____   11. A quick --- in basketball often means two points.

_____   12. Some people are able to --- on almost no food at all.

_____   13. After the --- both parties seemed pleased.

_____   14. It is difficult to --- of something one likes.

_____   15. The position of fund-raiser was ---, not elective.

_____   16. The devil is known for his --- when making bargains.

_____   17. The gyroscope seemed to be in --- most of the time.

_____   18. If the --- is false, the conclusion will fail.

_____   19. It is wise to --- one's investments.

_____   20. The --- dog slavered about his master's feet.

DIRECTIONS: Use your LATIN roots and affixes sheets; try to match the definitions with the words; look at the roots, prefixes, and suffixes for clues. Do NOT use a dictionary except as a last resort.

_____ APPLIQUÉ

_____ CIRCUMSTANCE

_____ COINCIDE

_____ CONVERT

_____ EMPLOY

_____ EXPOSE

_____ FERTILE

_____ INSPECT

_____ INTERSTICE

_____ INVIDIOUS

_____ MUTINY

_____ PATRONYMIC

_____ PENTHOUSE

_____ PERMISSION

_____ PERSECUTE

_____ REPEAL

_____ REVERT

_____ STAUNCH

_____ TORMENT

_____ TRAIT

1. n) apartment built on the roof of a building

2. v) occur at the same time; agree; take the same place at the same time; be alike

3. v) to leave unprotected; abandon; reveal; disclose

4. v) return; go back in action, thought or speech

5. n) a revolt against authority, especially sailors versus their officers

6. v) abolish; cancel; annul; withdraw officially

7. a) fastened on; said of one material sewed on another

8. n) a distinguishing quality or characteristic

9. v) to change; transform; turn; exchange
n) a person who changed

10. a) producing abundantly; rich; fruitful

11. v) to wrong; oppress cruelly; to injure or distress by harassment

12. a) exciting ill will or envy; giving offense

13. n) great pain or anguish, physical or mental
v) to cause agony; to harass

14. v) to make use of; to hire; to keep busy

15. n) condition, factor, or event; surrounding detail

16. v) stop the flow of blood or other body fluid
a) faithful; firm; trustworthy; strong

17. n) a small, narrow crack between things; crevice; crack; chink

18. n) a family name; surname
a) derived from the name of a father or ancestor

19. n) formal consent; leave; allowance

20. v) to look at carefully; examine critically; scrutinize

DIRECTIONS: Use your LATIN roots and affixes sheets; try to find the root in each vocabulary word. Write the root and its meaning; also circle the root in the vocabulary word.

vocabulary word	root	meaning
APPLIQUÉ	_____	_____
CIRCUMSTANCE	_____	_____
COINCIDE	_____	_____
CONVERT	_____	_____
EMPLOY	_____	_____
EXPOSE	_____	_____
FERTILE	_____	_____
INSPECT	_____	_____
INTERSTICE	_____	_____
INVIDIOUS	_____	_____
MUTINY	_____	_____
PATRONYMIC	_____	_____
PENTHOUSE	_____	_____
PERMISSION	_____	_____
PERSECUTE	_____	_____
REPEAL	_____	_____
REVERT	_____	_____
STAUNCH	_____	_____
TORMENT	_____	_____
TRAIT	_____	_____

DIRECTIONS: Use your LATIN roots and affixes sheets; try to find the word that is represented by the meanings of the roots and affixes. Write the word in the blank.

1. _____ between + to stand, set

2. _____ out, away + to place, put

3. _____ to stand, set

4. _____ to draw, drag

5. _____ father + name + like, related to

6. _____ with, together + upon + to fall, happen

7. _____ through + to follow + ??

8. _____ back, again + to turn

9. _____ through + to send + state, quality, act

10. _____ in, into + to look

11. _____ back, again + to push

12. _____ to carry, bear + able to

13. _____ around + to stand, set + state, quality

14. _____ to move + French ending

15. _____ with, together + to turn

16. _____ to, at, against + to fold

17. _____ to twist + state, quality, act

18. _____ in, into + to see + having the quality of

19. _____ to hang, weigh, pay + house

20. _____ in, into + to fold

DIRECTIONS: For each blank write one vocabulary word. All words will be used only once. Look for context clues in the sentence.

_____ 1. Captain Bligh was involved in a(n) ---.

_____ 2. The new store will --- over 80 people next year.

_____ 3. The broker's --- overlooked much of the city.

_____ 4. Our dog causes much --- for our three cats.

_____ 5. A single --- ruined our weekend camping trip.

_____ 6. --- is required before such action can take place.

_____ 7. Reformed addicts may --- to previous habits at times.

_____ 8. The --- technique can create interesting art on cloth.

_____ 9. The black loam was quite a(n) --- soil.

_____ 10. Tonto is a(n) --- friend of the Lone Ranger.

_____ 11. It is rare for two birthdays to --- in one family.

_____ 12. History proves that communists --- Christians.

_____ 13. The --- spoke much of his previous life of crime.

_____ 14. It is wise to --- a home before buying it.

_____ 15. Generosity was his outstanding ---.

_____ 16. The --- allowed a small draft into the room.

_____ 17. A person's last name is usually a(n) ---.

_____ 18. A major effort took place to --- the new tax.

_____ 19. A poor husband and father will --- his family to harm.

_____ 20. The slave's presence was --- to the pampered rich boy.

DIRECTIONS: Use your LATIN roots and affixes sheets; try to match the definitions with the words; look at the roots, prefixes, and suffixes for clues. Do NOT use a dictionary except as a last resort.

_____ COMPLEX

_____ CONVERSE

_____ DECADENCE

_____ EXPLICATE

_____ EXPOUND

_____ INSTITUTION

_____ INTROSPECTIVE

_____ INVISIBLE

_____ OMISSION

_____ PERPENDICULAR

_____ PROMOTE

_____ PROSECUTE

_____ PSEUDONYM

_____ PULSATE

_____ STATURE

_____ SUBVERSIVE

_____ SUFFER

_____ TORQUE

_____ TREATISE

_____ VOCIFEROUS

1. v) to set forth in detail; interpret

2. n) assumed name; false name; a pen name

3. a) hidden; out of sight; not apparent

4. n) a formal book or essay on some subject

5. n) height of body in normal standing position; development figuratively reached

6. a) vertical; upright; at right angles to

7. a) involved; intricate; not simple
   n) an obsession or fear; a group of buildings

8. n) a twisted metal collar or necklace; a force producing a twisting motion

9. n) establishment; established laws or customs; organization having religious, civic, or educational purposes

10. v) follow something to completion; carry on or practice; bring legal proceedings against

11. a) making a loud outcry; clamorous; shouting noisily

12. n) a falling away; a period of decline in morals, art, literature, etc.

13. n) something left out, not included, or neglected

14. a) tending to overthrow or destroy
    n) one who does the above

15. v) to make clear or explain

16. v) advance; raise to higher position; to further a cause

17. v) to talk or speak
    a) reversed in position; turned about

18. v) to undergo something painful or unpleasant; to allow or permit; tolerate

19. v) to beat or throb rhythmically; vibrate; quiver

20. a) inclined toward self-analysis and observation

DIRECTIONS: Use your LATIN roots and affixes sheets; try to find the root in each vocabulary word. Write the root and its meaning; also circle the root in the vocabulary word.

vocabulary word	root	meaning
COMPLEX	_____	_____
CONVERSE	_____	_____
DECADENCE	_____	_____
EXPLICATE	_____	_____
EXPOUND	_____	_____
INSTITUTION	_____	_____
INTROSPECTIVE	_____	_____
INVISIBLE	_____	_____
OMISSION	_____	_____
PERPENDICULAR	_____	_____
PROMOTE	_____	_____
PROSECUTE	_____	_____
PSEUDONYM	_____	_____
PULSATE	_____	_____
STATURE	_____	_____
SUBVERSIVE	_____	_____
SUFFER	_____	_____
TORQUE	_____	_____
TREATISE	_____	_____
VOCIFEROUS	_____	_____

DIRECTIONS: Use your LATIN roots and affixes sheets; try to find the word that is represented by the meanings of the roots and affixes. Write the word in the blank.

1. _____ down, away + to fall, happen + state, quality

2. _____ to push + to do

3. _____ under + to turn + one who

4. _____ out, away + to place, put

5. _____ for, forward + to follow + ?

6. _____ to twist

7. _____ in + to stand, set + state, quality

8. _____ to call + to carry, bear + having quality of

9. _____ with, together + to fold

10. _____ in, not + to see + able to

11. _____ to stand, set + state, quality

12. _____ to, toward + to send + state, quality

13. _____ with, together + to turn

14. _____ for, forward + to move

15. _____ under + to carry, bear

16. _____ through + to hang, weigh, pay + like, related to

17. _____ out, away + to fold + to do

18. _____ to draw, drag + to make, to act

19. _____ false + name

20. _____ inward + to look + state, quality

DIRECTIONS: For each blank write one vocabulary word. All words will be used only once. Look for context clues in the sentence.

_____   1. The speaker would --- on his favorite topic for hours.

_____   2. Some authors write under a(n) ---.

_____   3. A quiet person is likely to be somewhat --- in nature.

_____   4. Advertisers are paid to --- a product.

_____   5. --- elements in society can wreck a government.

_____   6. Good teachers will --- the material to their students.

_____   7. A heart that does not --- has serious problems.

_____   8. A right triangle has one --- corner.

_____   9. Today one can find a(n) --- on most any subject.

_____   10. A martyr is called to --- for his cause.

_____   11. It is tough to --- with lots of background noise.

_____   12. Mechanics use the --- wrench for precise tightening.

_____   13. Many people believe modern music is a sign of ---.

_____   14. A district attorney will --- the case.

_____   15. The criminal had a(n) --- about being followed.

_____   16. The crowd was --- in its denunciation of the man.

_____   17. The wind is ---, yet we can see its effects.

_____   18. The --- of one word changed the meaning of the essay.

_____   19. The candidate's moral --- was above reproach.

_____   20. The church is a venerable --- in Western societies.

DIRECTIONS: Use your LATIN roots and affixes sheets; try to match the definitions with the words; look at the roots, prefixes, and suffixes for clues. Do NOT use a dictionary except as a last resort.

_____ ABSTRACT

_____ DECIDUOUS

_____ IMPLICATE

_____ IMPOSE

_____ INSTANTANEOUS

_____ MISSIONARY

_____ PERSPECTIVE

_____ PREFERABLE

_____ PREVIEW

_____ PROPULSION

_____ PURSUE

_____ RECOMPENSE

_____ RECREANT

_____ REMOTE

_____ RENOWN

_____ SPECIOUS

_____ STATISTIC

_____ TORSION

_____ TRAVERSE

_____ VOCATION

1. n) one sent by the church to teach, preach, etc.

2. a) first choice; more desirable than others

3. a) seems good without being so; plausible but not genuine

4. a) crying for mercy; cowardly; disloyal
   n) a coward; traitor; disloyal person

5. v) to pass over; go across; to cross and recross

6. v) to follow in order to overtake, capture, etc.; to strive for; seek after; carry on

7. v) to twist or fold together; entangle; involve; to show to be a party

8. a) not concrete; theoretical
   n) summary; brief statement of the essence

9. v) to repay; make up for a loss
   n) repayment or remuneration

10. n) twisting; having one end firm and turning the other along a longitudinal axis

11. n) fame; great reputation; celebrity

12. a) immediate; without delay; done or happening in a moment

13. a) falling off at a certain season or stage; shedding leaves annually

14. n) a factual item; data of a numerical type

15. a) distant in space; far off; hidden away; secluded; faint or slight; not immediate

16. v) to show beforehand;
    n) private early showing

17. n) the career to which one is called; profession or trade

18. v) to place a burden or tax on; to force oneself on others; obtrude

19. n) a moving forward; a forward thrust or force

20. n) the showing of depth or distance on a flat drawing; view from a specific point and time

DIRECTIONS: Use your LATIN roots and affixes sheets; try to find the root in each vocabulary word. Write the root and its meaning; also circle the root in the vocabulary word.

vocabulary word	root	meaning
ABSTRACT	_____	_____
DECIDUOUS	_____	_____
IMPLICATE	_____	_____
IMPOSE	_____	_____
INSTANTANEOUS	_____	_____
MISSIONARY	_____	_____
PERSPECTIVE	_____	_____
PREFERABLE	_____	_____
PREVIEW	_____	_____
PROPULSION	_____	_____
PURSUE	_____	_____
RECOMPENSE	_____	_____
RECREANT	_____	_____
REMOTE	_____	_____
RENOWN	_____	_____
SPECIOUS	_____	_____
STATISTIC	_____	_____
TORSION	_____	_____
TRAVERSE	_____	_____
VOCATION	_____	_____

DIRECTIONS: Use your LATIN roots and affixes sheets; try to find the word that is represented by the meanings of the roots and affixes. Write the word in the blank.

1. _____ in, into + to put, place

2. _____ to twist + state, quality, act

3. _____ to send + state, quality + one who

4. _____ back, again + with + to hang, weigh, pay

5. _____ in, into + to fold + to do

6. _____ back, again + name

7. _____ through + to look + having the power of

8. _____ to call, voice + to do + state, quality, act

9. _____ for, forward + to follow

10. _____ down, away + to fall, happen + having quality of

11. _____ to look + having the quality of

12. _____ back, again + to move

13. _____ before + to carry, bear + able to be

14. _____ to stand, set + like, related to

15. _____ from, away + to draw, drag

16. _____ for, forward + to push + state, quality, act

17. _____ across + to turn

18. _____ before + to see

19. _____ back, again + to believe + one who

20. _____ in, into + to stand, set + having quality of

DIRECTIONS: For each blank write one vocabulary word. All words will be used only once. Look for context clues in the sentence.

_____   1. Theaters often show a(n) --- of coming attractions.

_____   2. Judas Iscariot is known as a famous ---.

_____   3. One type of --- tree is the birch family.

_____   4. Rock climbers often attempt to --- a rock face.

_____   5. The --- from Africa presented a talk at church.

_____   6. One vital --- is a person's pulse rate.

_____   7. Practical people do not go much for --- ideas.

_____   8. Sgt. Preston would --- his quarry to the North Pole.

_____   9. The chance of winning a million dollars is ---.

_____   10. One's --- of life tends to change with experience.

_____   11. Newer cars come with --- bars as standard equipment.

_____   12. The spy will --- all members of the terrorist squad.

_____   13. Nursing is a worthy --- for people to follow.

_____   14. The state wishes to --- a new tax on the people.

_____   15. Jet --- is a common force for driving airplanes.

_____   16. Most folks would say ice cream is --- to dry crackers.

_____   17. It was impossible to --- the small boy for his dog.

_____   18. The cowboy hero enjoys great --- among western fans.

_____   19. Seeing the prize caused a(n) --- change in the man.

_____   20. The --- document survived casual glances by the guards

DIRECTIONS: Use your LATIN roots and affixes sheets; try to match the definitions with the words; look at the roots, prefixes, and suffixes for clues. Do NOT use a dictionary except as a last resort.

_____ ATTRACT

_____ IMPOST

_____ INCIDENTAL

_____ INSISTENT

_____ MISCREANT

_____ MISSILE

_____ MULTIPLICITY

_____ PERSPICACIOUS

_____ PROPEL

_____ PROPENSITY

_____ PROVIDENTIAL

_____ REMOVE

_____ SECT

_____ SOMNIFEROUS

_____ SPECTACLE

_____ STATIC

_____ SYNONYM

_____ TORT

_____ UNIVERSE

_____ VOCAL

1. a) demanding; persistent in demands or assertions

2. n) a word having a similar meaning to another word in the same language

3. a) uttered, produced, or performed by the voice; spoken or sung

4. v) to push, drive, or force onward or ahead

5. n) a tax, especially on imported goods; a customs duty

6. a) inducing sleep; soporific

7. a) a natural inclination or tendency

8. a) villainous; evil
   n) evil person; villain; criminal

9. a) decreed by God; fortunate

10. n) a wrongful act or injury for which a civil action may be brought

11. n) group of people having common leadership, views, etc.

12. v) to draw to itself; to get attention; allure

13. n) electrical discharges that interfere with radio
    a) not moving or progressing; at rest; unmoving

14. n) all of creation; totality of existing things

15. n) a great number; quality of being many

16. v) to take something from where it is; to wipe out; to take off

17. a) acutely perceptive; shrewd; having keen insight

18. a) secondary or minor; happens in connection with something more important

19. n) something remarkable to look at; unusual sight

20. n) weapon or object designed to be shot or thrown

DIRECTIONS: Use your LATIN roots and affixes sheets; try to find the root in each vocabulary word. Write the root and its meaning; also circle the root in the vocabulary word.

vocabulary word	root	meaning
ATTRACT	_____	_____
IMPOST	_____	_____
INCIDENTAL	_____	_____
INSISTENT	_____	_____
MISCREANT	_____	_____
MISSILE	_____	_____
MULTIPLICITY	_____	_____
PERSPICACIOUS	_____	_____
PROPEL	_____	_____
PROPENSITY	_____	_____
PROVIDENTIAL	_____	_____
REMOVE	_____	_____
SECT	_____	_____
SOMNIFEROUS	_____	_____
SPECTACLE	_____	_____
STATIC	_____	_____
SYNONYM	_____	_____
TORT	_____	_____
UNIVERSE	_____	_____
VOCAL	_____	_____

DIRECTIONS: Use your LATIN roots and affixes sheets; try to find the word that is represented by the meanings of the roots and affixes. Write the word in the blank.

1. _____ for, forward + to push

2. _____ to look + that which

3. _____ bad + to believe + one who, like, related to

4. _____ one + to turn

5. _____ for, forward + to hang, weigh, pay + state, quality

6. _____ in, into + to fall, happen + that which + like

7. _____ to twist

8. _____ to stand, set + like, related to

9. _____ for, forward + to see + that which + like, related

10. _____ to call, voice + like, related to

11. _____ in, into + to place, put

12. _____ many + to fold + state, quality, act

13. _____ in, into + to stand, set + like, related to

14. _____ sleep + to carry, bear + having the quality of

15. _____ to, at, against + to draw, drag

16. _____ through + to look + quality of

17. _____ to follow

18. _____ with + name

19. _____ to send + like, related to

20. _____ back, again + to move

DIRECTIONS: For each blank write one vocabulary word. All words will be used only once. Look for context clues in the sentence.

_____ 1. The circus was a fine --- for the rural children.

_____ 2. The local public enemy number one was a true ---.

_____ 3. A rubber band will --- a paper wad many feet.

_____ 4. Beautiful is a(n) --- for pretty.

_____ 5. The lady was --- that her dog never strayed from home.

_____ 6. The local courts are filled with --- cases.

_____ 7. Having the fastest time was --- to winning the race.

_____ 8. The hecklers in the crowd were quite --- last night.

_____ 9. The --- on Swiss cuckoo clocks was 30 percent of wholesale.

_____ 10. A single --- arced over the hill onto the camp.

_____ 11. One religious --- believed that the guru was immortal.

_____ 12. The vast --- was all created by God.

_____ 13. A yellow flower will --- many honey bees.

_____ 14. The --- financier could find profits in odd places.

_____ 15. The alcoholic has a(n) --- for liquor of any type.

_____ 16. Jonah's rescue by the whale was a(n) --- act.

_____ 17. Paint thinner might --- the stain from the cloth.

_____ 18. Sleeping pills have a(n) --- effect on people.

_____ 19. The --- condition of the lizard fooled the bug.

_____ 20. There was a great --- of ants in the open jelly jar.

DIRECTIONS: Use your LATIN roots and affixes sheets; try to match the definitions with the words; look at the roots, prefixes, and suffixes for clues. Do NOT use a dictionary except as a last resort.

_____ AVERSE

_____ CONTRACT

_____ DESTINE

_____ HEMOSTASIS

_____ IMPOSTOR

_____ IMPULSIVE

_____ INCREDIBLE

_____ INFERENCE

_____ MANUMIT

_____ OCCASION

_____ OCTUPLE

_____ PROSPECT

_____ PROVISION

_____ REVOKE

_____ SEQUEL

_____ STANZA

_____ STIPEND

_____ TOPONYM

_____ TORTILLA

_____ VERSATILE

1. a) eight fold; consisting of eight parts

2. a) unbelievable; too improbable to be possible

3. n) group of lines forming one of the divisions of a poem or song

4. v) to rescind; cancel; withdraw

5. n) opportunity; a favorable time; a happening

6. n) flat, unleavened corn cake used as bread

7. v) to predetermine; to set apart for a purpose; intend

8. n) a preparing for; preparatory measure; food, goods, or supplies

9. n) regular or fixed payment for services; a salary or pension allowance

10. a) reluctant; unwilling; set against

11. v) to free from slavery; liberate

12. n) something that follows; a continuation

13. n) the stoppage of bleeding

14. n) the name of a place; a name indicating origin or locale

15. a) spontaneous; acting suddenly; driving forward

16. n) a logical conclusion; a deduction

17. n) agreement; covenant
    v) to get; acquire; incur; to shrink

18. n) a looking forward; a likely outcome or customer
    v) to explore or search for

19. a) competent in many things; able to turn easily from one job to another

20. n) a cheat or fraud; one pretending to be something or someone he is not

DIRECTIONS: Use your LATIN roots and affixes sheets; try to find the root in each vocabulary word. Write the root and its meaning; also circle the root in the vocabulary word.

vocabulary word	root	meaning
AVERSE	_____	_____
CONTRACT	_____	_____
DESTINE	_____	_____
HEMOSTASIS	_____	_____
IMPOSTOR	_____	_____
IMPULSIVE	_____	_____
INCREDIBLE	_____	_____
INFERENCE	_____	_____
MANUMIT	_____	_____
OCCASION	_____	_____
OCTUPLE	_____	_____
PROSPECT	_____	_____
PROVISION	_____	_____
REVOKE	_____	_____
SEQUEL	_____	_____
STANZA	_____	_____
STIPEND	_____	_____
TOPONYM	_____	_____
TORTILLA	_____	_____
VERSATILE	_____	_____

DIRECTIONS: Use your LATIN roots and affixes sheets; try to find the word that is represented by the meanings of the roots and affixes. Write the word in the blank.

1. _____ hand + to send

2. _____ to twist + Spanish ending

3. _____ in, not + to place, put + one who

4. _____ to stand, set + Italian ending

5. _____ to, toward + to fall, happen + state, quality

6. _____ from, away + to turn

7. _____ to turn + able to

8. _____ in, into + to push + having the power of

9. _____ coin + to hang, weigh, pay

10. _____ eight + to fold

11. _____ with, together + to draw, drag

12. _____ in, into + to carry, bear + state, quality

13. _____ to follow

14. _____ blood + to stand, set (standing)

15. _____ for, forward + to see + state, quality

16. _____ place + name

17. _____ for, forward + to look

18. _____ in, not + to believe + able to be

19. _____ back, again + to call, voice

20. _____ down, away + to stand, set

DIRECTIONS: For each blank write one vocabulary word. All words will be used only once. Look for context clues in the sentence.

_____ 1. It is correct to --- a privilege as punishment.

_____ 2. The paramedics worked to get the patient into ---.

_____ 3. The snowflake formed a basic --- pattern.

_____ 4. A good --- is the basis of a good taco.

_____ 5. The young business man was a fine --- for a sale.

_____ 6. Both parties signed the --- for the new building.

_____ 7. The --- of his first birthday was highly celebrated.

_____ 8. The teacher made --- for extra credit in history.

_____ 9. Wise men are --- to gambling with their money.

_____ 10. A famous --- means the city of brotherly love.

_____ 11. The jack of all trades is considered to be ---.

_____ 12. The magician's tricks were quite ---.

_____ 13. Some hit movies attempt a(n) --- for further profits.

_____ 14. Only God can --- the fate of a man.

_____ 15. The retiree did quite well on his weekly --- of $400.

_____ 16. It took six months for security to uncover the ---.

_____ 17. Lincoln's idea was to --- the slaves by decree.

_____ 18. The fourth --- of the poem is most people's favorite.

_____ 19. The boy's --- behavior caused many problems for him.

_____ 20. We decided what to do by --- rather than command.

DIRECTIONS: Use your LATIN roots and affixes sheets; try to match the definitions with the words; look at the roots, prefixes, and suffixes for clues. Do NOT use a dictionary except as a last resort.

_____ CONSTANT

_____ CONVERSANT

_____ DETRACT

_____ DISCREDIT

_____ HELIOSTAT

_____ IMPEL

_____ IMPOUND

_____ INTERMISSION

_____ METAPHOR

_____ OCCIDENT

_____ PERPLEX

_____ PROSPECTUS

_____ PROVOCATION

_____ REVISE

_____ SEQUENCE

_____ STANCHION

_____ SUSPEND

_____ TORTURE

_____ TRINOMIAL

_____ VERSUS

1. n) device with a mirror to reflect the sun's rays in one continuous direction

2. n) the coming of one thing after another; a series

3. n) countries west of Asia; western hemisphere

4. v) to take into legal custody; to gather or enclose water for irrigation

5. n) the inflicting of severe pain to get information or vengeance

6. a) familiar or acquainted with

7. prep) against; in contrast to

8. v) read over carefully to correct or improve; to change or amend

9. v) to push, drive or move forward; incite; urge

10. n) a statement outlining the main features of a new work or business enterprise

11. n) a figure of speech in which one thing is likened to another

12. a) unchanging; continual; remaining the same

13. n) upright bar or post used as a support; a device to confine a cow

14. v) to bar or exclude from office, position, etc.; to hang from above; to temporarily stop

15. n) interval of time between activities

16. n) mathematical expression of three terms connected by plus or minus signs

17. v) to take away; belittle

18. n) something that causes resentment or irritation

19. v) to puzzle; confuse; to make someone doubtful or uncertain

20. v) to disbelieve; disgrace; show reason to doubt
n) dishonor; damage

DIRECTIONS: Use your LATIN roots and affixes sheets; try to find the root in each vocabulary word. Write the root and its meaning; also circle the root in the vocabulary word.

vocabulary word	root	meaning
CONSTANT	_____	_____
CONVERSANT	_____	_____
DETRACT	_____	_____
DISCREDIT	_____	_____
HELIOSTAT	_____	_____
IMPEL	_____	_____
IMPOUND	_____	_____
INTERMISSION	_____	_____
METAPHOR	_____	_____
OCCIDENT	_____	_____
PERPLEX	_____	_____
PROSPECTUS	_____	_____
PROVOCATION	_____	_____
REVISE	_____	_____
SEQUENCE	_____	_____
STANCHION	_____	_____
SUSPEND	_____	_____
TORTURE	_____	_____
TRINOMIAL	_____	_____
VERSUS	_____	_____

DIRECTIONS: Use your LATIN roots and affixes sheets; try to find the word that is represented by the meanings of the roots and affixes. Write the word in the blank.

1. _____ in, into + to place, put

2. _____ to twist + state, quality, act

3. _____ between + to send + state, quality, act

4. _____ for, forward + to call, voice + to do + state, act

5. _____ down + to draw, drag

6. _____ to stand, set + French ending

7. _____ with + to stand, set + that which

8. _____ to turn

9. _____ for, forward + to look + Latin ending

10. _____ in, into + to push

11. _____ three + name + like, related to

12. _____ change + to carry, bear

13. _____ to follow + state, quality

14. _____ with + to turn + like, related to

15. _____ through + to fold

16. _____ sun + to stand, set

17. _____ back, again + to see

18. _____ to, toward + to fall, happen + state, quality

19. _____ under + to hang, weigh, pay

20. _____ away, negative + to believe + Latin ending

DIRECTIONS: For each blank write one vocabulary word. All words will be used only once. Look for context clues in the sentence.

_____   1. A(n) --- was used to warm the small instrument shack.

_____   2. The court heard a case entitled Brown --- Green.

_____   3. After four hours we only had a twenty-minute ---.

_____   4. The algebra problem had a variable and one ---.

_____   5. The --- from the mutual fund looked very rewarding.

_____   6. The police came to --- the stolen property.

_____   7. Finding the proper --- often breaks the code.

_____   8. The cow bolted from the --- when released.

_____   9. Simple puzzles often --- wise people.

_____   10. It is usually best to --- a first draft.

_____   11. A blemish on the apple does not --- from the taste.

_____   12. Some people seem --- on almost any subject.

_____   13. Factoring a(n) --- in algebra takes some skill.

_____   14. For some time the Orient disliked the ---.

_____   15. The right stimulus will --- a person to try.

_____   16. The rack and the iron maiden were implements of ---.

_____   17. The poet used a beautiful --- to describe the swan.

_____   18. His remark was the --- that set off the argument.

_____   19. The politician attempted to --- his opponent.

_____   20. The judge agreed to --- the hearing for five days

DIRECTIONS: Use your LATIN roots and affixes sheets; try to match the definitions with the words; look at the roots, prefixes, and suffixes for clues. Do NOT use a dictionary except as a last resort.

_____ AGNOMEN

_____ CONSTITUENT

_____ CREED

_____ DISTRACT

_____ EMIT

_____ EXPULSION

_____ GYROSTATICS

_____ INTERPOSE

_____ IRREVOCABLE

_____ OFFERTORY

_____ PLAIT

_____ PROPOUND

_____ RECIDIVIST

_____ RESPECT

_____ SEQUESTER

_____ STADIUM

_____ SUPERVISE

_____ SUSPENSE

_____ TROUSSEAU

_____ VERTEBRA

1. n) a forcing out; condition of being thrown out

2. n) bride's outfit of clothes, linen, etc.

3. n) nickname or added epithet

4. v) set apart; separate; confiscate; take over

5. a) unalterable; cannot be undone or recalled

6. n) brief statement of religious belief; statement of principles or opinions

7. n) place for outdoor games or meetings surrounded by many seats for spectators

8. n) a flattened fold; a pleat; a braid
   v) to press cloth into folds; to braid

9. v) to show esteem or honor for; relate to
   n) deference; honor; esteem

10. n) branch of physics dealing with rotating bodies and their tendency tomaintain their plane of rotation

11. v) to send out; give forth; utter; issue

12. n) any of the single bones in the spinal column

13. n) being undetermined or undecided, usually with feelings of anxiety and apprehension

14. v) to set forth; propose; put forward

15. n) one who votes for his representative
    a) serving as part of the whole

16. v) to place or come between; to interrupt

17. n) part of the service when collection is taken; the collection itself

18. v) oversee or direct; superintend

19. v) turn the mind away; confuse; harass

20. n) person who goes back to crime; habitual criminal

DIRECTIONS: Use your LATIN roots and affixes sheets; try to find the root in each vocabulary word. Write the root and its meaning; also circle the root in the vocabulary word.

vocabulary word	root	meaning
AGNOMEN	_____	_____
CONSTITUENT	_____	_____
CREED	_____	_____
DISTRACT	_____	_____
EMIT	_____	_____
EXPULSION	_____	_____
GYROSTATICS	_____	_____
INTERPOSE	_____	_____
IRREVOCABLE	_____	_____
OFFERTORY	_____	_____
PLAIT	_____	_____
PROPOUND	_____	_____
RECIDIVIST	_____	_____
RESPECT	_____	_____
SEQUESTER	_____	_____
STADIUM	_____	_____
SUPERVISE	_____	_____
SUSPENSE	_____	_____
TROUSSEAU	_____	_____
VERTEBRA	_____	_____

DIRECTIONS: Use your LATIN roots and affixes sheets; try to find the word that is represented by the meanings of the roots and affixes. Write the word in the blank.

1. _____ out, away + to push + state, quality, act

2. _____ back, again + to fall, happen + one who

3. _____ to twist (French)

4. _____ circle + to stand, set + like, related to

5. _____ above, over + to see

6. _____ to fold

7. _____ out, away + to send

8. _____ to turn

9. _____ for, forward + to place, put

10. _____ to believe

11. _____ under + to hand, weigh, pay

12. _____ to, at + name + having the quality of

13. _____ to + to carry, bear + having the quality of

14. _____ to stand, set + Latin ending

15. _____ between + to place, put

16. _____ back, again + to look

17. _____ away, negative + to draw, drag

18. _____ to follow

19. _____ not + back, again + to call, voice + able to

20. _____ with + to stand, set + that which, one who

DIRECTIONS: For each blank write one vocabulary word. All words will be used only once. Look for context clues in the sentence.

_____ 1. The --- of $274.15 went to foreign missions.

_____ 2. To --- oneself among armed combatants is scary.

_____ 3. The local football --- was jammed with fans.

_____ 4. Memorizing a(n) --- teaches basic faith to children.

_____ 5. Mother will usually --- the garden activities.

_____ 6. Outside noises often --- one from one's studies.

_____ 7. The three-time offender was termed a(n) ---.

_____ 8. Bright new clothes filled the bride's ---.

_____ 9. --- was the punishment for cutting class.

_____ 10. The field of --- contributed to space navigation.

_____ 11. The wrangler wanted to --- his cows from the others.

_____ 12. Eric's --- was "the red."

_____ 13. Many a(n) --- writes his congressman at times.

_____ 14. Bess did --- a love knot in her hair.

_____ 15. The lowest --- in man's back is called the tail bone.

_____ 16. Death is usually a(n) --- condition.

_____ 17. The speaker will --- his thoughts on the problem.

_____ 18. The sprayer did not --- enough mixture to be useful.

_____ 19. Money and --- do not necessarily go together.

_____ 20. The --- of the radio drama kept us avidly listening.

DIRECTIONS: Use your LATIN roots and affixes sheets; try to match the definitions with the words; look at the roots, prefixes, and suffixes for clues. Do NOT use a dictionary except as a last resort.

_____ ACCREDIT

_____ ANNIVERSARY

_____ ANONYMOUS

_____ APPEND

_____ CONTRAST

_____ DISMISS

_____ ENTREAT

_____ EXPEL

_____ EXTANT

_____ INVOCATION

_____ JUXTAPOSITION

_____ PARAPHERNALIA

_____ PLEXUS

_____ PROVOST

_____ RESPITE

_____ RHEOSTAT

_____ SPECULATE

_____ TRUSS

_____ VERTEX

_____ VIDEO

1. n) being side by side or close together

2. n) the picture phase of broadcasting
   a) having to do with the picture

3. n) device for regulating electric current by varying resistance without opening the circuit

4. n) the highest point; summit; top; apex

5. v) to send away; eject; remove from office

6. n) act of calling on God for help, etc.; the prayer at the beginning of a service

7. v) to attach; affix; add as a supplement

8. v) think about; ponder; meditate; to buy stocks, land, hoping to gain with quite some risk

9. n) the official in charge; superintendent

10. a) with no name known or acknowledged

11. n) an interwoven system of parts; a network of nerves, muscles, vessels, etc.

12. a) still existing; not lost or destroyed

13. v) to show differences in comparison
    n) a difference

14. v) to beg; beseech; to ask earnestly for

15. v) to bundle or tie; to support or strengthen with a framework

16. n) yearly return of the date of some event

17. n) delay or postponement; temporary interval of relief or rest

18. n) personal belongings; collection of articles; equipment; apparatus; trappings; gear

19. v) to drive out by force; to make leave; deprive of rights

20. v) to authorize; to bring into favor

DIRECTIONS: Use your LATIN roots and affixes sheets; try to find the root in each vocabulary word. Write the root and its meaning; also circle the root in the vocabulary word.

vocabulary word	root	meaning
ACCREDIT	_____	_____
ANNIVERSARY	_____	_____
ANONYMOUS	_____	_____
APPEND	_____	_____
CONTRAST	_____	_____
DISMISS	_____	_____
ENTREAT	_____	_____
EXPEL	_____	_____
EXTANT	_____	_____
INVOCATION	_____	_____
JUXTAPOSITION	_____	_____
PARAPHERNALIA	_____	_____
PLEXUS	_____	_____
PROVOST	_____	_____
RESPITE	_____	_____
RHEOSTAT	_____	_____
SPECULATE	_____	_____
TRUSS	_____	_____
VERTEX	_____	_____
VIDEO	_____	_____

DIRECTIONS: Use your LATIN roots and affixes sheets; try to find the word that is represented by the meanings of the roots and affixes. Write the word in the blank.

1. _____ near + to place, put + state, quality

2. _____ to, toward + to believe + ??

3. _____ away, negative + to send

4. _____ to see

5. _____ in, into + to draw, drag

6. _____ current + to stand, set

7. _____ beyond + to carry, bear + ??

8. _____ year + to turn + like, related to

9. _____ in, into + to call, voice + state, quality, act

10. _____ to twist (French)

11. _____ to fold + Latin ending

12. _____ against + to stand, set

13. _____ to look + to do

14. _____ out, away + to push

15. _____ for, forward + to place, put

16. _____ without, not + name + having the quality of

17. _____ back, again + to look

18. _____ to turn

19. _____ out, away + to stand, set

20. _____ to, toward + to hang, weigh, pay

DIRECTIONS: For each blank write one vocabulary word. All words will be used only once. Look for context clues in the sentence.

_____   1. The fighter was hit squarely in the solar ---.

_____   2. At the --- we could see for miles in all directions.

_____   3. Students often hope the teacher will --- them early.

_____   4. The postscript is used to --- a message on a letter.

_____   5. The meeting began with a(n) --- by a local pastor.

_____   6. Most people --- about the weather.

_____   7. An apparent --- of tactics existed between the foes.

_____   8. A man should remember his wife on their wedding ---.

_____   9. A potentiometer is a variable ---.

_____   10. The three-minute break was a much-appreciated ---.

_____   11. The woman was forced to --- the bandit for her son.

_____   12. The major donor preferred to remain ---.

_____   13. A single --- held the sagging bridge.

_____   14. The boy wanted to --- his dinner over the boat's side.

_____   15. The ham and eggs were in --- on the plate.

_____   16. Radio is somewhat like TV without the --- portion.

_____   17. After the bombing run only two buildings remained ---.

_____   18. The examiners would not --- the young applicant.

_____   19. The soldier had quite a bit of survival --- with him.

_____   20. The --- marshal of Sussex was Lord Henry.

DIRECTIONS: Use your LATIN roots and affixes sheets; try to match the definitions with the words; look at the roots, prefixes, and suffixes for clues. Do NOT use a dictionary except as a last resort.

_____ ADVERSE

_____ AEROSTAT

_____ ANTONYM

_____ CLAIRVOYANCE

_____ COMPENDIUM

_____ COMPLICATE

_____ CREDENCE

_____ DEMISE

_____ EPONYM

_____ EVOKE

_____ OPPONENT

_____ PERIPHERY

_____ PLIABLE

_____ PURPOSE

_____ RESTIVE

_____ RETROSPECT

_____ SPECTER

_____ STABILIZE

_____ VERTICAL

_____ VISAGE

1. n) summary or abstract; concise and comprehensive treatise or summary

2. n) person who is against one; one who opposes; adversary

3. v) to call forth; summon; elicit

4. n) belief, especially in the report of another

5. a) hostile; opposed; unfavorable; harmful

6. n) contemplation of the past; thinking of the past

7. v) to make firm; to keep from fluctuating

8. n) name of person who is source for a national or institutional name (Penn - Pennsylvania)

9. a) balky; contrary; unruly; refusing to go forward

10. n) word whose meaning is the opposite of another word

11. n) apparition; most often an imagined object of fear or dread

12. v) to aim, intend, resolve, or plan
    n) an aim or intention; the end in view

13. v) to make difficult; to twist together

14. a) easily bent or molded; flexible; easily influenced or persuaded

15. a) directly overhead; at the zenith; straight up and down

16. n) perimeter; environs; surrounding space; boundary line

17. n) dirigible, balloon, or lighter than air craft

18. n) the face; countenance

19. n) death; transfer of estate or authority by will or lease

20. n) alleged ability to see things not in sight; supposed perception

DIRECTIONS: Use your LATIN roots and affixes sheets; try to find the root in each vocabulary word. Write the root and its meaning; also circle the root in the vocabulary word.

vocabulary word	root	meaning
ADVERSE	_____	_____
AEROSTAT	_____	_____
ANTONYM	_____	_____
CLAIRVOYANCE	_____	_____
COMPENDIUM	_____	_____
COMPLICATE	_____	_____
CREDENCE	_____	_____
DEMISE	_____	_____
EPONYM	_____	_____
EVOKE	_____	_____
OPPONENT	_____	_____
PERIPHERY	_____	_____
PLIABLE	_____	_____
PURPOSE	_____	_____
RESTIVE	_____	_____
RETROSPECT	_____	_____
SPECTER	_____	_____
STABILIZE	_____	_____
VERTICAL	_____	_____
VISAGE	_____	_____

DIRECTIONS: Use your LATIN roots and affixes sheets; try to find the word that is represented by the meanings of the roots and affixes. Write the word in the blank.

1. _____ down, away + to send

2. _____ backward + to look

3. _____ to turn + like, related to

4. _____ to believe + state, quality, act

5. _____ upon + name

6. _____ to fold + able to be

7. _____ air + to stand, set

8. _____ with, together + to fold + to do

9. _____ to look + that which

10. _____ around + to carry, bear + state, quality, act

11. _____ opposite + name

12. _____ for, forward + to place, put

13. _____ out, away + to call

14. _____ to, at, against + to turn

15. _____ to see + state, quality

16. _____ with, together + to hang, weigh, pay + Latin ending

17. _____ to stand, set + able to + to do

18. _____ back, again + to stand, set + that which

19. _____ clear + to see + state, quality, act

20. _____ to, at, against + to place, put + one who

DIRECTIONS: For each blank write one vocabulary word. All words will be used only once. Look for context clues in the sentence.

_____ 1. The news of his --- came too late for us to respond.

_____ 2. The basic --- of mankind is to glorify God.

_____ 3. The --- weather conditions hindered the maneuvers.

_____ 4. The victorious man's --- shone with happiness.

_____ 5. The additional restrictions would --- matters greatly.

_____ 6. There seemed to be a dark --- that rose in his mind when he thought of his sad childhood.

_____ 7. The French invented and flew an early ---.

_____ 8. The simple are --- in the hands of the cunning.

_____ 9. The cliff was almost perfectly --- at one spot.

_____ 10. Happy is one --- for sad.

_____ 11. The speaker asked questions to --- crowd response.

_____ 12. Yesterday's mistakes seem obvious in ---.

_____ 13. Goliath was a fearsome --- for the Israelites to face.

_____ 14. An anchor is used to --- a boat's position.

_____ 15. The --- cited all the known sources on the subject.

_____ 16. William Penn is the --- for Pennsylvania

_____ 17. The young boy was always on the --- of the group.

_____ 18. The king's ring gave --- to the messenger's report.

_____ 19. The mule was --- when brought to the plow.

_____ 20. The Chaldeans of King Nebuchadnezzar's court falsely claimed --- about his dream.

DIRECTIONS: Use your LATIN roots and affixes sheets; try to match the definitions with the words; look at the roots, prefixes, and suffixes for clues. Do NOT use a dictionary except as a last resort.

_____ ADVERSITY

_____ APOSTASY

_____ COGNOMEN

_____ COMPENSATE

_____ COMPLICITY

_____ COMPROMISE

_____ CREDENTIAL

_____ DEVICE

_____ ECSTATIC

_____ EQUIVOCATE

_____ PHOSPHORESCENT

_____ PLIGHT

_____ PORTRAY

_____ POSITIVE

_____ REPOSITORY

_____ RESTITUTION

_____ SPECIALIZE

_____ SPECTRUM

_____ VERTIGO

_____ VISIBLE

1. n) predicament; awkward or dangerous situation

2. n) a partnership in wrongdoing

3. n) reparation; making good for loss or damage

4. n) that which entitles to confidence; often a certificate of position

5. n) dizziness or giddiness

6. n) an abandoning of what one believed in

7. a) giving light without heat

8. v) to make a picture of; depict; delineate

9. n) settlement in which both sides give up some demands
   v) to settle by giving up some demands

10. v) to make particular; to direct or concentrate on one thing

11. v) hedge; use vague terms; be purposely ambiguous

12. n) misfortune; calamity; wretched state

13. n) the range of colored bands in light; a range of something

14. a) can be seen by the eye; can be observed with the mind; manifest; evident

15. n) a plan; scheme; trick; mechanical contrivance; a design or emblem

16. n) box, chest, or room for safekeeping; place where things are kept

17. n) the family name; surname

18. a) characterized by emotions of great joy

19. v) make up for; counterbalance; make amends; pay for

20. a) sure; definite; confident; assured

DIRECTIONS: Use your LATIN roots and affixes sheets; try to find the root in each vocabulary word. Write the root and its meaning; also circle the root in the vocabulary word.

vocabulary word	root	meaning
ADVERSITY	_____	_____
APOSTASY	_____	_____
COGNOMEN	_____	_____
COMPENSATE	_____	_____
COMPLICITY	_____	_____
COMPROMISE	_____	_____
CREDENTIAL	_____	_____
DEVICE	_____	_____
ECSTATIC	_____	_____
EQUIVOCATE	_____	_____
PHOSPHORESCENT	_____	_____
PLIGHT	_____	_____
PORTRAY	_____	_____
POSITIVE	_____	_____
REPOSITORY	_____	_____
RESTITUTION	_____	_____
SPECIALIZE	_____	_____
SPECTRUM	_____	_____
VERTIGO	_____	_____
VISIBLE	_____	_____

DIRECTIONS: Use your LATIN roots and affixes sheets; try to find the word that is represented by the meanings of the roots and affixes. Write the word in the blank.

1. _____ with, together + for, forward + to send

2. _____ equal + to call, voice + to do, make

3. _____ to, at, against + to turn + state, quality, act

4. _____ to fold

5. _____ to see + able to

6. _____ with, together + to fold + state, quality, act

7. _____ to look + like, related to + to do

8. _____ light + to carry, bear + becoming

9. _____ to look + Latin ending

10. _____ with, together + name + having quality of

11. _____ back, again + to place, put + place where

12. _____ to believe + state, quality + like, related to

13. _____ to place, put + having the power of

14. _____ with, together + to hang, weigh, pay + to do, make

15. _____ back, again + to stand, set + state, quality, act

16. _____ out, away + to stand, set + like, related to

17. _____ to turn

18. _____ away + to stand, set + state, quality, act

19. _____ for, forward + to draw, drag

20. _____ down, away + to see

DIRECTIONS: For each blank write one vocabulary word. All words will be used only once. Look for context clues in the sentence.

_____ 1. The rainbow revealed the whole color ---.

_____ 2. The --- swamp gas gave an eerie glow in the darkness.

_____ 3. The normal --- was already full with documents.

_____ 4. The man showed a(n) ---, which gave him access to the high security area.

_____ 5. The girl's --- attitude helped her to do well.

_____ 6. The alderman's --- showed in his sinful actions.

_____ 7. Looking down from high places can cause ---.

_____ 8. A common --- in America is Smith.

_____ 9. A faint track was --- at the edge of the trail.

_____ 10. The rock climber's --- was seen by the park ranger.

_____ 11. The --- of the thief and the bank teller came out only after much testimony.

_____ 12. A simple --- was used to evade the alarm systems.

_____ 13. Modern man tends to --- in a chosen field of work.

_____ 14. The boy thought it best to --- when asked about the recent prank in the hallway.

_____ 15. The --- of the outcast was seen in his shabby dress.

_____ 16. When the package came, the girl was --- about it.

_____ 17. It is hard to --- for harsh words spoken in anger.

_____ 18. A good artist can --- an image clearly on paper.

_____ 19. $100 was quite a(n) --- on the owner's part.

_____ 20. Complete --- amounted to a large sum of money.

DIRECTIONS: Use your LATIN roots and affixes sheets; try to match the definitions with the words; look at the roots, prefixes, and suffixes for clues. Do NOT use a dictionary except as a last resort.

_____ ADVERTISE

1. n) a word with the same pronunciation as another but with a different meaning and spelling

_____ ADVISE

2. a) trustworthy; can be believed; plausible

_____ BELVEDERE

3. v) to withstand; oppose; fend off; stand firm against

_____ COMMIT

4. a) separated; far; having a gap between; cool in manner; aloof

_____ CONVOCATION

5. n) small summerhouse on a height or gallery built for giving a view of the scenery

_____ CREDIBLE

6. v) to draw out; prolong; lengthen in duration

_____ CRYPTONYM

7. v) counsel; recommend; inform; consult

_____ DEPENDABLE

8. n) a whirling mass of water; whirlpool; whirlwind

_____ DESIST

9. n) carriage or bearing of the body; a pose; a stand or attitude relative to something

_____ DISTANT

10. a) fourfold; four times as many
    v) to multiply by four

_____ EXPEND

11. n) a calling together; assembling by summons

_____ HOMONYM

12. a) can be relied upon; trustworthy

_____ POSTURE

13. v) to consume by using; use up

_____ PROFFER

14. v) to give in trust; consign; to do or perpetrate; to pledge

_____ PROTRACT

15. v) to mention, describe or define in detail; state exactly

_____ QUADRUPLE

16. n) a secret name

_____ RESIST

17. n) a mean or evil feeling for another; a grudge; malice or ill will

_____ SPECIFY

18. v) to offer, usually something intangible

_____ SPITE

19. v) stop; cease; abstain

_____ VORTEX

20. v) to call to public attention

DIRECTIONS: Use your LATIN roots and affixes sheets; try to find the root in each vocabulary word. Write the root and its meaning; also circle the root in the vocabulary word.

vocabulary word	root	meaning
ADVERTISE	_____	_____
ADVISE	_____	_____
BELVEDERE	_____	_____
COMMIT	_____	_____
CONVOCATION	_____	_____
CREDIBLE	_____	_____
CRYPTONYM	_____	_____
DEPENDABLE	_____	_____
DESIST	_____	_____
DISTANT	_____	_____
EXPEND	_____	_____
HOMONYM	_____	_____
POSTURE	_____	_____
PROFFER	_____	_____
PROTRACT	_____	_____
QUADRUPLE	_____	_____
RESIST	_____	_____
SPECIFY	_____	_____
SPITE	_____	_____
VORTEX	_____	_____

DIRECTIONS: Use your LATIN roots and affixes sheets; try to find the word that is represented by the meanings of the roots and affixes. Write the word in the blank.

1. _____ out, away + to hang, weigh, pay

2. _____ with, together + to call, voice + state, quality

3. _____ to turn

4. _____ to look + to do

5. _____ to, at, against + to turn + to make, act

6. _____ same + name

7. _____ away, negative + to stand, set

8. _____ to believe + able to be

9. _____ for, forward + to draw, drag

10. _____ to, at, against + to see

11. _____ for, forward + to carry, bear

12. _____ back, again + to stand, set

13. _____ with, together + to send

14. _____ to look

15. _____ down, away, not + to stand, set

16. _____ hidden + name

17. _____ four + to fold

18. _____ to place, put + that which, state, quality

19. _____ beautiful, fine + to see

20. _____ down, away + to hang, weigh, pay + able to be

DIRECTIONS: For each blank write one vocabulary word. All words will be used only once. Look for context clues in the sentence.

_____ 1. His former girlfriend's attitude was quite ---.

_____ 2. A bear cannot --- honey when he smells it.

_____ 3. The ship was caught in the --- and lost.

_____ 4. It is unwise to --- all one's energy at the start of a long contest.

_____ 5. The spy used his --- when sending coded messages.

_____ 6. It is often wise to --- to get a good price for goods.

_____ 7. A liar will --- almost anything to get his way.

_____ 8. Because of --- the man beat his neighbor's dog.

_____ 9. To join one had to give a(n) --- profession of faith.

_____ 10. When earnings ---, one makes some real money.

_____ 11. Four men will --- to do the job for the next year.

_____ 12. The agent could not --- the exact harvest yet.

_____ 13. Old dad is always --- when it comes to going fishing.

_____ 14. The --- was held in a large hall so all could attend.

_____ 15. The --- for weigh only has three letters.

_____ 16. We admired the surroundings from the ---.

_____ 17. The boy was told to --- from his annoying activity.

_____ 18. In an effort to not --- the meeting any longer than necessary, the man held his peace.

_____ 19. The authorities continually --- people to stay away from dangerous situations in emergencies.

_____ 20. Slumping in one's seat is not good ---.

DIRECTIONS: Use your LATIN roots and affixes sheets; try to match the definitions with the words; look at the roots, prefixes, and suffixes for clues. Do NOT use a dictionary except as a last resort.

_____ ADMISSION

_____ ANIMADVERT

_____ AVOW

_____ COMMISSARY

_____ CONSISTENCY

_____ CREDITOR

_____ DENOMINATION

_____ DESTITUTE

_____ DISPENSE

_____ EXPENSE

_____ IGNOMINY

_____ PROPONENT

_____ PROTRACTOR

_____ RECONSTITUTE

_____ REFEREE

_____ REPLICATE

_____ SPECIMEN

_____ SUPPOSITION

_____ TRANSPOSE

_____ VORTICAL

1. n) person to whom another is indebted

2. n) the paying out of money; cost or fee; loss or drain

3. v) to fold; bend back; (rare — to repeat)

4. n) name of a class of things; class or kind having specific value; a religious sect

5. a) moving in a whirling pattern

6. n) allowing to enter; access; a conceding or confessing

7. n) a semi-circle instrument with gradations used for drawing and measuring angles

8. v) declare openly; admit frankly; confess; acknowledge

9. v) to restore to original form by adding water

10. v) to change the usual or normal position for another; in music to write/play in another key

11. n) firmness or thickness of a liquid; agreement, in harmony; conformity with previous practice

12. v) distribute; give out; deal out; excuse

13. n) one of a group as a sample for all; a typical part

14. v) remark critically; comment on, usually with disapproval

15. a) lacking; poor; living in complete poverty

16. n) a theory; hypothesis; something regarded as true

17. n) person given a duty by authority; a store in camp for food and supplies

18. n) one who makes a proposal or supports a cause

19. n) person to whom anything is given for a decision; umpire; judge

20. n) disgrace; shame and dishonor; infamy

DIRECTIONS: Use your LATIN roots and affixes sheets; try to find the root in each vocabulary word. Write the root and its meaning; also circle the root in the vocabulary word.

vocabulary word	root	meaning
ADMISSION	_____	_____
ANIMADVERT	_____	_____
AVOW	_____	_____
COMMISSARY	_____	_____
CONSISTENCY	_____	_____
CREDITOR	_____	_____
DENOMINATION	_____	_____
DESTITUTE	_____	_____
DISPENSE	_____	_____
EXPENSE	_____	_____
IGNOMINY	_____	_____
PROPONENT	_____	_____
PROTRACTOR	_____	_____
RECONSTITUTE	_____	_____
REFEREE	_____	_____
REPLICATE	_____	_____
SPECIMEN	_____	_____
SUPPOSITION	_____	_____
TRANSPOSE	_____	_____
VORTICAL	_____	_____

DIRECTIONS: Use your LATIN roots and affixes sheets; try to find the word that is represented by the meanings of the roots and affixes. Write the word in the blank.

1. _____ back, again + with, together + to stand, set

2. _____ down, away, not + to stand, set

3. _____ not, without + name + state, quality

4. _____ with, together + to stand, set + state, quality

5. _____ to turn + like, related to

6. _____ with, together + to send + like, related to

7. _____ back, again + to carry, bear + one who

8. _____ away, negative + to hang, weigh, pay

9. _____ to, at, against + to send + state, quality

10. _____ across + to place, put

11. _____ spirit + to, at, against + to turn

12. _____ back, again + to fold + to do

13. _____ to believe + Latin part + one who

14. _____ under + to place, put + state, quality, act

15. _____ for, forward + to push + one who

16. _____ out, away + to hang, weigh, pay

17. _____ for, forward + to draw, drag + one who, that which

18. _____ to, at + to call, voice

19. _____ down, away + name + to do + state, quality, act

20. _____ to look + something done

DIRECTIONS: For each blank write one vocabulary word. All words will be used only once. Look for context clues in the sentence.

_____   1. Half the town belonged to one --- or another.

_____   2. George Washington was a strong --- of freedom.

_____   3. Some people can --- music as they play it.

_____   4. At 5:30 p.m. we began to --- the food to the crew.

_____   5. The campers had to --- their dried food with water.

_____   6. The --- of his crime made quite an impact on him.

_____   7. A frank --- of the facts is the best way to make a clean breast of the situation.

_____   8. The --- at the fort was shut due to lack of supplies.

_____   9. The man would not --- to his gambling activities.

_____   10. Most of the tribe held to the --- that they were invincible in battle.

_____   11. Feeding eight children was quite a(n) ---.

_____   12. The horse was a fine --- of the breed.

_____   13. The windstorm spun in a(n) --- manner.

_____   14. The final decision was up to the --- on third base.

_____   15. The tattered man appeared to be ---.

_____   16. The --- was coming at noon for his payment.

_____   17. The math test called for the use of a(n) ---.

_____   18. The camp coffee's --- reminded one of syrup instead of water.

_____   19. It takes a good crease to --- heavy cardboard in a straight line.

_____   20. A nitpicker will --- about almost anyone at any time.

GREEK WORKSHEETS

DIRECTIONS: Use your GREEK roots and affixes sheets; try to match the definitions with the words; look at the roots, prefixes, and suffixes for clues. Do NOT use a dictionary except as a last resort.

_____ ALTIMETER

_____ ANARCHIST

_____ ANDROGYNOUS

_____ CYCLONOSCOPE

_____ DIAGRAM

_____ ENGENDER

_____ GENEALOGY

_____ GEOCENTRIC

_____ HEMATOLOGY

_____ HEXAGON

_____ HYDRANGEA

_____ ISOBAR

_____ MIMEOGRAPH

_____ ORTHOGAMY

_____ PYROLYSIS

_____ SAXOPHONE

_____ STETHOMETER

_____ THEOCRACY

_____ TOPOGRAPHER

_____ ZOOLOGY

1. n) the study of family ancestry

2. n) machine for making copies with a stencil

3. n) chemical decomposition by heat

4. n) measured or viewed from the earth's center; regarding the earth as the center of all

5. a) an organism with both male and female organs

6. n) the study of animal life

7. n) a line on a map connecting points of equal pressure at the same time

8. v) a plant of the saxifrage family

9. n) one who believes no government is best

10. n) government under the immediate direction of God

11. n) geometrical figure; sketch, drawing, or plan explaining a thing by outlining its parts, etc.

12. n) one who draws maps indicating surface features

13. n) device used to measure the expansion of the chest or abdomen in respiration

14. v) to bring about; produce; cause

15. n) a plane figure with six angles and six sides

16. n) self-fertilization in plants or animals

17. n) instrument for measuring height above ground

18. n) a group of single reed, keyed instruments with a curved, metal body invented by A.J. Sax

19. n) device used to find the center of a cyclone

20. n) the study of blood and its diseases

DIRECTIONS: Use your GREEK roots and affixes sheets; try to find the root in each vocabulary words. Write the root and its meaning; also circle the root in the vocabulary word.

vocabulary word	root	meaning
ALTIMETER	_____	_____
ANARCHIST	_____	_____
ANDROGYNOUS	_____	_____
CYCLONOSCOPE	_____	_____
DIAGRAM	_____	_____
ENGENDER	_____	_____
GENEALOGY	_____	_____
GEOCENTRIC	_____	_____
HEMATOLOGY	_____	_____
HEXAGON	_____	_____
HYDRANGEA	_____	_____
ISOBAR	_____	_____
MIMEOGRAPH	_____	_____
ORTHOGAMY	_____	_____
PYROLYSIS	_____	_____
SAXOPHONE	_____	_____
STETHOMETER	_____	_____
THEOCRACY	_____	_____
TOPOGRAPHER	_____	_____
ZOOLOGY	_____	_____

DIRECTIONS: Use your GREEK roots and affixes sheets; try to find the word that is represented by the meanings of the roots and affixes. Write the word in the blank.

1. _____ in, into + cause, kind, race + that which

2. _____ God + to rule + state, quality, act

3. _____ water + vessel

4. _____ to copy, imitate + to write

5. _____ cause, kind, race + study of

6. _____ high, extremity + measure

7. _____ six + angle, corner

8. _____ equal + pressure, weight

9. _____ circle + to look

10. _____ chest, breast + measure

11. _____ fire + to free + condition, act

12. _____ man + woman + having the quality of

13. _____ animal + study of

14. _____ blood + study of

15. _____ place + to write + state, quality, act

16. _____ through, between + to write

17. _____ invented by A.J. Sax + sound

18. _____ earth + center + like, related to

19. _____ straight, right + marriage + state, quality, act

20. _____ not, without + first, to rule + one who

DIRECTIONS: For each blank write one vocabulary word. All words will be used only once. Look for context clues in the sentence.

_____ 1. A(n) --- is used by bees as a basic design for combs.

_____ 2. Some plants are considered to be ---.

_____ 3. Cooking usually involves some type of --- in changing the characteristics of food.

_____ 4. The study of minerals and vegetables is not part of ---.

_____ 5. Teachers may use the --- to make many copies of a paper for utilization in the classroom.

_____ 6. The --- produces a sound that was popular in the big band era earlier this century.

_____ 7. Looking for your family roots involves ---.

_____ 8. Fruit trees that don't need cross-pollination have the property of ---.

_____ 9. The --- tried to kill the president.

_____ 10. A skilled --- can create a map filled with good information.

_____ 11. The --- showed a seven-inch increase when the man took a deep breath.

_____ 12. The --- on the weather map surrounded the county.

_____ 13. Until Copernicus most people's ideas about the planets were --- in nature.

_____ 14. The plane's --- showed that we were dangerously close to the surface of the planet.

_____ 15. Christian activists are often accused of trying to install a(n) --- for the national government.

_____ 16. The --- is used by weathermen to find storm centers.

_____ 17. The gardener cared for the --- very well.

_____ 18. The lab technician was skilled in --- and could perform the tests on the samples very quickly.

_____ 19. An exploded --- is very helpful when attempting to take apart or repair anything mechanical.

_____ 20. The boy hoped to --- the girl's love by paying close attention to her wants and giving her gifts.

DIRECTIONS: Use your GREEK roots and affixes sheets; try to match the definitions with the words; look at the roots, prefixes, and suffixes for clues. Do NOT use a dictionary except as a last resort.

_____ ANACHRONISM

_____ ANDROGEN

_____ ANTIPYRETIC

_____ BIGAMIST

_____ DICTAPHONE

_____ EPISCOPAL

_____ EULOGY

_____ GENTLEMAN

_____ GRAPHOLOGY

_____ GYNARCHY

_____ HYDRANT

_____ ISOTOPE

_____ MEGAPHONE

_____ MICROGRAPH

_____ MILLIMETER

_____ PERIGEE

_____ PRIMOGENITOR

_____ PROGRAM

_____ STEREOMETRY

_____ TRILOGY

1. n) a tool to do very small writing or engraving

2. a) of or governed by bishops

3. n) study of handwriting, esp. as related to telling character, aptitudes, etc.

4. n) a set of three related plays or books that form a larger work

5. n) something occurring out of its proper place and time

6. n) a man of good birth and social standing; one attending a person of rank; well-bred

7. n) a measurement equal to 1/1000th of a meter

8. n) one who is married to at least two people at the same time

9. n) two or more forms of an element having similar properties but different weights

10. n) ancestor; forefather; earliest of the tribe

11. n) writing or speech in praise of some event or person, the person usually being dead

12. n) art of determining the dimensions and volumes of solid figures

13. n) that which reduces a fever

14. n) point closest to the center in an orbital path

15. n) list of events, pieces, performers, etc.; a plan of procedure
    v) to plan out a series of events

16. n) government by a woman or women

17. n) male hormone or similar substance that promotes masculine characteristics

18. n) funnel-shaped device for increasing the volume of a voice

19. v) a large discharge pipe with a valve to get water; a fireplug

20. n) machine for recording and reproducing words spoken into it for later transcription

DIRECTIONS: Use your GREEK roots and affixes sheets; try to find the root in each vocabulary words. Write the root and its meaning; also circle the root in the vocabulary word.

vocabulary word	root	meaning
ANACHRONISM	_____	_____
ANDROGEN	_____	_____
ANTIPYRETIC	_____	_____
BIGAMIST	_____	_____
DICTAPHONE	_____	_____
EPISCOPAL	_____	_____
EULOGY	_____	_____
GENTLEMAN	_____	_____
GRAPHOLOGY	_____	_____
GYNARCHY	_____	_____
HYDRANT	_____	_____
ISOTOPE	_____	_____
MEGAPHONE	_____	_____
MICROGRAPH	_____	_____
MILLIMETER	_____	_____
PERIGEE	_____	_____
PRIMOGENITOR	_____	_____
PROGRAM	_____	_____
STEREOMETRY	_____	_____
TRILOGY	_____	_____

DIRECTIONS: Use your GREEK roots and affixes sheets; try to find the word that is represented by the meanings of the roots and affixes. Write the word in the blank.

1. _____ against, opposite + fire + like, related to

2. _____ good, well + word, discourse

3. _____ thousand + measure

4. _____ to write + study of

5. _____ small + to write

6. _____ two + marriage + one who

7. _____ first + cause, kind, race + one who

8. _____ up, back, again + time + state, quality, act

9. _____ water + that which

10. _____ solid, 3-dimensional + measure + state, quality

11. _____ three + word, discourse

12. _____ around + earth

13. _____ on, outside + to look + like, related to

14. _____ for, before, forward + to write

15. _____ cause, kind, race + French form + man

16. _____ to speak + sound

17. _____ great, million + sound

18. _____ woman + first, to rule

19. _____ man + cause, kind, race

20. _____ equal + place

DIRECTIONS: For each blank write one vocabulary word. All words will be used only once. Look for context clues in the sentence.

_____   1. Richard Cory was thought to be a(n) --- by most of the townspeople.

_____   2. Cheerleaders will often use a(n) --- so that the crowd can hear them.

_____   3. The art of --- is used to figure the capacity of cylinders and other such containers.

_____   4. The minister delivered a beautiful --- in honor of the past life of Mr. Goodman.

_____   5. Cold water is a remedy that has --- properties.

_____   6. You can't tell the players without a(n) ---.

_____   7. Uranium has more than one ---.

_____   8. The doctor injected the necessary --- into the patient.

_____   9. A satellite in an elliptical orbit comes closest to the earth at a point called the ---.

_____   10. A church government with bishops giving oversight reflects a(n) --- structure.

_____   11. A knight in armor would be a(n) --- today.

_____   12. In most towns a car is not allowed to park in front of a fire ---.

_____   13. J.R.R. Tolkien wrote a(n) --- of novels about hobbits, dwarves, and elves.

_____   14. A(n) --- neglects to see that God created marriage to be between one man and one woman.

_____   15. If the length of something is measured by the ---, you can be sure it is quite small.

_____   16. The fabled Amazon women were thought to be a(n) ---.

_____   17. Efficient businessmen often use a(n) --- in their car while commuting to and from work.

_____   18. Adam is the --- of the human race.

_____   19. Engravers working on very small objects can use a(n) --- to good advantage.

_____   20. Some handwriting experts claim --- can reveal personality characteristics.

DIRECTIONS: Use your GREEK roots and affixes sheets; try to match the definitions with the words; look at the roots, prefixes, and suffixes for clues. Do NOT use a dictionary except as a last resort.

_____ ANTIPHONY

_____ ARCHANGEL

_____ CRYPTOGRAM

_____ CYTOLOGY

_____ EPILOGUE

_____ GENDER

_____ GEODE

_____ GYNOPHOBIA

_____ HYDRAULIC

_____ ISOPYRE

_____ LITHOGRAPH

_____ MICROMETER

_____ PHILANDER

_____ POLYGRAPH

_____ PRIMOGENITURE

_____ PROLOGUE

_____ PSYCHOGENIC

_____ SYMMETRY

_____ TECHNOCRACY

_____ TRAVELOGUE

1. n) a sexual class or kind; a grammatical category

2. n) a print or copy made from a stone or metal plate

3. n) an introduction to a poem or play

4. n) a lecture describing travels, usually accompanied with pictures

5. v) to be excessively flirty; to be insincere at love

6. n) something written in code or cipher

7. n) an abnormal fear of women

8. n) the opposition of sounds; harmony produced by sounds in opposition

9. n) the right of the eldest son to inherit his father's estate

10. n) sameness of opposite parts; alike on both sides

11. a) operated by the movement and force of liquid

12. a) originating in the mind; caused by mental conflicts

13. n) the study of the function, structure, and life history of cells

14. n) a tool used to measure very small distances

15. n) angel of the highest rank; chief angel

16. n) type of opal containing iron and other impurities

17. n) government by experts; system controlled by scientists and engineers

18. n) a stone with a cavity lined with crystals

19. n) closing section added to a novel, play, etc., that provides further information or comment

20. n) a device for reproducing writings or drawings; device for recording simultaneous changes in blood pressure, pulse rate, respiration, etc.

DIRECTIONS: Use your GREEK roots and affixes sheets; try to find the root in each vocabulary words. Write the root and its meaning; also circle the root in the vocabulary word.

vocabulary word	root	meaning
ANTIPHONY	_____	_____
ARCHANGEL	_____	_____
CRYPTOGRAM	_____	_____
CYTOLOGY	_____	_____
EPILOGUE	_____	_____
GENDER	_____	_____
GEODE	_____	_____
GYNOPHOBIA	_____	_____
HYDRAULIC	_____	_____
ISOPYRE	_____	_____
LITHOGRAPH	_____	_____
MICROMETER	_____	_____
PHILANDER	_____	_____
POLYGRAPH	_____	_____
PRIMOGENITURE	_____	_____
PROLOGUE	_____	_____
PSYCHOGENIC	_____	_____
SYMMETRY	_____	_____
TECHNOCRACY	_____	_____
TRAVELOGUE	_____	_____

DIRECTIONS: Use your GREEK roots and affixes sheets; try to find the word that is represented by the meanings of the roots and affixes. Write the word in the blank.

1. _____ many + to write

2. _____ equal + fire

3. _____ first, to rule + angel (messenger)

4. _____ earth + resembling

5. _____ against, opposite + sound + state, quality, act

6. _____ stone + to write

7. _____ to love + man

8. _____ cell + study of

9. _____ with, together + measure

10. _____ hidden + to write

11. _____ first + cause, kind, race + state, quality, act

12. _____ woman + to fear + condition

13. _____ art, skill + to rule + state, quality, act

14. _____ water + pipe, flute + like, related to

15. _____ on, outside + word, discourse

16. _____ small + measure

17. _____ travel + word, discourse

18. _____ mind + cause, kind, race + like, related to

19. _____ cause, kind, race + that which

20. _____ for, before, forward + word, discourse

DIRECTIONS: For each blank write one vocabulary word. All words will be used only once. Look for context clues in the sentence.

_____ 1. Heavy loads can easily be lifted with a(n) --- jack.

_____ 2. The missionary gave a(n) --- of his recent trip to Africa.

_____ 3. A butterfly displays --- in its two halves.

_____ 4. A man who will --- is not being considerate or morally correct in how he treats women.

_____ 5. The biologist specialized in --- at the research lab.

_____ 6. Much of today's sickness arises from --- causes.

_____ 7. The exterior of a(n) --- does not reveal its internal beauty.

_____ 8. The English practiced --- for many years, so the great English estates were not often broken up.

_____ 9. --- can produce pleasing or displeasing sounds.

_____ 10. The --- copied the ransom note perfectly.

_____ 11. Previous to the play one actor delivered the ---.

_____ 12. Biblical --- is male and female.

_____ 13. Michael and Gabriel are examples of a(n) ---.

_____ 14. The prospector found a beautiful --- in the sands of the Nevada desert.

_____ 15. A seller of women's apparel had better not suffer from ---.

_____ 16. A(n) --- at the end of a novel often is helpful to clear up some aspect of the plot.

_____ 17. Those who believe a(n) --- is the best form of rule usually see themselves as the experts.

_____ 18. The mechanic uses a(n) --- to check dimensions on crankshafts and certain other surfaces.

_____ 19. The picture was a(n) ---, not an original.

_____ 20. A common use of the --- is for a secret military message.

DIRECTIONS: Use your GREEK roots and affixes sheets; try to match the definitions with the words; look at the roots, prefixes, and suffixes for clues. Do NOT use a dictionary except as a last resort.

_____ APHONIC

_____ CHRONOGRAM

_____ DIGAMY

_____ ECOLOGIST

_____ GENESIS

_____ GEOGRAPHER

_____ GONIOMETER

_____ GYROSCOPE

_____ HYDRODYNAMICS

_____ INDIGENOUS

_____ ISOTROPIC

_____ LEXICOGRAPHY

_____ METEOROLOGY

_____ MONOGRAPH

_____ PHILANTHROPY

_____ POLYPHONIC

_____ PROGENITOR

_____ PYROSIS

_____ TOPOLOGY

_____ ZOOMETRY

1. n) one who specializes in describing the surface of the earth

2. n) native; born, growing, or produced naturally in a given region or country

3. n) the desire to help mankind as evidenced by acts of charity, etc.

4. n) inscription in which certain prominent letters express a Roman numeral date

5. n) study of place names in relation to their history

6. n) the study of weather and climate

7. n) one who studies the environment

8. a) having physical properties that are the same regardless of the direction of measurement

9. n) instrument for measuring angles, esp. of solids

10. n) wheel mounted in a ring so the axis is free to turn in any direction yet the spinning wheel maintains its own plane of rotation

11. n) a second legal marriage; having a second mate after the death or divorce of the first

12. n) the beginning or origin

13. n) condition of a burning sensation in the stomach and esophagus with belching acid fluid; heartburn

14. n) a forefather; ancestor in a direct line

15. n) branch of physics dealing with motion and action of water and other fluids

16. n) measurement and comparison of relative sizes of different parts of animals

17. n) the writing or compiling of a dictionary

18. n) a book, paper, or article about one subject

19. a) not sounded or pronounced

20. a) having or making many sounds

DIRECTIONS: Use your GREEK roots and affixes sheets; try to find the root in each vocabulary words. Write the root and its meaning; also circle the root in the vocabulary word.

vocabulary word	root	meaning
APHONIC	_____	_____
CHRONOGRAM	_____	_____
DIGAMY	_____	_____
ECOLOGIST	_____	_____
GENESIS	_____	_____
GEOGRAPHER	_____	_____
GONIOMETER	_____	_____
GYROSCOPE	_____	_____
HYDRODYNAMICS	_____	_____
INDIGENOUS	_____	_____
ISOTROPIC	_____	_____
LEXICOGRAPHY	_____	_____
METEOROLOGY	_____	_____
MONOGRAPH	_____	_____
PHILANTHROPY	_____	_____
POLYPHONIC	_____	_____
PROGENITOR	_____	_____
PYROSIS	_____	_____
TOPOLOGY	_____	_____
ZOOMETRY	_____	_____

DIRECTIONS: Use your GREEK roots and affixes sheets; try to find the word that is represented by the meanings of the roots and affixes. Write the word in the blank.

1. _____ fire + condition, act

2. _____ animal + measure + state, quality, act

3. _____ many + sound + like, related to

4. _____ word, speech + to write + state, quality, act

5. _____ ring, circle + to look

6. _____ time + to write

7. _____ within + cause, kind, race + having quality of

8. _____ house + word, study + one who

9. _____ not, without + sound + like, related to

10. _____ beyond, change + hovering in the air + study of

11. _____ to love + man, human + state, quality, act

12. _____ earth + to write + one who

13. _____ water + power + science, system

14. _____ equal + to turn + like, related to

15. _____ angle, corner + measure

16. _____ place + study of

17. _____ two + marriage + state, quality, act

18. _____ cause, kind, race + state, quality, act

19. _____ one + to write

20. _____ for, before, forward + cause, kind, race + one who

DIRECTIONS: For each blank write one vocabulary word. All words will be used only once. Look for context clues in the sentence.

_____

_____

_____

_____

_____

_____

_____

_____

_____

_____

_____

_____

_____

_____

_____

_____

_____

_____

_____

_____

1. The students brought in many varieties of dogs for their --- project.

2. The condition of --- often leaves a bad taste in a person's mouth.

3. Noah Webster was a high point in the field of ---.

4. Ships of the past have often used the --- to stabilize their compasses.

5. The --- population was opposed to the newcomers.

6. The man's public --- was a cover-up for his guilt.

7. Many interesting facts about an area can be learned by delving into the --- of the region.

8. A good --- can produce a map anyone can follow.

9. Most people would like to have a famous --- in their family history.

10. In some African cultures, --- is still common.

11. The phrase, MerCy MiXed with LoVe, is a(n) --- holding the numeral MCMXLV which stands for 1940.

12. The professor wrote a short --- on limited atonement.

13. A regular band produces --- sounds.

14. The famous silent e is a(n) --- letter.

15. --- compounds have like physical properties regardless of the direction of measurement.

16. Understanding --- is helpful in designing fish habitats in streams.

17. The --- for the project came from a magazine article read by one of the members of the club.

18. Pond culture is a favorite small study for a(n) ---.

19. One wonders if the pyramid builders used a(n) ---.

20. A working knowledge of --- increases the margin of success when predicting the weather.

DIRECTIONS: Use your GREEK roots and affixes sheets; try to match the definitions with the words; look at the roots, prefixes, and suffixes for clues. Do NOT use a dictionary except as a last resort.

_____ ACROGRAPHY

_____ APOLOGUE

_____ ARCHDUKE

_____ CACOPHONY

_____ DOXOLOGY

_____ GENE

_____ GEODETIC

_____ HELIOSCOPE

_____ HYDROELECTRIC

_____ ISOCHROMATIC

_____ KILOMETER

_____ MONOGRAM

_____ MORPHOLOGY

_____ NITROGEN

_____ PHILOGYNIST

_____ PLUTOCRACY

_____ POLYANDRY

_____ PROGENY

_____ PSYCHOGRAPH

_____ THERMOMETER

1. n) practice of having two or more husbands at the same time

2. n) study of form and structure; in linguistics, the study of form and structure of words

3. a) of locating exact points on the earth's surface

4. n) a thing or part that is comparable with another

5. n) a distance measurement unit equal to one thousand meters

6. n) a chief duke, esp. a prince in the former Austrian royal family

7. n) any of several hymns of praise to God

8. n) chart outlining relative strengths of personality traits

9. n) one who loves or is fond of women

10. n) dissonance; discordant sound

11. n) a device for looking at the sun without eye damage

12. n) instrument used to measure temperatures

13. a) having the same color

14. n) offspring; children; descendants

15. n) that which transmits hereditary traits

16. n) a design with letters

17. n) a colorless, odorless, gaseous element forming nearly 4/5 of the atmosphere

18. n) government by the rich or wealthy

19. n) process for producing designs in relief on metal by tracing on chalk

20. a) having to do with electricity produced by water power or friction of a stream

DIRECTIONS: Use your GREEK roots and affixes sheets; try to find the root in each vocabulary words. Write the root and its meaning; also circle the root in the vocabulary word.

vocabulary word	root	meaning
ACROGRAPHY	_____	_____
APOLOGUE	_____	_____
ARCHDUKE	_____	_____
CACOPHONY	_____	_____
DOXOLOGY	_____	_____
GENE	_____	_____
GEODETIC	_____	_____
HELIOSCOPE	_____	_____
HYDROELECTRIC	_____	_____
ISOCHROMATIC	_____	_____
KILOMETER	_____	_____
MONOGRAM	_____	_____
MORPHOLOGY	_____	_____
NITROGEN	_____	_____
PHILOGYNIST	_____	_____
PLUTOCRACY	_____	_____
POLYANDRY	_____	_____
PROGENY	_____	_____
PSYCHOGRAPH	_____	_____
THERMOMETER	_____	_____

DIRECTIONS: Use your GREEK roots and affixes sheets; try to find the word that is represented by the meanings of the roots and affixes. Write the word in the blank.

1. _____ earth + divide + like, related to

2. _____ first, to rule + duke

3. _____ thousand + measure

4. _____ many + man, human + state, quality, act

5. _____ to love + woman + one who

6. _____ form + study of

7. _____ from, away + word, discourse

8. _____ equal + color + like, related to

9. _____ mind + to write

10. _____ opinion, praise + word, discourse, study

11. _____ niter + cause, kind, race

12. _____ heat + measure

13. _____ high, extremity + to write + state, quality, act

14. _____ cause, kind, race

15. _____ for, before, forward + cause, kind, race + state

16. _____ sun + to look

17. _____ bad + sound + state, quality, act

18. _____ one + to write

19. _____ wealth + to rule + state, quality, act

20. _____ water + electric

DIRECTIONS: For each blank write one vocabulary word. All words will be used only once. Look for context clues in the sentence.

_____   1. Linguists and sculptors both utilize ---.

_____   2. --- best describes the sounds of an orchestra while it is tuning up.

_____   3. The nurse uses a(n) --- to check symptoms on many patients under her care.

_____   4. Almost every man could qualify for being a(n) ---.

_____   5. An accurate --- can tell a number of things about a person and their apparent actions and motives.

_____   6. The --- is shorter than a mile and is used as a common measurement for distance in many countries.

_____   7. Metal sculptors and artists probably use ---.

_____   8. Varying amounts of --- is contained in fertilizers.

_____   9. The --- is commonly sung in church services.

_____   10. God never intended --- as a way of life.

_____   11. Without a(n) --- it is dangerous to look at the sun, especially through lenses.

_____   12. High levels of income and property foster a(n) ---.

_____   13. Gills are the --- to lungs.

_____   14. The Pacific Northwest generates much --- power due to all of its rivers.

_____   15. The United States --- Survey team produces many maps.

_____   16. The beginning letter of each chapter was a beautiful ---.

_____   17. World War I was started when a(n) --- was killed.

_____   18. A shift of just one --- changes the makeup of the next generation.

_____   19. The --- of one family numbered over 300 after only three generations.

_____   20. A chameleon and his background are --- when they blend together.

DIRECTIONS: Use your GREEK roots and affixes sheets; try to match the definitions with the words; look at the roots, prefixes, and suffixes for clues. Do NOT use a dictionary except as a last resort.

_____ ANAGRAM

_____ ANTIPHON

_____ AUTOGAMY

_____ CHRONOSCOPE

_____ CONGENITAL

_____ DEGENERATE

_____ DIALOGUE

_____ GENERALIZE

_____ GEOLOGIST

_____ HEXAMETER

_____ HOMOGRAPH

_____ HYDROLYSIS

_____ ISOGENOUS

_____ ORTHOGONAL

_____ PEDOMETER

_____ PSYCHOLOGIST

_____ PYROPHOBIA

_____ SEISMOGRAPH

_____ SPIROMETER

_____ THERIANTHROPIC

1. a) existing as such at birth; resulting from heredity

2. n) device that measures the approximate distance walked by recording the number of steps taken

3. v) state an overall precept or idea

4. n) chemical decomposition of a compound due to its reaction to water ions

5. n) self-fertilization as in a flower getting pollen from its own stamens

6. n) instrument for recording the intensity, time, and direction of earthquakes

7. n) a line of verse with six metrical feet

8. a) refers to made up combinations of human and animal forms

9. n) a word or phrase made from another by rearranging its letters

10. n) one who studies the mind and human behavior

11. v) sink below a former condition; deteriorate
a) or n) referring to a fallen condition

12. n) device for measuring the breathing capacity of the lungs

13. n) a hymn, psalm, etc., chanted or sung in responsive, alternating parts

14. n) one who studies the crust of the earth

15. n) a word with the same spelling as another but with a different meaning and origin

16. n) a talking together; conversation

17. a) having to do with right angles; rectangular

18. n) instrument for measuring very small intervals of time

19. n) an irrational fear of fire

20. a) having the same origin

DIRECTIONS: Use your GREEK roots and affixes sheets; try to find the root in each vocabulary words. Write the root and its meaning; also circle the root in the vocabulary word.

vocabulary word	root	meaning
ANAGRAM	_____	_____
ANTIPHON	_____	_____
AUTOGAMY	_____	_____
CHRONOSCOPE	_____	_____
CONGENITAL	_____	_____
DEGENERATE	_____	_____
DIALOGUE	_____	_____
GENERALIZE	_____	_____
GEOLOGIST	_____	_____
HEXAMETER	_____	_____
HOMOGRAPH	_____	_____
HYDROLYSIS	_____	_____
ISOGENOUS	_____	_____
ORTHOGONAL	_____	_____
PEDOMETER	_____	_____
PSYCHOLOGIST	_____	_____
PYROPHOBIA	_____	_____
SEISMOGRAPH	_____	_____
SPIROMETER	_____	_____
THERIANTHROPIC	_____	_____

DIRECTIONS: Use your GREEK roots and affixes sheets; try to find the word that is represented by the meanings of the roots and affixes. Write the word in the blank.

1. _____ straight, right + angle, corner + like, related to

2. _____ beast + man, human + like, related to

3. _____ cause, kind, race + like, related to + to make

4. _____ foot + measure

5. _____ same + to write

6. _____ self + marriage + state, quality, act

7. _____ fire + to fear + condition

8. _____ up, back, again + to write

9. _____ through, between + word, discourse

10. _____ time + to look

11. _____ breath, life + measure

12. _____ against, opposite + sound

13. _____ to shake + to write

14. _____ six + measure

15. _____ away, down, negative + cause, kind + to make

16. _____ water + to free + condition, act

17. _____ mind + study of + one who

18. _____ with, together + cause, kind, race + like

19. _____ earth + study of + one who

20. _____ equal + cause, kind, race + having the quality of

DIRECTIONS: For each blank write one vocabulary word. All words will be used only once. Look for context clues in the sentence.

_____ 1. After being trapped in a forest fire, the man suffered from ---.

_____ 2. The --- showed that the athlete had great lungs.

_____ 3. The mine had a resident --- to check over the ore samples that were brought in.

_____ 4. A garden left to itself will --- into a weedy tangle in a short time.

_____ 5. Siblings are --- since they have the same parents.

_____ 6. Writing --- into a book requires knowledge of quotation marks and their attendant punctuation.

_____ 7. A(n) --- must be adjusted for your stride to give a near accurate reading.

_____ 8. The more traditional churches use the --- regularly in their services.

_____ 9. The effect of --- on some items is disintegration.

_____ 10. A square is a(n) --- figure.

_____ 11. A stop watch might qualify as a(n) ---.

_____ 12. The --- placed the intensity of the quake at 4.9 on the Richter scale.

_____ 13. Mary is a(n) --- of army.

_____ 14. The --- gave his patient many different mental tests.

_____ 15. The poem was written in iambic ---.

_____ 16. To --- without considering all aspects is dangerous.

_____ 17. The centaur is an example of a mythological --- creature.

_____ 18. A plant exhibiting --- does not really need bees or wind to spread pollen.

_____ 19. The word bow is an example of a(n) ---.

_____ 20. A(n) --- defect may be reversible through medical treatment or therapy of some sort.

DIRECTIONS: Use your GREEK roots and affixes sheets; try to match the definitions with the words; look at the roots, prefixes, and suffixes for clues. Do NOT use a dictionary except as a last resort.

_____ ARCHENEMY

_____ AUTOBIOGRAPHY

_____ BIOGENESIS

_____ GENERALLY

_____ GEOMANCY

_____ HOLOGRAPH

_____ HOROSCOPE

_____ HYDROPONICS

_____ ISODYNAMIC

_____ LOGOGRAM

_____ LYCANTHROPE

_____ METER

_____ OCHLOCRACY

_____ PETROLOGY

_____ PHONETIC

_____ PHOTOGENIC

_____ PYROMETER

_____ SOMATOLOGY

_____ STENOGRAPHER

_____ TELEPHONE

1. n) the development of living organisms from other living organisms

2. n) a document written entirely in the handwriting of the author

3. n) a letter, character, or symbol used to represent an entire word ($ for dollar)

4. a) of speech sounds and their producing and recording

5. n) government by the mob; mob rule

6. n) the study of the physical nature of man

7. n) a chief enemy; Satan

8. n) instrument for conveying sounds over distances

9. a) artistically suited for being photographed

10. n) a self-written history of one's own life

11. n) method of growing plants in nutrient rich solutions instead of soil

12. adv) in most instances; widely; of most people

13. n) one skilled in taking dictation by shorthand and later transcribing to normal writing

14. n) a person who believes he is a wolf; werewolf

15. n) false prophecy by supposed figures formed when a handful of earth is cast on the ground

16. n) rhythm in verse or music; unit of length equal to 39.37 inches; instrument for measuring

17. n) made up chart of planet and star positions by which some profess to tell future events and even personality characteristics

18. n) the study of rocks

19. n) instrument used to measure very high heat

20. a) having equal force

DIRECTIONS: Use your GREEK roots and affixes sheets; try to find the root in each vocabulary words. Write the root and its meaning; also circle the root in the vocabulary word.

vocabulary word	root	meaning
ARCHENEMY	_____	_____
AUTOBIOGRAPHY	_____	_____
BIOGENESIS	_____	_____
GENERALLY	_____	_____
GEOMANCY	_____	_____
HOLOGRAPH	_____	_____
HOROSCOPE	_____	_____
HYDROPONICS	_____	_____
ISODYNAMIC	_____	_____
LOGOGRAM	_____	_____
LYCANTHROPE	_____	_____
METER	_____	_____
OCHLOCRACY	_____	_____
PETROLOGY	_____	_____
PHONETIC	_____	_____
PHOTOGENIC	_____	_____
PYROMETER	_____	_____
SOMATOLOGY	_____	_____
STENOGRAPHER	_____	_____
TELEPHONE	_____	_____

DIRECTIONS: Use your GREEK roots and affixes sheets; try to find the word that is represented by the meanings of the roots and affixes. Write the word in the blank.

1. _____ word, discourse, study + to write

2. _____ sound + like, related to

3. _____ narrow + to write + one who

4. _____ hour + to look

5. _____ wolf + man, human

6. _____ body + study of

7. _____ first, to rule + enemy

8. _____ from afar + sound

9. _____ measure

10. _____ cause, kind, race + like + in the manner of

11. _____ self + life + to write + state, quality, act

12. _____ light + cause, kind, race + like, related to

13. _____ earth + divination

14. _____ equal + power + like, related to

15. _____ life + cause, kind, race + state, quality, act

16. _____ whole + to write

17. _____ water + labor + science, system

18. _____ mob + to rule + state, quality, act

19. _____ fire + measure

20. _____ rock + study of

DIRECTIONS: For each blank write one vocabulary word. All words will be used only once. Look for context clues in the sentence.

_____   1. Rockhounds read many books dealing with ---.

_____   2. Space technicians used a(n) --- to check the reentry temperature on the space shuttles.

_____   3. People in northern climates can use --- to help produce tomatoes in cool weather.

_____   4. The --- is a fantasy figure found in horror stories.

_____   5. Common consent means the idea is --- agreed upon.

_____   6. Two opposing forces pushing or pulling against one another and getting nowhere are said to be ---.

_____   7. «The --- chart at the beginning of dictionaries is often called the key to pronunciation.

_____   8. A good --- will not only take quick and accurate notes but will also produce an error free document.

_____   9. The --- is much like the democracy since neither protects the rights of the minority except by whim.

_____   10. The last will and testament was a(n) --- of the man who left it.

_____   11. The young man's pictures revealed him to be quite ---.

_____   12. The --- of the United States in the Pacific theater in WWII was Japan.

_____   13. Though it was against God's will, the gypsy tried to use --- to predict the weather.

_____   14. Teenage girls have a fondness for talking on the --- at almost any time.

_____   15. The field of --- does not deal with the spiritual aspects of man.

_____   16. Booker T. Washington wrote his own ---.

_____   17. The --- on the gas tank was accurate to the ounce.

_____   18. Many people mistakenly check their daily --- instead of God's Word to find direction for their lives.

_____   19. One common --- in small business is the @ sign.

_____   20. All humans but Adam are a product of ---.

DIRECTIONS: Use your GREEK roots and affixes sheets; try to match the definitions with the words; look at the roots, prefixes, and suffixes for clues. Do NOT use a dictionary except as a last resort.

_____ APOGAMY

_____ AUTOGRAPH

_____ CHRONOLOGY

_____ DERMATOGEN

_____ GENERATE

_____ GEOMETRIC

_____ GYNECOLOGY

_____ HELIOMETER

_____ HEXAGRAM

_____ HYDROTROPISM

_____ KALEIDOSCOPE

_____ LOGARITHM

_____ MICROPHONE

_____ MISANTHROPE

_____ NECROLOGY

_____ PENTAGON

_____ POLYGENESIS

_____ PYRE

_____ SOTERIOLOGY

_____ STEREOGRAPHY

1. n) device for measuring the angular distance between two stars

2. n) device for intensifying weak sounds by electromagnetics

3. n) art of representing solids on a plane surface

4. n) development of a plant without the union of sexual organs or cells

5. n) tubelike instrument containing loose bits of colored glass reflected by mirrors to form patterns when viewed in rotation

6. n) a woodpile on which a dead body is burned

7. n) a layer of dividing cells from which the epidermis is formed

8. n) the theory that different species are descended from ultimate different ancestors

9. v) to produce; procreate; beget; bring into being

10. n) list of people who died in a certain place or time; obituary

11. a) characterized by straight lines, triangles, circles, or similar regular forms

12. n) tendency of a plant to grow or turn in the direction of moisture

13. n) a signature, personally written

14. n) study of the application of the work of redemption

15. n) the study and treatment of women's health

16. n) a six-pointed star

17. n) one who hates people

18. n) science of measuring time in fixed periods; list or table of dates in proper sequence

19. v) a plane figure with five sides and angles

20. n) the exponent of the power to which a fixed number must be raised in order to produce a given number

DIRECTIONS: Use your GREEK roots and affixes sheets; try to find the root in each vocabulary words. Write the root and its meaning; also circle the root in the vocabulary word.

vocabulary word	root	meaning
APOGAMY	_____	_____
AUTOGRAPH	_____	_____
CHRONOLOGY	_____	_____
DERMATOGEN	_____	_____
GENERATE	_____	_____
GEOMETRIC	_____	_____
GYNECOLOGY	_____	_____
HELIOMETER	_____	_____
HEXAGRAM	_____	_____
HYDROTROPISM	_____	_____
KALEIDOSCOPE	_____	_____
LOGARITHM	_____	_____
MICROPHONE	_____	_____
MISANTHROPE	_____	_____
NECROLOGY	_____	_____
PENTAGON	_____	_____
POLYGENESIS	_____	_____
PYRE	_____	_____
SOTERIOLOGY	_____	_____
STEREOGRAPHY	_____	_____

DIRECTIONS: Use your GREEK roots and affixes sheets; try to find the word which is represented by the meanings of the roots and affixes. Write the word in the blank.

1. _____ many + cause, kind, race + state, quality, act

2. _____ six + to write

3. _____ safety, salvation + study of

4. _____ death, dead + study of

5. _____ beautiful + form + to look

6. _____ from, away + marriage + state, quality, act

7. _____ water + to turn + state, quality, act

8. _____ skin + cause, kind, race

9. _____ five + angle, corner

10. _____ to hate + man, human

11. _____ woman + study of

12. _____ sun + measure

13. _____ earth + measure + like, related to

14. _____ fire

15. _____ time + study of

16. _____ cause, kind, race + to make, to do

17. _____ self + to write

18. _____ small + sound

19. _____ solid, 3-dimensional + to write + state, quality

20. _____ word, discourse + number

DIRECTIONS: For each blank write one vocabulary word. All words will be used only once. Look for context clues in the sentence.

_____ 1. The Vikings would use a ship for the funeral --- of a great warrior.

_____ 2. Public speakers are cautioned to speak into the --- so that the audience can clearly hear them.

_____ 3. The --- section of the newspaper is large after a serious epidemic or disaster.

_____ 4. The --- is often called the Star of David.

_____ 5. --- causes the roots of a tree to grow toward a stream or pond.

_____ 6. Fans will often seek the --- of a famous personality.

_____ 7. The --- contained red, blue, yellow, white, and green colors in its many designs.

_____ 8. His line drawings had a very --- quality to them.

_____ 9. Astronomers can use a(n) --- to figure distances in space.

_____ 10. The --- of Civil War battles is important for seeing how one event led to another.

_____ 11. Since God created all the animals, a Christian should accept --- as a basic truth.

_____ 12. Plant propagation by grafting and tip-layering shows the quality of ---.

_____ 13. The gash penetrated the --- beneath the skin.

_____ 14. Artists and draftsmen have developed --- to make their drawings more lifelike.

_____ 15. A good motor will --- a great deal of power.

_____ 16. The --- did not seem to have any friends at all.

_____ 17. The --- is the basis for slide rule computations.

_____ 18. --- deals with how Christ participates in the salvation process.

_____ 19. A famous --- is the military building in Washington, DC., so named because of its shape.

_____ 20. One specializing in --- knows many things about the care and preservation of women

DIRECTIONS: Use your GREEK roots and affixes sheets; try to match the definitions with the words; look at the roots, prefixes, and suffixes for clues. Do NOT use a dictionary except as a last resort.

_____ ANDROPHOBIA

_____ ARCHIMAGE

_____ AUTOGENESIS

_____ CHROMATOLOGY

_____ GENERATION

_____ GENRE

_____ GEOPHAGY

_____ HELIOGRAPH

_____ HYDROUS

_____ ISOCRACY

_____ LOGIC

_____ METRIC

_____ MICROSCOPE

_____ MONOPHONIC

_____ POLYGAMIST

_____ PYROGRAPHY

_____ SPECTROLOGY

_____ SPHEROMETER

_____ SYLLOGISM

_____ TELEGRAM

1. n) the eating of earth

2. n) instrument for looking at very small objects

3. n) the study of light waves

4. n) considered a powerful wizard, though the Bible forbids witchcraft

5. a) containing water; watery

6. n) instrument used to measure the surface curvature of rounded bodies

7. n) one who is married to more than one person at the same time

8. n) the science or method of correct reasoning

9. a) of sound reproduction through a single channel to one or more speakers

10. n) a message sent by wire

11. n) a type of work in literature or art

12. n) the process of burning designs on wood or leather

13. n) an abnormal fear of men

14. n) device for measuring intensity of sunlight; a mirror for signaling using the sun's rays

15. n) scientific study of colors; chromatics

16. a) of, involving, or used in measuring; designating the system of measurement based on the meter

17. n) a political system where everyone has equal power

18. n) reasoning in which two statements (premises) are made with logical conclusions drawn from them

19. n) act of creating offspring; period of about 30 years; all people born at a given time

20. n) spontaneous generation with no outside source; self-genesis

DIRECTIONS: Use your GREEK roots and affixes sheets; try to find the root in each vocabulary words. Write the root and its meaning; also circle the root in the vocabulary word.

vocabulary word	root	meaning
ANDROPHOBIA	_____	_____
ARCHIMAGE	_____	_____
AUTOGENESIS	_____	_____
CHROMATOLOGY	_____	_____
GENERATION	_____	_____
GENRE	_____	_____
GEOPHAGY	_____	_____
HELIOGRAPH	_____	_____
HYDROUS	_____	_____
ISOCRACY	_____	_____
LOGIC	_____	_____
METRIC	_____	_____
MICROSCOPE	_____	_____
MONOPHONIC	_____	_____
POLYGAMIST	_____	_____
PYROGRAPHY	_____	_____
SPECTROLOGY	_____	_____
SPHEROMETER	_____	_____
SYLLOGISM	_____	_____
TELEGRAM	_____	_____

DIRECTIONS: Use your GREEK roots and affixes sheets; try to find the word which is represented by the meanings of the roots and affixes. Write the word in the blank.

1. _____ earth + to eat + state, quality, act

2. _____ self + cause, kind, race + state, quality, act

3. _____ word, discourse, study + like, related to

4. _____ to look + study of

5. _____ many + marriage + one who

6. _____ small + to look

7. _____ first, to rule + mage

8. _____ equal + to rule + state, quality, act

9. _____ with, together + word, discourse + state, quality

10. _____ cause, kind, race + to make, to do + state, quality

11. _____ one + sound + like, related to

12. _____ from afar + to write

13. _____ man, human + to fear + condition

14. _____ cause, kind, race

15. _____ ball + measure

16. _____ sun + to write

17. _____ color + study of

18. _____ measure + like, related to

19. _____ fire + to write + state, quality, act

20. _____ water + having the quality of

DIRECTIONS: For each blank write one vocabulary word. All words will be used only once. Look for context clues in the sentence.

_____ 1. The --- usually involves two basic statements and one conclusion made from them

_____ 2. A photographer needs to know some --- to get good quality pictures in Technicolor or black and white.

_____ 3. Historical novels are just one --- of novel.

_____ 4. A(n) --- is great in theory but would be difficult to manage since no one need take orders from anyone.

_____ 5. The phenomenon of --- often occurs during famines.

_____ 6. King David was a(n) --- though God intended marriage to be between one man and one woman.

_____ 7. Evolution attempts to make people accept ---, and that life can come from nothing.

_____ 8. It is good to use --- when making important decisions.

_____ 9. The message from his uncle in Tupelo came by ---.

_____ 10. Under the --- the wasp appeared to be a monster.

_____ 11. In one --- the immigrants were successfully integrated into the community.

_____ 12. Artistic belt makers are often skilled in ---.

_____ 13. In some ancient books a --- is a formidable character to encounter.

_____ 14. The prism is a device used in --- to explain color in light wave lengths.

_____ 15. Fresh fruit usually has a(n) --- quality to it.

_____ 16. The engineer uses the --- when measuring the interior of the large wine vat.

_____ 17. A rape experience could cause a girl to develop ---.

_____ 18. The --- system gave a fair sound but lacked the fullness of more modern digital systems.

_____ 19. Part of the scout's equipment was a(n) --- for flashing messages back to base camp.

_____ 20. Many automobiles today take --- size wrenches instead of standard sizes found on American-made cars.

DIRECTIONS: Use your GREEK roots and affixes sheets; try to match the definitions with the words; look at the roots, prefixes, and suffixes for clues. Do NOT use a dictionary except as a last resort.

_____ ACROGEN

_____ ANTHROPOCENTRIC

_____ BIBLIOGRAPHY

_____ BIOLOGY

_____ CHRONOMETER

_____ COSMOLOGY

_____ ENDOGAMY

_____ EPIGEOUS

_____ ERGOMETER

_____ GENERATOR

_____ HETEROGRAPHY

_____ HYDROGEN

_____ ISOMETRIC

_____ NOMOLOGY

_____ PHONEME

_____ POLYGON

_____ PSYCHOMETRY

_____ PYRITE

_____ STETHOSCOPE

_____ TELEGRAPH

1. a) growing on or above the ground after germination

2. n) having equality of measurement

3. n) iron sulfide; fool's gold; a natural yellow mineral that is a common sulfur source

4. n) spelling that differs from current standard usage

5. n) apparatus or system for sending messages by electric impulses over wire or radio waves

6. n) the study of living things

7. n) theory or philosophy of the nature and principles of the universe

8. n) a plane figure with several sides and angles

9. n) list of writings on one subject or of one author

10. n) a single sound represented in transcription by a given symbol

11. n) instrument used to examine the heart and lungs by listening to the sounds they make

12. n) device for measuring the amount of energy used

13. n) a highly accurate watch or clock

14. n) machine for producing energy gas or steam; machine for converting energy into electricity; a dynamo

15. n) marrying within one's own tribe or social group

16. n) the science of law and lawmaking

17. n) flowerless plant growing and producing only at its tips (e.g., ferns/ mosses)

18. n) inflammable, colorless, odorless gas that is the lightest of all known natural substances

19. a) ungodly belief that considers man as the central fact or final aim of the universe

20. n) measurement of the mental processes

DIRECTIONS: Use your GREEK roots and affixes sheets; try to find the root in each vocabulary words. Write the root and its meaning; also circle the root in the vocabulary word.

vocabulary word	root	meaning
ACROGEN	_____	_____
ANTHROPOCENTRIC	_____	_____
BIBLIOGRAPHY	_____	_____
BIOLOGY	_____	_____
CHRONOMETER	_____	_____
COSMOLOGY	_____	_____
ENDOGAMY	_____	_____
EPIGEOUS	_____	_____
ERGOMETER	_____	_____
GENERATOR	_____	_____
HETEROGRAPHY	_____	_____
HYDROGEN	_____	_____
ISOMETRIC	_____	_____
NOMOLOGY	_____	_____
PHONEME	_____	_____
POLYGON	_____	_____
PSYCHOMETRY	_____	_____
PYRITE	_____	_____
STETHOSCOPE	_____	_____
TELEGRAPH	_____	_____

DIRECTIONS: Use your GREEK roots and affixes sheets; try to find the word that is represented by the meanings of the roots and affixes. Write the word in the blank.

1. _____ work, power + measure

2. _____ equal + measure + like, related to

3. _____ time + measure

4. _____ fire + having the quality of

5. _____ high, extremity + cause, kind, race

6. _____ other + to write + state, quality, act

7. _____ many + angle, corner

8. _____ book + to write + state, quality, act

9. _____ law, order + study of

10. _____ inside + marriage + state, quality, act

11. _____ sound + something done

12. _____ life + study of

13. _____ from afar + to write

14. _____ mind + measure + state, quality, act

15. _____ man, human + center + like, related to

16. _____ cause, kind, race + to make, to do + that which

17. _____ chest, breast + to look

18. _____ universe, harmony + study of

19. _____ water + cause, kind, race

20. _____ on, outside + earth + having the quality of

DIRECTIONS: For each blank write one vocabulary word. All words will be used only once. Look for context clues in the sentence.

_____ 1. Pharisees and lawyers are versed in ---.

_____ 2. A famous picture shows a Plains Indian at a(n) --- pole, listening to the "talking trees."

_____ 3. Corn is an example of a(n) --- plant.

_____ 4. Schwa, the upside down e, is a famous ---.

_____ 5. At times it takes a creative mind to decipher the --- found on a student's paper.

_____ 6. A properly researched paper should include a(n) --- of source materials.

_____ 7. The IQ tests are used in ---.

_____ 8. Cutting off all the tips of a(n) --- does not help it grow.

_____ 9. The practice of --- often results in genetic problems today.

_____ 10. Both botany and zoology are covered in a basic --- course in school.

_____ 11. The --- is a standard item in a doctor's kit.

_____ 12. The typical humanist is --- in his beliefs.

_____ 13. Many a greenhorn has been fooled by ---.

_____ 14. The gasoline --- provides electricity to supply most of the needs of one household.

_____ 15. Much of --- is speculation even today since space is so vast and unknown.

_____ 16. A balloon filled with --- will rise in the air.

_____ 17. Examples of a(n) --- are the rhombus and trapezoid.

_____ 18. Grandfather's railroad Elgin watch was a(n) --- of precision and beauty.

_____ 19. A(n) --- fixed to the machine was supposed to register a reading in foot-pounds of force.

_____ 20. --- exercise requires very little equipment.

DIRECTIONS: Use your GREEK roots and affixes sheets; try to match the definitions with the words; look at the roots, prefixes, and suffixes for clues. Do NOT use a dictionary except as a last resort.

_____ ANTHROPOID

_____ ARCHITECT

_____ ASYMMETRICAL

_____ AUTOCRATIC

_____ BIOGRAPHER

_____ CHRONICLE

_____ DEHYDRATE

_____ GENERIC

_____ GENTEEL

_____ GEOPHYSICS

_____ HOMOGENEOUS

_____ HYDROGRAPHY

_____ IDEOLOGY

_____ ISOMER

_____ MONOLOGUE

_____ PHONOSCOPE

_____ PHOTOMETRY

_____ PORNOGRAPHY

_____ TECHNOLOGY

_____ TOMOGRAPHY

1. a) despotic; dictatorial; self-willed

2. n) the study of practical or industrial arts

3. n) device to exhibit properties of a sounding body, used to evaluate string quality (violins)

4. a) excessively or pretentiously well-bred, polite, refined, etc.

5. n) the measurement of light intensity

6. n) the study of ideas; doctrines, opinions, or way of thinking of an individual, group, etc.

7. n) person who designs and draws plans for buildings

8. n) a long speech by one speaker; soliloquy

9. v) to remove the water from

10. n) X-ray photography that films one plane only and blanks the others out

11. a) manlike; resembling men

12. n) one who writes histories of individual lives

13. n) science of weather, winds, tides, etc., and their effect upon the earth

14. n) study, description, and mapping of oceans, lakes, rivers, esp. for commerce and navigation

15. n) writings or images meant to create lustful, impure thoughts

16. a) universal; applies to the whole group

17. a) the same in structure, quality, etc.; identical

18. a) having differences on both sides when divided in half

19. n) historical record according to date; a narrative history
    v) to tell or write the history of; record

20. n) two chemical compounds having the same elements in proportion by weight but differing in chemical and physical properties

DIRECTIONS: Use your GREEK roots and affixes sheets; try to find the root in each vocabulary words. Write the root and its meaning; also circle the root in the vocabulary word.

vocabulary word	root	meaning
ANTHROPOID	_____	_____
ARCHITECT	_____	_____
ASYMMETRICAL	_____	_____
AUTOCRATIC	_____	_____
BIOGRAPHER	_____	_____
CHRONICLE	_____	_____
DEHYDRATE	_____	_____
GENERIC	_____	_____
GENTEEL	_____	_____
GEOPHYSICS	_____	_____
HOMOGENEOUS	_____	_____
HYDROGRAPHY	_____	_____
IDEOLOGY	_____	_____
ISOMER	_____	_____
MONOLOGUE	_____	_____
PHONOSCOPE	_____	_____
PHOTOMETRY	_____	_____
PORNOGRAPHY	_____	_____
TECHNOLOGY	_____	_____
TOMOGRAPHY	_____	_____

DIRECTIONS: Use your GREEK roots and affixes sheets; try to find the word that is represented by the meanings of the roots and affixes. Write the word in the blank.

1. _____ sound + to look

2. _____ art, skill + study of

3. _____ prostitute + to write + state, quality, act

4. _____ to cut + to write + state, quality, act

5. _____ cause, kind, race + French form

6. _____ self + to rule + like, related to

7. _____ idea + study of

8. _____ one + word, discourse

9. _____ light + measure + state, quality, act

10. _____ away, down, negative + water + to make, to do

11. _____ man, human + resembling

12. _____ same + cause, kind, race + having the quality of

13. _____ not, without + with, together + measure + like

14. _____ life + to write + one who

15. _____ first, to rule + builder

16. _____ water + to write + state, quality, act

17. _____ earth + nature, natural + science, system

18. _____ cause, kind, race + like, related to

19. _____ equal + part

20. _____ time + like, related to

DIRECTIONS: For each blank write one vocabulary word. All words will be used only once. Look for context clues in the sentence.

_____   1. The --- given by the actor was actually both interesting and informative.

_____   2. --- is useful at times for making a medical diagnosis.

_____   3. A general knowledge of --- enables one to predict the effects of storms and tides.

_____   4. Modern --- affords mankind many conveniences.

_____   5. The basic --- of the pro-life people holds to the sanctity of human life.

_____   6. Samuel Pepys was Ben Jonson's ---.

_____   7. In order to distinguish one --- from another, a chemist must look at structure and appearance.

_____   8. The field of --- has produced many useful charts and maps for shipping purposes.

_____   9. An old --- shed new light on the battle.

_____   10. The --- planned for a later addition to the house.

_____   11. When most houses are divided in half, the two halves are ---.

_____   12. The root word found in --- is often translated as fornication in the New Testament, and expressly forbidden.

_____   13. Automatic light metering on cameras is a good example of how --- has developed.

_____   14. Schools often try to put pupils in --- groupings.

_____   15. The mayor's son had a(n) --- air about him.

_____   16. The ape is considered a(n) --- in some ways.

_____   17. It is can be wise to buy the --- brands of some items.

_____   18. The violin repairman used his --- to check the new shipment of gut and wire strings.

_____   19. Exposure to direct heat causes things to --- by varying degrees according to their composition.

_____   20. Whether a head of state or head of family, a(n) --- authority can make life rather miserable.

DIRECTIONS: Use your GREEK roots and affixes sheets; try to match the definitions with the words; look at the roots, prefixes, and suffixes for clues. Do NOT use a dictionary except as a last resort.

_____ ANALOGY

_____ ANTHROPOGENESIS

_____ CACOGRAPHY

_____ CHRONOLOGICAL

_____ EPIGRAPHY

_____ EUPHONIC

_____ EXOGAMY

_____ GENEROUS

_____ GENTILE

_____ HYDROLOGY

_____ METRONOME

_____ MISOGYNIST

_____ MORPHOGENESIS

_____ NOMOGRAPHY

_____ PARAPSYCHOLOGY

_____ PERISCOPE

_____ PHONOTYPE

_____ PYROMANCY

_____ TELEOLOGY

_____ TRIGONOMETRY

1. n) one who hates women

2. a) having a pleasant sound

3. n) study of water and its distribution, especially its underground sources

4. n) structural changes during the development of an organism

5. n) study investigating the psychological aspects of supposedly supernatural events

6. a) noble-minded; willing to give; ample; large

7. n) the branch of math that deals with angles, sides, and ratios of right triangles

8. n) a person who is not Jewish

9. a) arranged in order of occurrence

10. n) inscriptions as a group; study dealing with decoding, interpreting, and classifying inscriptions

11. n) custom of marrying only outside the clan, family, or tribe

12. n) a phonetic symbol used in printing

13. n) study of man's origin and development

14. n) viewing tube with mirrors found on submarines

15. n) bad handwriting; incorrect spelling

16. n) the study of final causes

17. n) device that beats time at a desired rate, as for piano practice

18. n) similarity in some respects between things otherwise unlike; a point by point comparison for purposes of explanation

19. n) the false art of predicting the future by trying to read flames

20. n) the writing or drafting of laws

DIRECTIONS: Use your GREEK roots and affixes sheets; try to find the root in each vocabulary words. Write the root and its meaning; also circle the root in the vocabulary word.

vocabulary word	root	meaning
ANALOGY	_____	_____
ANTHROPOGENESIS	_____	_____
CACOGRAPHY	_____	_____
CHRONOLOGICAL	_____	_____
EPIGRAPHY	_____	_____
EUPHONIC	_____	_____
EXOGAMY	_____	_____
GENEROUS	_____	_____
GENTILE	_____	_____
HYDROLOGY	_____	_____
METRONOME	_____	_____
MISOGYNIST	_____	_____
MORPHOGENESIS	_____	_____
NOMOGRAPHY	_____	_____
PARAPSYCHOLOGY	_____	_____
PERISCOPE	_____	_____
PHONOTYPE	_____	_____
PYROMANCY	_____	_____
TELEOLOGY	_____	_____
TRIGONOMETRY	_____	_____

DIRECTIONS: Use your GREEK roots and affixes sheets; try to find the word that is represented by the meanings of the roots and affixes. Write the word in the blank.

1. _____ time + word, discourse, study + like, related to

2. _____ to hate + woman + one who

3. _____ fire + divination

4. _____ outside + marriage + state, quality, act

5. _____ cause, kind, race + like, related to

6. _____ measure + law, order

7. _____ beside, variation + mind + study of

8. _____ up, back, again + word, discourse, study

9. _____ around + to look

10. _____ form + cause, kind, race + state, quality, act

11. _____ on, outside + to write + state, quality, act

12. _____ three + angle, corner + measure + state, quality

13. _____ man, human + cause, kind, race + state, quality

14. _____ sound + model

15. _____ water + study of

16. _____ from afar + study of

17. _____ cause, kind, race + having the quality of

18. _____ good, well + sound + like, related to

19. _____ law, order + to write + state, quality, act

20. _____ bad + to write + state, quality, act

DIRECTIONS: For each blank write one vocabulary word. All words will be used only once. Look for context clues in the sentence.

_____ 1. The symbol was a(n) --- not often seen in print.

_____ 2. Christ dissolved the wall between Jew and --- for the Christians at least.

_____ 3. The origin of the universe is a topic in ---.

_____ 4. --- studies false sciences and claims made by charlatans.

_____ 5. The --- clicked on steadily as the girl practiced.

_____ 6. The teacher drew a clear --- between his method of studying for a test and training for a race.

_____ 7. With experience, well drillers have a good sense of --- for their local areas.

_____ 8. The --- account of the event revealed a hidden cause of the final conflict.

_____ 9. The view through the --- showed an enemy convoy ahead.

_____ 10. Legislators and some lawyers believe they are the only ones who understand ---.

_____ 11. People from most Western cultures practice --- when selecting a mate.

_____ 12. Mother always gave each of us a(n) --- helping of vegetables on our dinner plates.

_____ 13. The blending of voices produced a(n) --- experience.

_____ 14. The false prophet used --- in his attempt to fool the king, though God clearly forbid this.

_____ 15. The --- caused the paper to be almost unreadable.

_____ 16. Through the use of ---, the linguist was able to decipher the meaning of the runes.

_____ 17. The Bible has much to say about --- in Genesis.

_____ 18. It is doubtful that a confirmed --- will marry.

_____ 19. Surveyors make heavy use of ---.

_____ 20. The --- of the frog shows some interesting changes.

DIRECTIONS: Use your GREEK roots and affixes sheets; try to match the definitions with the words; look at the roots, prefixes, and suffixes for clues. Do NOT use a dictionary.

_____ ANALOGUE

_____ ANTHROPOLOGIST

_____ ARISTOCRAT

_____ BAROMETER

_____ CALLIGRAPHY

_____ EXOGENOUS

_____ GENTLE

_____ GEOTHERMIC

_____ GRAPHICS

_____ HEXARCHY

_____ HYDROMETER

_____ ISOMORPHIC

_____ MONOGENISM

_____ OCEANOGRAPHY

_____ ORTHOSCOPIC

_____ PHONICS

_____ PHOTOGRAPH

_____ PYROGENIC

_____ STEREOPHONIC

_____ TETROLOGY

1. n) science of sound; use of elementary sounds and their symbols to teach reading and enunciation

2. n) a group of six friendly or allied states or governments

3. n) instrument for measuring the specific gravity of a liquid

4. n) a set of four related dramas or literary works

5. a) developing from without; originating externally

6. n) art of making drawings according to mathematical rules; computer drawings or visuals

7. a) of sound reproduction through multiple channels to produce directional sound effects

8. n) image or picture produced by a film sensitive to light

9. a) giving a true flat image without distortion

10. n) member of the privileged upper class; nobleman

11. n) branch of geography dealing with the oceans

12. a) having to do with the heat of the earth's interior

13. n) beautiful handwriting

14. a) having qualities considered appropriate to birth; polite; tame; easily handled; gradual

15. n) a thing or part that is comparable with another

16. a) producing or produced by heat or fever

17. n) the belief that all humans descended from a single ancestor or pair of ancestors

18. a) having similar or identical structure or appearance

19. n) instrument that measures atmospheric pressure

20. n) one who studies mankind

DIRECTIONS: Use your GREEK roots and affixes sheets; try to find the root in each vocabulary words. Write the root and its meaning; also circle the root in the vocabulary word.

vocabulary word	root	meaning
ANALOGUE	_____	_____
ANTHROPOLOGIST	_____	_____
ARISTOCRAT	_____	_____
BAROMETER	_____	_____
CALLIGRAPHY	_____	_____
EXOGENOUS	_____	_____
GENTLE	_____	_____
GEOTHERMIC	_____	_____
GRAPHICS	_____	_____
HEXARCHY	_____	_____
HYDROMETER	_____	_____
ISOMORPHIC	_____	_____
MONOGENISM	_____	_____
OCEANOGRAPHY	_____	_____
ORTHOSCOPIC	_____	_____
PHONICS	_____	_____
PHOTOGRAPH	_____	_____
PYROGENIC	_____	_____
STEREOPHONIC	_____	_____
TETROLOGY	_____	_____

DIRECTIONS: Use your GREEK roots and affixes sheets; try to find the word which is represented by the meanings of the roots and affixes. Write the word in the blank.

1. _____ water + measure

2. _____ cause, kind, race + French form

3. _____ fire + cause, kind, race + like, related to

4. _____ up, back, again + word, discourse

5. _____ equal + form + like, related to

6. _____ solid, 3-dimensional + sound + like, related to

7. _____ to write + science, system

8. _____ sound + science, system

9. _____ pressure, weight + measure

10. _____ one + cause, kind, race + state, quality, act

11. _____ light + to write

12. _____ ocean + to write + state, quality, act

13. _____ outside + cause, kind, race + having quality of

14. _____ four + word, discourse, study

15. _____ earth + heat + like, related to

16. _____ best + to rule

17. _____ beautiful + to write + state, quality, act

18. _____ straight, right + to look + state, quality, act

19. _____ man, human + word, discourse, study + one who

20. _____ six + first, to rule + state, quality, act

DIRECTIONS: For each blank write one vocabulary word. All words will be used only once. Look for context clues in the sentence.

_____ 1. The best reading program is one that uses ---.

_____ 2. The modern --- playback systems give one the sensation of attending a live concert.

_____ 3. Heat rashes are usually the result of --- action.

_____ 4. The writer produced a(n) --- about two alien worlds.

_____ 5. The --- in the computer program were very lifelike.

_____ 6. A quick look at the --- confirmed that a storm was moving in fast.

_____ 7. The Bible gives evidence to support --- with the story of Adam and Eve.

_____ 8. The --- drawing made an accurate template.

_____ 9. The man carried his wife's --- with him at all times.

_____ 10. The horse was quite --- with young children.

_____ 11. When looking at comparative animal structures, the human arm is a(n) --- to the foreleg of many mammals.

_____ 12. The --- is useful to check the amount of sugar by weight in a solution.

_____ 13. The man in purple is a(n) --- and member of king's personal advisory cabinet.

_____ 14. --- is often used for decorative purposes on plaques.

_____ 15. The person leading the expedition to the remote tribe was a(n) --- of international renown.

_____ 16. Identical twins could be described as ---.

_____ 17. Six European nations formed a(n) --- for mutual aid, growth, and protection.

_____ 18. A geyser is a good example of --- action.

_____ 19. The study of --- has led to many discoveries about the sea that have helped mankind.

_____ 20. The problem was --- to the group originally, but it ultimately affected them quite seriously.

DIRECTIONS: Use your GREEK roots and affixes sheets; try to match the definitions with the words; look at the roots, prefixes, and suffixes for clues. Do NOT use a dictionary except as a last resort.

_____ ANALOGOUS

_____ ANHYDROUS

_____ ANTHROPOMETRY

_____ ATMOMETER

_____ CARDIOGRAM

_____ CRONY

_____ DIAGONAL

_____ EPIGRAPH

_____ EXOGEN

_____ GAMETE

_____ GENETICS

_____ HOMOGENIZE

_____ HOROLOGY

_____ HYDROSCOPE

_____ MATRIARCH

_____ ORTHOGRAPHY

_____ PHILOLOGY

_____ PHONOLITE

_____ PICTOGRAPH

_____ POLYGYNY

1. a) extending on a slant between opposite corners

2. n) the science or art of measuring time or making timepieces

3. n) the love of learning and literature; the study of written records

4. a) without water; dry

5. n) a seed plant that grows by adding layers to the outside

6. n) an igneous rock of alkali feldspar and nephelite that rings when struck; clinkstone

7. n) a mother who rules her family or tribe

8. n) the study of heredity and variation

9. n) a device for seeing things far below the water's surface

10. n) the practice of having two or more wives at the same time

11. n) a close friend

12. n) correct spelling

13. a) similar or comparable in some respects

14. n) inscription on a building, monument, etc.; motto or quote at the beginning of a book, chapter, etc.

15. n) instrument that measures the amount of water evaporation

16. v) to make uniform by blending

17. n) a cell that unites with another to form a new cell

18. n) a picture representing an idea; hieroglyph

19. n) a record of the heart's action on a graph

20. n) the science of measuring the human body and its parts

DIRECTIONS: Use your GREEK roots and affixes sheets; try to find the root in each vocabulary words. Write the root and its meaning; also circle the root in the vocabulary word.

vocabulary word	root	meaning
ANALOGOUS	_____	_____
ANHYDROUS	_____	_____
ANTHROPOMETRY	_____	_____
ATMOMETER	_____	_____
CARDIOGRAM	_____	_____
CRONY	_____	_____
DIAGONAL	_____	_____
EPIGRAPH	_____	_____
EXOGEN	_____	_____
GAMETE	_____	_____
GENETICS	_____	_____
HOMOGENIZE	_____	_____
HOROLOGY	_____	_____
HYDROSCOPE	_____	_____
MATRIARCH	_____	_____
ORTHOGRAPHY	_____	_____
PHILOLOGY	_____	_____
PHONOLITE	_____	_____
PICTOGRAPH	_____	_____
POLYGYNY	_____	_____

DIRECTIONS: Use your GREEK roots and affixes sheets; try to find the word that is represented by the meanings of the roots and affixes. Write the word in the blank.

1. _____ to paint + to write

2. _____ breath + measure

3. _____ time + state, quality, act

4. _____ marriage + Greek form

5. _____ through, between + angle, corner + like, related to

6. _____ mother + first, to rule

7. _____ man, human + measure + state, quality, act

8. _____ cause, kind, race + science, system

9. _____ many + woman + state, quality, act

10. _____ hour + study of

11. _____ heart + to write

12. _____ straight, right + to write + state, quality, act

13. _____ not, without + water + having the quality of

14. _____ to love + word, discourse, study of

15. _____ outside + cause, kind, race

16. _____ sound + stone

17. _____ up, back, again + word + having the quality of

18. _____ water + to look

19. _____ on, outside + to write

20. _____ same + cause, kind, race + to make, to act

DIRECTIONS: For each blank write one vocabulary word. All words will be used only once. Look for context clues in the sentence.

_____ 1. The --- line ran from one corner to another.

_____ 2. A person would use --- to determine the average physical characteristics of an Irishman.

_____ 3. Mendel studied --- when he worked with peas.

_____ 4. One who practices --- will read many books.

_____ 5. Queen Victoria served as the --- of England.

_____ 6. The proverbial Swiss watchmaker is one thought to be skilled in ---.

_____ 7. The desert sand was --- for miles around.

_____ 8. The --- is the basis for all living reproduction.

_____ 9. The --- of a skull and crossbones on a label generally means the bottle's contents are poisonous.

_____ 10. Heart specialists can use the --- to pinpoint problems in their patients.

_____ 11. The --- could be useful in searching for sunken treasure or other objects lost at sea.

_____ 12. The practice of --- is ungodly since it violates God's idea of marriage.

_____ 13. The two situations were not ---, so no profitable comparisons could be made.

_____ 14. His --- from college days kept him informed of the happenings at his old school.

_____ 15. The --- gave a clear sound as he hit it with his rock pick.

_____ 16. Above the door of the building was a(n) --- saying, "We've got it, we'll get it, or it's not to be had."

_____ 17. The --- showed a huge rise when the temperature soared to over one hundred degrees.

_____ 18. Most creameries --- the milk they sell.

_____ 19. A spelling paper with all items correct shows a good command of ---.

_____ 20. The plant with many seeds may be a(n) ---.

DIRECTIONS: Use your GREEK roots and affixes sheets; try to match the definitions with the words; look at the roots, prefixes, and suffixes for clues. Do NOT use a dictionary except as a last resort.

_____ ANTHROPOMORPHISM

_____ BUREAUCRACY

_____ CENTIMETER

_____ GENIAL

_____ GENUINE

_____ GEOTROPISM

_____ GRAPHITE

_____ HIERARCHY

_____ HYDROPATHY

_____ IDEOGRAPH

_____ ILLOGICAL

_____ INGENUE

_____ ISONOMY

_____ NEUROLOGY

_____ PANTOGRAPH

_____ PERIMETER

_____ PHONOGRAPH

_____ PYROMANIAC

_____ TELESCOPE

_____ THEOLOGY

1. n) one who has a strong impulse to set destructive fires

2. n) a symbol representing an idea (@, *, =)

3. a) not reasonable; based on or using faulty reasoning

4. n) the study of God and religious doctrines

5. n) movement or growth of a living organism in response to the force of earth's gravity

6. n) the treatment of disease by the use of water

7. n) device that makes distant objects appear closer than they really are

8. n) the outer boundary of a figure or area; the total length of the boundary

9. n) a mechanical device for reproducing a drawing to various scales

10. n) unit of measure equal to 1/100th meter

11. n) the study of the structure and diseases of the nervous system

12. n) system of church government in graded ranks; people or things arranged in order of rank

13. a) real; not fake or artificial; authentic; of original stock; sincere and frank

14. n) soft, black carbon used for lead in pencils

15. n) the attributing of human characteristics to objects, plants, or animals

16. n) instrument that produces sound from the tracings on a flat disk

17. n) equality of laws, rights, and privileges

18. n) an inexperienced, innocent, and unworldly young woman

19. a) good for life and growth; cheerful; amiable; friendly; sympathetic; cordial

20. n) government by departments and officials following an inflexible routine; red tape

DIRECTIONS: Use your GREEK roots and affixes sheets; try to find the root in each vocabulary words. Write the root and its meaning; also circle the root in the vocabulary word.

vocabulary word	root	meaning
ANTHROPOMORPHISM	_____	_____
BUREAUCRACY	_____	_____
CENTIMETER	_____	_____
GENIAL	_____	_____
GENUINE	_____	_____
GEOTROPISM	_____	_____
GRAPHITE	_____	_____
HIERARCHY	_____	_____
HYDROPATHY	_____	_____
IDEOGRAPH	_____	_____
ILLOGICAL	_____	_____
INGENUE	_____	_____
ISONOMY	_____	_____
NEUROLOGY	_____	_____
PANTOGRAPH	_____	_____
PERIMETER	_____	_____
PHONOGRAPH	_____	_____
PYROMANIAC	_____	_____
TELESCOPE	_____	_____
THEOLOGY	_____	_____

DIRECTIONS: Use your GREEK roots and affixes sheets; try to find the word that is represented by the meanings of the roots and affixes. Write the word in the blank.

1. _____ nerve + study of

2. _____ sound + to write

3. _____ sacred + first, to rule + state, quality, act

4. _____ not + word, discourse + like, related to

5. _____ cause, kind, race + like, related to

6. _____ water + feeling, disease + state, quality, act

7. _____ all + to write

8. _____ from afar + to look

9. _____ equal + law, order + state, quality, act

10. _____ earth + to turn + state, quality, act

11. _____ around + measure

12. _____ man, human + form + state, quality, act

13. _____ cause, kind, race + like, related to

14. _____ God + study of

15. _____ fire + craving, insanity + related to

16. _____ desk + to rule + state, quality, act

17. _____ in, into + cause, kind, race

18. _____ to write + having the quality of

19. _____ idea + to write

20. _____ hundred + measure

DIRECTIONS: For each blank write one vocabulary word. All words will be used only once. Look for context clues in the sentence.

_____ 1. Under God we all stand equal under the law; we all exist in a condition of ---.

_____ 2. The five friends were quite a(n) --- group.

_____ 3. Pastors generally have studied some formal ---.

_____ 4. The --- allowed the technician to increase the size of the figure by three times.

_____ 5. The sea captain put the --- to his eye to check the flag of the ship on the horizon.

_____ 6. The man's argument was so --- that not a single person who heard him would accept his point.

_____ 7. The writer often used --- to describe the way the animals acted in her story.

_____ 8. A good doctor has a working knowledge of ---.

_____ 9. The hatband was made of --- rattlesnake skin.

_____ 10. It was great fun to listen to the --- and hear the big bands play all the old songs.

_____ 11. The --- of the church included clerics, bishops, and archbishops.

_____ 12. The guards patrolled the --- of the compound.

_____ 13. The local --- was frustrating to deal with but could be made to come around with persistent effort.

_____ 14. To use --- in all cases of sickness would not make good sense at all.

_____ 15. The hardness of the --- is generally shown by a number near the eraser on the pencil.

_____ 16. The country girl was thought to be a(n) --- since she seemed to know nothing of the city ways.

_____ 17. One --- is a little more than 3/8ths of an inch.

_____ 18. The long berry canes loop over to the ground as a result of ---.

_____ 19. After some investigation it was determined that the forest fires had been set by a(n) ---.

_____ 20. Mathematics makes constant use of one --- when writing a normal equation.

DIRECTIONS: Use your GREEK roots and affixes sheets; try to match the definitions with the words; look at the roots, prefixes, and suffixes for clues. Do NOT use a dictionary except as a last resort.

_____ ANTHROPOPATHY   1. a) being married to one woman at a time

_____ APOLOGY   2. n) a class; kind; sort; group of things with common distinguishing characteristics

_____ CHOREOGRAPHY   3. n) formal written or spoken defense; expression of regret for a fault or injury; asking pardon

_____ CHRONIC   4. n) the study of the development of speech sounds

_____ CYCLOMETER   5. n) an abnormal fear of the water

_____ GENITAL   6. n) a distinct section of writing begun on a new line and often indented

_____ GENUS   7. n) the attributing of human feelings and passions to non-human beings or objects

_____ GRAMMAR   8. n) a line of verse having five metrical feet or measures

_____ HETEROGAMY   9. n) one who studies or is an authority on God and His relations to the universe

_____ HYDROPHOBIA   10. n) system of rules for speaking or writing a language

_____ INGENUOUS   11. n) dancing, esp. ballet dancing; the art of devising dancing routines

_____ ISOGONAL   12. n) device that sounds an alarm due to high heat

_____ MONOGYNOUS   13. a) of or relating to reproductive organs

_____ PARAGRAPH   14. a) naive; open; candid; simple; artless; noble

_____ PATRIARCH   15. n) instrument that measures the arcs of circles

_____ PENTAMETER   16. n) area the mind can cover; range of view; extent of action, observation, inquiry, etc.

_____ PHONOLOGY   17. a) recurring; constant; lasting a long time

_____ PYROSTAT   18. n) the father and ruler of a family or tribe; father or founder; man of great dignity and age

_____ SCOPE   19. n) reproduction where sexual and asexual generations alternate; indirect pollination

_____ THEOLOGIAN   20. a) having equal angles

DIRECTIONS: Use your GREEK roots and affixes sheets; try to find the root in each vocabulary words. Write the root and its meaning; also circle the root in the vocabulary word.

vocabulary word	root	meaning
ANTHROPOPATHY	_____	_____
APOLOGY	_____	_____
CHOREOGRAPHY	_____	_____
CHRONIC	_____	_____
CYCLOMETER	_____	_____
GENITAL	_____	_____
GENUS	_____	_____
GRAMMAR	_____	_____
HETEROGAMY	_____	_____
HYDROPHOBIA	_____	_____
INGENUOUS	_____	_____
ISOGONAL	_____	_____
MONOGYNOUS	_____	_____
PARAGRAPH	_____	_____
PATRIARCH	_____	_____
PENTAMETER	_____	_____
PHONOLOGY	_____	_____
PYROSTAT	_____	_____
SCOPE	_____	_____
THEOLOGIAN	_____	_____

DIRECTIONS: Use your GREEK roots and affixes sheets; try to find the word that is represented by the meanings of the roots and affixes. Write the word in the blank.

1. _____ water + to fear + condition

2. _____ father + first, to rule

3. _____ to look

4. _____ cause, kind, race + Latin form

5. _____ in, into + cause, kind, race + having quality of

6. _____ fire + standing

7. _____ man, human + feeling, disease + state, quality, act

8. _____ God + word, discourse, study + on who

9. _____ equal + angle, corner + like, related to

10. _____ time + like, related to

11. _____ from, away + word, discourse, study

12. _____ five + measure

13. _____ circle + measure

14. _____ other + marriage + state, quality, act

15. _____ to dance + to write + state, quality, act

16. _____ cause, kind, race + like, related to

17. _____ to write

18. _____ one + woman + having the quality of

19. _____ sound + study of

20. _____ beside, variation + to write

DIRECTIONS: For each blank write one vocabulary word. All words will be used only once. Look for context clues in the sentence.

_____ 1. Iambic --- is the common line structure in English blank verse.

_____ 2. Dealing with astrophysics was beyond the --- of the basic math teacher.

_____ 3. A smoke alarm is not necessarily a(n) ---.

_____ 4. John Calvin was an important --- during the Reformation period.

_____ 5. Certain plants reproduce by the process of ---.

_____ 6. Malaria is a(n) --- disease because it keeps coming back again and again.

_____ 7. Most married men in the United States are ---.

_____ 8. Grandfather was the --- of the family after he reached 58 years of age.

_____ 9. --- is used to help analyze tone in human speech.

_____ 10. The amateurs were unable to give all the proper --- names for the various animals they classified.

_____ 11. Poets who ascribe human feelings to trees and animals are practicing a form of ---.

_____ 12. The young man was quite --- in his mannerisms and dealings with other people.

_____ 13. The --- of the dance troupe was evidently quite complex since the movements were timed with precision.

_____ 14. The arc of the circle was measured by the ---.

_____ 15. The note from the count demanded a public --- for supposed affront suffered at the court.

_____ 16. A rectangle has the quality of being ---.

_____ 17. Not wanting to swim or get wet may be a sign of ---.

_____ 18. The study of --- is unfortunately not too interesting to the vast majority of students.

_____ 19. The introductory --- of an essay should contain a thesis statement.

_____ 20. God designed the --- organs so that life could continue on Earth.

DIRECTIONS: Use your GREEK roots and affixes sheets; try to match the definitions with the words; look at the roots, prefixes, and suffixes for clues. Do NOT use a dictionary except as a last resort.

_____ ANTHROPOPHAGY 1. n) metric measure of length equal to 1/10th meter

_____ APOGEE 2. n) great mental capacity and inventive ability; a person with such talent

_____ CYCLOGRAPH 3. n) measurement of the range and power of vision

_____ DECIMETER 4. n) one who habitually doubts or questions; one who doubts the doctrines of Christianity

_____ DEMOCRATIC 5. n) cleverness; originality; skill

_____ DERMATOLOGY 6. a) spiritually reborn; renewed; restored v) cause spiritual rebirth through religious conversion; to form again; cause to be renewed

_____ ERGOGRAPH 7. n) a plane figure of four sides with opposite sides equal and parallel

_____ GENIUS 8. n) the point farthest from the center of orbit

_____ HYDROPHONE 9. n) branch of medicine dealing with the skin and its diseases

_____ INGENUITY 10. n) art of making or using fireworks; a dazzling display

_____ ISOSCELES 11. n) a state ruled or governed by a king, queen, or emperor

_____ LOGOMACHY 12. n) cannibalism

_____ MONARCHY 13. n) designates a triangle with two equal sides

_____ OPTOMETRY 14. n) a camera that can take a complete picture of one-half a sphere

_____ PARALLELOGRAM 15. n) one who studies diseases

_____ PATHOLOGIST 16. n) device for detecting and registering distance and direction of sound carried by water

_____ PYROTECHNICS 17. n) instrument for measuring and reading the amount of work done in muscular exertion

_____ REGENERATE 18. a) of rule by the people

_____ SKEPTIC 19. n) harmony of sounds or colors; an extended musical piece for full orchestra

_____ SYMPHONY 20. n) a battle of words only; an argument about words

DIRECTIONS: Use your GREEK roots and affixes sheets; try to find the root in each vocabulary words. Write the root and its meaning; also circle the root in the vocabulary word.

vocabulary word	root	meaning
ANTHROPOPHAGY	_____	_____
APOGEE	_____	_____
CYCLOGRAPH	_____	_____
DECIMETER	_____	_____
DEMOCRATIC	_____	_____
DERMATOLOGY	_____	_____
ERGOGRAPH	_____	_____
GENIUS	_____	_____
HYDROPHONE	_____	_____
INGENUITY	_____	_____
ISOSCELES	_____	_____
LOGOMACHY	_____	_____
MONARCHY	_____	_____
OPTOMETRY	_____	_____
PARALLELOGRAM	_____	_____
PATHOLOGIST	_____	_____
PYROTECHNICS	_____	_____
REGENERATE	_____	_____
SKEPTIC	_____	_____
SYMPHONY	_____	_____

DIRECTIONS: Use your GREEK roots and affixes sheets; try to find the word that is represented by the meanings of the roots and affixes. Write the word in the blank.

1. _____ water + sound

2. _____ one + first, to rule

3. _____ people + to rule + like, related to

4. _____ back, again + cause, kind, race + to make, to do

5. _____ man, human + to eat + state, quality, act

6. _____ equal + leg

7. _____ feeling, disease + word, study + one who

8. _____ circle + to write

9. _____ eye, sight + measure + state, quality, act

10. _____ work, power + to write

11. _____ beside, variation + mutual + to write

12. _____ ten + measure

13. _____ with, together + sound + state, quality, act

14. _____ fire + art, skill + science, system

15. _____ from, away + earth

16. _____ in, into + cause, kind, race + state, quality

17. _____ to look + like, related to

18. _____ skin + study of

19. _____ word, discourse + battle

20. _____ cause, kind, race + Latin form

DIRECTIONS: For each blank write one vocabulary word. All words will be used only once. Look for context clues in the sentence.

_____

_____

_____

_____

_____

_____

_____

_____

_____

_____

_____

_____

_____

_____

_____

_____

_____

_____

_____

_____

1. As his muscles strained, the --- quivered but held at the same reading.

2. Houdini showed remarkable --- in his novel solutions to the many escape problems he encountered.

3. Some missionaries have had to try and share the Gospel with people who practiced ---.

4. Their dispute was limited to a(n) ---.

5. A rectangle is a unique --- in that all four of its angles are the same.

6. The communications satellite was over 140 miles from the earth at its ---.

7. The display of --- on the Fourth of July was quite spectacular and could be seen for some distance.

8. The --- triangle has certain peculiar properties.

9. The orchestra performed a(n) --- written by Brahms.

10. The --- would be used to capture a complete picture of half the world from space.

11. A person with foresight might choose --- as their future profession.

12. Polio, chicken pox, and mumps are all concerns of the ---.

13. The --- method of government has numerous pitfalls although it is often highly praised.

14. Only the Lord Himself can truly --- a lost sinner.

15. The length of one --- is just under four inches.

16. The sonar systems in submarines are a type of ---.

17. The --- has difficulty in accepting any new ideas.

18. Rashes would be a subject of study in ---.

19. England's form of government is a constitutional ---.

20. Edison gave very little evidence of his --- while he was young.

DIRECTIONS: Use your GREEK roots and affixes sheets; try to match the definitions with the words; look at the roots, prefixes, and suffixes for clues. Do NOT use a dictionary except as a last resort.

_____ ANDROCRACY

_____ APOLOGETICS

_____ ASTROLOGY

_____ DEMOGRAPHY

_____ EPIGRAM

_____ ETYMOLOGY

_____ GENOCIDE

_____ HETEROGENEOUS

_____ HYDROPLANE

_____ INGENIOUS

_____ ISOTHERM

_____ LOGOGRIPH

_____ MONOGAMOUS

_____ OLIGARCHY

_____ PARAMETER

_____ PENTAGRAM

_____ PHONOMETER

_____ PYROTOXIN

_____ SPECTROSCOPE

_____ SYNCHRONIZE

1. a) differing in structure, quality, etc.; dissimilar; unlike

2. n) a riddle

3. n) the origin and development of words; tracing that development using linguistics

4. n) line on a map connecting points of equal temperature at the same time

5. n) government where a few hold the ruling power

6. n) a five-pointed star

7. n) information about a body of people

8. n) device used to measure the intensity and vibration frequency of sound

9. n) a constant with variable values; a condition established for a given situation

10. n) government run by a man or men

11. n) a short poem

12. a) cleverness; originality; skill

13. n) a poison that induces a fever

14. v) to make occur at the same time

15. n) branch of theology that defends the faith

16. a) being married to one person

17. n) optical instrument used for forming light waves for study

18. n) the systematic killing of a people or nation (probably ok)

19. n) a biblically prohibited belief teaching that heavenly bodies influence human characteristics and history

20. n) small, light motorboat that skims the water

DIRECTIONS: Use your GREEK roots and affixes sheets; try to find the root in each vocabulary words. Write the root and its meaning; also circle the root in the vocabulary word.

vocabulary word	root	meaning
ANDROCRACY	_____	_____
APOLOGETICS	_____	_____
ASTROLOGY	_____	_____
DEMOGRAPHY	_____	_____
EPIGRAM	_____	_____
ETYMOLOGY	_____	_____
GENOCIDE	_____	_____
HETEROGENEOUS	_____	_____
HYDROPLANE	_____	_____
INGENIOUS	_____	_____
ISOTHERM	_____	_____
LOGOGRIPH	_____	_____
MONOGAMOUS	_____	_____
OLIGARCHY	_____	_____
PARAMETER	_____	_____
PENTAGRAM	_____	_____
PHONOMETER	_____	_____
PYROTOXIN	_____	_____
SPECTROSCOPE	_____	_____
SYNCHRONIZE	_____	_____

DIRECTIONS: Use your GREEK roots and affixes sheets; try to find the word that is represented by the meanings of the roots and affixes. Write the word in the blank.

1. _____ people + to write + state, quality, act

2. _____ few + first, to rule + state, quality, act

3. _____ fire + poison + like, related to

4. _____ other + cause, kind, race + having the quality of

5. _____ in, into + cause, kind, race + having quality of

6. _____ word, discourse + fish net

7. _____ true + study of

8. _____ man, human + to rule + state, quality, act

9. _____ five + to write

10. _____ one + marriage + having the quality of

11. _____ on, outside + to write

12. _____ with, together + time + to make, to act

13. _____ from, away + word, discourse + science, system

14. _____ sound + measure

15. _____ equal + heat

16. _____ to look + to look

17. _____ water + flat

18. _____ cause, kind, race + to kill, cut

19. _____ beside, variation + measure

20. _____ star + study of

DIRECTIONS: For each blank write one vocabulary word. All words will be used only once. Look for context clues in the sentence.

_____ 1. The --- was difficult to solve without an extra clue.

_____ 2. The fifty students were quite --- in many of their interests and experiences.

_____ 3. The juice on the arrow tip was a dangerous ---.

_____ 4. The one thousand men who comprised the ruling class were the basis of the ---.

_____ 5. The Bible stresses a(n) --- relationship in marriage.

_____ 6. The --- was used in the physics lab to help the students understand light wave theory.

_____ 7. The solution was quite --- in that no one had thought in those terms before.

_____ 8. A large --- was outlined in chalk on the floor of the room.

_____ 9. Political candidates will usually study the --- of their election area.

_____ 10. A small group of generals formed the core of the --- that ruled the nation.

_____ 11. One particular --- was calibrated in decibels to check noise levels.

_____ 12. The basic --- of investing is having the money available and being able to lose it.

_____ 13. The Jews accused the Nazis of committing --- against them.

_____ 14. It is best to --- actions in order to coordinate an attack.

_____ 15. The --- was easy to move through the shallows.

_____ 16. Many people are bound by the fear of --- , concerned that the stars and planets guide their fate.

_____ 17. The three lines of verse comprised a(n) ---.

_____ 18. This whole series of lessons has been based on ---.

_____ 19. Cornelius Van Til developed --- from the reformed Christian position.

_____ 20. The --- on the weather map surrounded the whole southern section of the state.

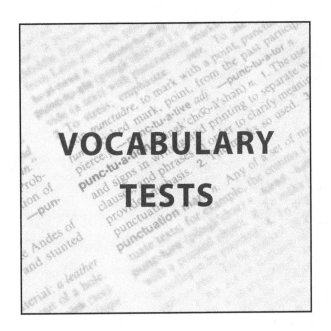

VOCABULARY TESTS

Directions: Work from the definitions to the words. Place each definition number in the correct blank. Some definitions will not fit in any blank. Some words may not have a matching definition; write NONE in the blank by those words. A very few words may have two correct definitions; if so, place both numbers in the blank to get credit. No definition will be used twice.

Definitions

DIRECTIONS: Work from this page to the answer sheet. Place each definition number in a correct blank; no # will be used more than once; some will not be used at all. If no # matches a blank, write NONE in the blank. A few words may have two correct numbers in their blanks.

1. a blessing; a giving of thanks
2. pipe or channel for moving liquids
3. to hinder the progress of; obstruct
4. skill; dexterity; lack of difficulty
5. having an evil influence; likely to cause death; harmful
6. a government gift of money for aid
7. living; to give life or motion to
8. sickness; disease; an ailment
9. to refuse to take; discard
10. false front; building front
11. to break an oath; to lie under oath
12. to replace; cause to be set aside
13. to speed up the progress
14. a 1000-year period
15. place where two lines meet or cross
16. a dwelling house; apartments or buildings owned by another
17. a private meeting
18. to die
19. a patron; one who gives help
20. renter; occupant; one who occupies
21. to be enough or adequate
22. to throw in-between; interrupt with
23. slander; speak evil of
24. an unprovoked attack or warlike act
25. trickery; skill or ingenuity
26. to write beforehand; order
27. original; first copy
28. a trimming of the toenails

29. device that regulates the flow by means of a membrane, flap, or lid
30. lure; persuade to do wrong
31. undernourishment from lack of food or improper diet
32. to give up rights on oath; recant
33. to reveal; uncover; make known
34. surround; to shut in all around
35. lacking in distinctive qualities; hard to classify
36. yearly; comes once a year
37. strong hatred; ill will; enmity
38. to enroll in the armed forces
39. fat; obese; stout
40. yearly return of a date or an event
41. enunciation; wording; expression
42. note added to the main work as an afterthought at the end
43. portion or area divided for military reasons
44. a 100th anniversary
45. timid; cowardly
46. a principle, doctrine, or belief held as truth
47. one devoted to a habit
48. any two-footed mammal
49. the degree of a slope; a slope
50. twisted; coiled; spiraled
51. delude; lead astray; mislead
52. set free; release from bondage
53. a rule of conduct; a moral rule
54. to cut in two
55. recurs year after year
56. arched bridge over a span to carry a road or track

57. nobleminded; generous in spirit
58. stinking; having a bad or foul odor
59. a refraining from some or all food, drink, or other pleasure
60. clique; group within a group
61. accustomed to sit most times
62. easily affected or influenced by
63. a small platform to speak from
64. words engraved on some surface
65. a heading or title found on articles or illustrations
66. agreeing completely; united in opinion; everyone agrees
67. to serve as chairman; rule over
68. formal statement of opinion
69. the curved path of an object hurtling through space
70. remainder; that which is left after a part is removed
71. wrongdoing or misconduct in handling funds while in office
72. free from fear, care, or danger
73. real; actual
74. wall built into the water to restrain currents to protect piers, harbors, etc.
75. to make firm or fast; to protect
76. container; vessel; used to hold something else
77. a happy trail in the moonlight
78. beam that holds floor planks
79. to act as judge; give judgment
80. easily accepts suggestions
81. concerned with only the obvious
82. never stopping; constant
83. happening every two years

ANSWER SHEET LATIN VOCABULARY TEST 1-9

___ ABJURE

___ ABSTINENCE

___ ADDICT

___ AGGRESSION

___ ADJUDICATE

___ ANIMATE

___ ANIMOSITY

___ ANNIVERSARY

___ ARTIFICE

___ BENEDICTION

___ BENEFACTOR

___ BIENNIAL

___ BISECT

___ CAPTION

___ CENTENNIAL

___ CONCLAVE

___ CONDUIT

___ CONVOLUTED

___ CORPULENT

___ DECEASE

___ DECEIVE

___ DEGREE

___ DICTION

___ DICTUM

___ DISCLOSE

___ EMANCIPATE

___ ENCLOSE

___ EXPEDITE

___ FACADE

___ FACILITY

___ FACSIMILE

___ FACTION

___ GRADIENT

___ IMPEDE

___ INCESSANT

___ INDUCT

___ INSCRIPTION

___ INTERJECT

___ INTERSECTION

___ JETTY

___ JOIST

___ MAGNANIMOUS

___ MALADY

___ MALFEASANCE

___ MALIGN

___ MALIGNANT

___ MALNUTRITION

___ MILLENIUM

___ NONDESCRIPT

___ PERJURY

___ PODIUM

___ POSTSCRIPT

___ PRECEPT

___ PRESCRIBE

___ PRESIDE

___ PUSILLANIMOUS

___ RECEPTACLE

___ RECEPTIVE

___ RESIDUE

___ SECTOR

___ SECURE

___ SEDENTARY

___ SEDUCE

___ SICKLE

___ SUBSIDY

___ SUFFICE

___ SUPERFICIAL

___ SUPERSEDE

___ SUSCEPTIBLE

___ TENANT

___ TENEMENT

___ TRAJECTORY

___ UNANIMOUS

___ VALVE

___ VIADUCT

Definitions

DIRECTIONS: Work from this page to the answer sheet. Place each definition number in a correct blank; no # will be used more than once; some will not be used at all. If no # matches a blank, write NONE in the blank. A few words may have two correct numbers in their blanks.

1. belong to, be connected or associated

2. a candy, ice cream, preserves

3. a turning aside from the main subect

4. a decree, official proclamation

5. to cut across; divide by cutting

6. misshapen; abnormally shaped

7. a walled-in area

8. to combine; include; merge; unite into one group

9. a list of ancestors; descent; lineage

10. a position that brings profit with little work

11. one who receives good things, esp. an inheritance

12. upright drum around which cables are wound

13. highly competent; skilled

14. honest; habitually truthful

15. to admit as true; to grant as a right

16. exit; a way out

17. an order or command; will of the people expressed to their representatives

18. a three-legged cauldron, stool, support, etc.

19. accuse; to bring criminal charges against

20. confirm; substantiate; prove to be true

21. shut out; deny the right to redeem (a mortgage)

22. to kidnap

23. a walker; one who goes on foot

24. phlebotomy; bloodletting for therapy

25. in concise form; a gel container holding medicine

26. to forbid or restrain an action or use

27. the face; visage; facial expression; approval

28. bleak; dreary; depressing; gloomy

29. very slight or subtle; not easily sensed by the mind

30. to hear and decide; to act as judge; give judgment

31. a small platform (as for a lecturer)

32. to set free; release from bondage

33. richness or splendor; grandeur; stately beauty

34. diminish; to move, go, or slope backward

35. to write carelessly or illegibly

36. to give as a reason or proof

37. miserable; wretched; degraded

38. dull; prosaic; lacking imagination

39. formal statement of opinion; a saying or adage

40. a very small particle; any of the blood cells

41. to follow, as in office; come after; gain a favorable result

42. prior or previous; that which comes before

43. a curse or slander; a calling down of evil

44. a private meeting

45. beam that holds up floor panels

46. building, offices, apartments held by another

47. inflamed area in body tissues containing pus

48. lavish; generosity in giving

49. a guess; predicting on incomplete or uncertain evidence

50. a moving backward; retreating; declining

51. characterized by treachery or slyness

52. a farewell; something said in parting

53. a finish; end; conclusion

54. a phase; a cut side of a gem; a side or aspect

55. calm or composed; serious and unemotional

56. to sin; go beyond a limit; break a law or command

57. to be enough or adequate

58. has the appearance of being true

59. amount by which a sum is less than what is required

60. something contained in an envelope

61. accustomed to sit much of the time

62. surrounding; situated around the sides

63. rub out; erase; make inconspicuous

64. kind or kindly; inclined to do good; charitable

65. device or artifice; deception; plan to avoid the unpleasant

66. an opening; mouth or outlet of a tube or cavity; vent

67. timid; cowardly

68. a dead body, usually of a person

69. hard to manage; obstinate

70. near or close; adjoining

71. small tongs or pliers for grasping, compressing, and pulling

72. to infer or decide something

73. entrance; a way in

74. busy; diligent; persevering

75. a hermit; one who lives a solitary, secluded life

76. a favor or request; blessing or welcome benefit

77. prevent; make impossible (esp. in advance)

78. assent; agree to; enter upon the duties of

79. roomy; spacious

80. a steward or buyer of provisions for an institution

81. interpret new ideas by help of past experience

82. wise and careful; showing sound judgment

83. something added; equipment

84. a 1000-year period; any period of peace and prosperity

85. fat; obese; stout

86. to hinder the progress of; obstruct

87. large; bulky; full

88. one who flees his home or country to seek safety elsewhere

89. to belong; be connected with

90. a ceasing or stopping

91. talkative; described by a great flow of words

92. impudent or insolent; not relevant to the matter

93. a number, letter, or symbol written underneath

94. one who disagrees

95. a criminal; an evil doer

96. hundredth anniversary or its celebration

97. strong hatred; ill will; enmity; open or active hostility

98. make a written copy; adapt music for a different instrument or voice

99. having the intended result; effective

100. good natured; med. doing no harm

___ ABDUCT	___ CIRCUMJACENT	___ EFFICACIOUS
___ ABJECT	___ CLOSURE	___ EGRESS
___ ABSCESS	___ CONCEDE	___ EMANCIPATE
___ ACCEDE	___ CONCESSION	___ ENCLOSURE
___ ADDUCE	___ CONCLAVE	___ FACET
___ ADJACENT	___ CONFECTION	___ FORCEPS
___ ADJUDICATE	___ CONJECTURE	___ FORECLOSE
___ ANIMOSITY	___ CORPSE	___ IMPEDE
___ ANTECEDENT	___ CORPULENT	___ IMPERCEPTIBLE
___ APPERCEIVE	___ CORPUS	___ IMPERTINENT
___ APPERTAIN	___ CORPUSCLE	___ INCORPORATE
___ APPURTENANCE	___ COUNTENANCE	___ INDICT
___ ASSIDUOUS	___ DECEPTION	___ INGRESS
___ BENEVOLENT	___ DEDUCE	___ INSIDIOUS
___ BENIGN	___ DEFICIT	___ INTERDICT
___ BOON	___ DICTUM	___ JOIST
___ CAPACIOUS	___ DIGRESSION	___ JUDICIOUS
___ CAPSTAN	___ DISMAL	___ MAGNIFICENCE
___ CAPSULE	___ DISSIDENT	___ MALEDICTION
___ CENTENNIAL	___ EDICT	___ MALEFACTOR
___ CESSATION	___ EFFACE	___ MALFORMED

___ MANCIPLE

___ MANDATE

___ MILLENNIUM

___ MUNIFICENCE

___ OCCLUSION

___ ORIFICE

___ PEDESTRIA

___ PEDIGEE

___ PERTAIN

___ PODIUM

___ PRECLUDE

___ PROFICIENT

___ PUSILLANIMOUS

___ RECEDE

___ RECLUSE

___ REFRACTORY

___ REFUGEE

___ RETINUE

___ RETROGRADE

___ SCRIBBLE

___ SEDATE

___ SEDENTARY

___ SINECURE

___ SUBSCRIPT

___ SUBTERFUGE

___ SUFFICE

___ TRANSCRIBE

___ TRANSECT

___ TRANSGRESS

___ TRIPOD

___ VALEDICTION

___ VENESECTION

___ VERACIOUS

___ VERIFY

___ VERISIMILITUDE

___ VOLUBLE

___ VOLUMINOUS

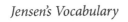

Definitions

DIRECTIONS: Work from this page to the answer sheet. Place each definition number in a correct blank; no # will be used more than once; some will not be used at all. If no # matches a blank, write NONE in the blank. A few words may have two correct numbers in their blanks.

1. fame, great reputation; celebrity

2. one sent by the church to teach, preach, etc.

3. seems good without being so

4. view from a specific point and time

5. assumed name; false name; pen name

6. requester of a job, help, aid, etc.

7. crying for mercy; cowardly; disloyal

8. profession or trade; career to which one is called

9. involved; intricate; not simple

10. twisted metal collar; a twisting force

11. pass over; go across; cross and recross

12. follow after to capture; strive for; seek after

13. twist or fold together; show to be a party

14. something left out, not included, or neglected

15. make a clear explanation

16. forward thrust or force; moving forward

17. force oneself on others; place a tax or burden on

18. family name; surname; derived from a father

19. immediate; without delay; done in a moment

20. summary; brief statement of the essence

21. overly submissive; servile; too willing to serve

22. make use of; hire; to keep busy

23. advance; raise to a higher position

24. a dead body; a corpse

25. easily managed or taught; obedient; docile

26. a bad sign or prophecy

27. system of names used in a branch of learning

28. about to happen

29. guess; conjecture; idea formed without proof

30. tall jar with narrow neck and two handles near the top

31. think out; plan; invent; contrive

32. an element; a part; ingredient

33. previous statement serving as basis for argument

34. double dealing; hypocritical cunning or deception

35. of or affecting the whole organism

36. in name but not in fact; slight compared to expectations

37. honor; courteous regard; yielding in opinion or wishes

38. a pulling over a surface; adhesive friction

39. small, steep waterfall; a shower

40. ductile; tensile; can be drawn out in length

41. put a wrong name on the wrong person or thing

42. belongs outside; extraneous

43. swinging; hanging freely

44. truce or temporary cessation of fighting

45. irresponsible; lax in performance of duty

46. bestow; discuss; converse; exchange ideas

47. flow or rhythm; beat; measured movement

48. leave unprotected; reveal; disclose; abandon

49. occur at the same time

50. draw back in; withdraw; recant

51. side of a coin with the main image

52. producing abundantly; rich; fruitful

53. revolt vs. authority, esp. sailors vs. officers

54. shedding leaves annually

55. show beforehand; private early showing

56. first choice; more desirable than others

57. factual item; data of a numerical type

58. reply; remuneration; make up for a loss

59. period of decline in morals, art, literature, etc.

60. clamorous; making a loud outcry

61. tending to overthrow or destroy; one who does so

62. turned about; reversed in position; to speak

63. formal book or essay on a subject

64. take across a river or narrow body of water

65. showing depth or distance on a flat drawing

66. distant in space; far off; faint or slight

67. bring to completion; bring legal proceedings against

68. small, narrow crack; crevice; chink

69. great pain or anguish; cause agony; harass

70. house or apartment composed of two units

71. turmoil; agitation; confusion; disturbance

72. path or trail; barely observable quality

73. sharp in taste; sour; small pastry filled with jam, etc.

74. turn aside; deflect; amuse; entertain

75. essential; belonging to; inherent

76. disgusting; offensive; causing strong dislike

77. group of building; an obsession or fear

78. regular payment made during retirement

79. required; obligatory; coercive; forced

80. thoughtful or reflective, often with sadness

81. that which is scorned; contemptible

82. continue; refuse to quit; endure

83. remain barely alive; continue to just exist

84. mixture of decaying vegetable refuse, manure, etc.

85. see in the mind; form a mental image

86. distinguishing quality or characteristic

87. deform; force out of shape by bending, twisting, etc.

88. exciting ill will or envy; giving offense

89. launch or leap; ancient military device for throwing large objects

90. witty reply; turn an insult or deed back on a person

91. bend inward; one who dwells on himself

92. stop the blood flow; faithful; strong

93. change; transform; turn; person who changed

94. vary; give variety to; make different

95. beat or throb rhythmically; vibrate; quiver

96. strong liking or fondness for; inclination; taste

97. signaling system using lights, flags, and arms

98. get money by violence, threats, etc.

99. not concrete; theoretical

100. negligent; heedless; unintentional

ANSWER SHEET LATIN II VOCABULARY TEST 1-9

___ ABSTRACT	___ DECADENCE	___ INSTANTANEOUS
___ AMPHORA	___ DECIDUOUS	___ INTERSTICE
___ APPLICANT	___ DEFERENCE	___ INTRINSIC
___ ARMISTICE	___ DESPICABLE	___ INTROVERT
___ ASPECT	___ DEVISE	___ INVIDIOUS
___ AUSPICE	___ DIVERSIFY	___ MISNOMER
___ CADAVER	___ DIVERT	___ MISSIONARY
___ CADENCE	___ DUPLEX	___ MUTINY
___ CADENZA	___ DUPLICITY	___ NOMINAL
___ CASCADE	___ EMPLOY	___ OBSEQUIOUS
___ CATAPULT	___ ENVISAGE	___ OBVERSE
___ COINCIDE	___ EXPLICATE	___ OMISSION
___ COMMOTION	___ EXPOSE	___ PATRONYMIC
___ COMPLEX	___ EXTORT	___ PENCHANT
___ COMPONENT	___ EXTRINSIC	___ PENDULOUS
___ COMPOST	___ FERRY	___ PENSION
___ COMPULSORY	___ FERTILE	___ PENSIVE
___ CONFER	___ IMPENDING	___ PERSIST
___ CONTORT	___ IMPLICATE	___ PERSPECTIVE
___ CONVERSE	___ IMPOSE	___ PREFERABLE
___ CONVERT	___ INADVERTENT	___ PREMISE

___ PREVIEW

___ PROMOTE

___ PROPULSION

___ PROSECUTE

___ PSEUDONYM

___ PULSATE

___ PURSUE

___ RECOMPENSE

___ RECREANT

___ REMISS

___ REMOTE

___ RENOWN

___ REPULSIVE

___ RETORT

___ RETRACT

___ SEMAPHORE

___ SPECIOUS

___ STATISTIC

___ STATURE

___ STAUNCH

___ SUBSIST

___ SUBVERSIVE

___ SURMISE

___ SYSTEMIC

___ TART

___ TORMENT

___ TORQUE

___ TORSION

___ TRACE

___ TRACTABLE

___ TRACTILE

___ TRAIT

___ TRAVERSE

___ TREATISE

___ TRIPLEX

___ VOCATION

___ VOCIFEROUS

Definitions

DIRECTIONS: Work from this page to the answer sheet. Place each definition number in a correct blank; no # will be used more than once; some will not be used at all. If no # matches a blank, write NONE in the blank. A few words may have two correct numbers in their blanks..

1. stubborn, resisting remedy or reason
2. stop the flow of blood or body fluid
3. something left out or neglected
4. making a loud outcry; clamoring
5. seems good without being so
6. a twisted metal collar
7. all of creation; all existing things
8. predetermine; set apart for a purpose
9. competent in many things
10. regular or fixed payment; pension
11. one pretending to be something he isn't
12. a paying out of money; a cost or drain
13. a religious group or body
14. allowing to enter; a confessing
15. restore to original by adding water
16. thickness of liquid; in agreement
17. one of a group as a sample for all
18. lacking; poor; in complete poverty
19. a store in a camp for supplies and food
20. umpire; judge
21. to call to public attention
22. can be believed; plausible
23. multiply by four; four times as many
24. a secret name
25. carriage of the body; attitude or stand
26. awkward or dangerous situation

27. an abandoning of what one believed in
28. place where things are kept
29. a plan; scheme; mechanical contrivance
30. family name; surname
31. word meaning the opposite of another
32. directly overhead; straight up and down
33. lighter than air craft; a balloon
34. to call forth; summon; elicit
35. on the edges; environs; boundary line
36. make firm; keep from fluctuating
37. yearly return date of some event
38. to make leave; drive out by force
39. to tie; support with a framework
40. attach or add as a supplement; affix
41. temporary interval of relief; a delay
42. beg; beseech; ask earnestly for
43. nickname or added epithet
44. cannot be undone or recalled
45. set apart; separate; confiscate
46. familiar or acquainted with
47. change or amend; read over to improve
48. western hemisphere
49. to take away; belittle
50. imagined object of fear or dread
51. small, steep waterfall; a shower
52. servile; overly submissive

53. faithful; firm; loyal; strong

54. entangle or involve; show to be a party

55. inducing sleep; soporific

56. supposed perception

57. force producing a twisting motion

58. set free from slavery; liberate

59. name of a place

60. false name; pen name; assumed name

61. person to whom another is indebted

62. instrument for drawing or measuring angles

63. moving in a whirling pattern

64. villain; criminal; evil person

65. malice or ill will; a mean feeling for another

66. distribute; give out; deal out

67. remark critically; comment negatively

68. theory; something regarding as true

69. one who makes a proposal

70. disgrace; shame; dishonor; infamy

71. a calling together; assembly by summons

72. whirlpool; whirling mass of water

73. consume by using up

74. stop; cease; abstain

75. give in trust; pledge

76. range of colors in light

77. characterized by emotions of great joy

78. a partnership in wrongdoing

79. giddiness or dizziness

80. giving light without heat

81. the face; countenance

82. make difficult; twist together

83. balky; contrary; refusing to go forward

84. easily bent, molded or influenced

85. death; transfer of estate by will

86. able to see things not in sight

87. no known or acknowledged name

88. highest point; apex; summit; top

89. side by side or close together

90. heat measuring and regulating device

91. personal belongings; gear; equipment

92. official in charge; superintendent

93. give forth; utter; issue

94. habitual criminal; goes back to crime

95. bride's outfit of clothes, linens, etc.

96. take into legal custody

97. thing used to hold a cow

98. to puzzle; confuse; make doubtful

99. against; in contrast to

100. still existing; not destroyed

ANSWER SHEET LATIN II VOCABULARY TEST 1-18

___ ADMISSION	___ CREDIBLE	___ IMPLICATE
___ ADVERTISE	___ CREDITOR	___ IMPOSTER
___ AEROSTAT	___ CRYPTONYM	___ IMPOUND
___ AGNOMEN	___ DEMISE	___ IRREVOCABLE
___ ANIMADVERT	___ DENOMINATION	___ JUXTAPOSITION
___ ANNIVERSARY	___ DESIST	___ MANUMIT
___ ANONYMOUS	___ DESTINE	___ MISCREANT
___ ANTONYM	___ DESTITUTE	___ OBSEQUIOUS
___ APOSTACY	___ DETRACT	___ OBSTINATE
___ APPEND	___ DEVICE	___ OCCIDENT
___ AVOW	___ DISPENSE	___ OMISSION
___ BELVEDERE	___ ECSTATIC	___ PARAPHERNALIA
___ CASCADE	___ EMIT	___ PERIPHERY
___ CLAIRVOYANCE	___ ENTREAT	___ PERPLEX
___ COGNOMEN	___ EVOKE	___ PERSPICACIOUS
___ COMMISSARY	___ EXPEL	___ PLEXUS
___ COMPLICATE	___ EXPEND	___ PLIABLE
___ COMPLICITY	___ EXPENSE	___ PLIGHT
___ CONSISTENCY	___ EXTANT	___ POSTURE
___ CONVERSANT	___ HOMONYM	___ PROPONENT
___ CONVOCATION	___ IGNOMINY	___ PROTRACTOR

___ PSEUDONYM

___ QUADRUPLE

___ RECIDIVIST

___ RECONSTITUTE

___ REFEREE

___ REPLICATE

___ REPOSITORY

___ RESPITE

___ RESTIVE

___ REVISE

___ RHEOSTAT

___ SEQUESTER

___ SOMNIFEROUS

___ SPECIMEN

___ SPECIOUS

___ SPECTER

___ SPECTRUM

___ SPITE

___ STABILIZE

___ STANCHION

___ STAUNCH

___ STIPEND

___ SUPPOSITION

___ TOPONYM

___ TORQUE

___ TROUSSEAU

___ TRUSS

___ UNIVERSE

___ VERSATILE

___ VERSUS

___ VERTEX

___ VERTICAL

___ VERTIGO

___ VISAGE

___ VOCIFEROUS

___ VORTEX

___ VORTICAL

Definitions

DIRECTIONS: Work from this page to the answer sheet. Place each definition number in a correct blank; no # will be used more than once; some will not be used at all. If no # matches a blank, write NONE in the blank. A few words may have two correct numbers in their blanks..

1. writing and compiling a dictionary

2. any of several hymns of praise to God

3. a design with letters

4. offspring; children; descendants

5. irrational fear of fire

6. a werewolf

7. one who hates people

8. existing since birth

9. government under the immediate direction of God

10. obituary; list of dead people

11. measures the height above ground

12. non-English system of measurement

13. political system where all are equal

14. type of work in literature or art

15. an organism with both male and female organs

16. plane figure with six sides and angles

17. sees the earth as the center of all

18. to bring about, produce, or cause

19. chemical decomposition by heat

20. study of family history

21. study of the application of the work of redemption

22. electromagnetic device for intensifying weak sounds

23. historical record according to date

24. something out of its proper time

25. that which reduces a fever

26. funnel-shaped device to raise voice volume

27. government by a woman or women

28. to be insincere at love

29. additional comment at the end of a play

30. device to measure curved surfaces

31. machine that records voice for later transcription

32. rule by experts or engineers

33. one who studies the environment

34. something written in code or cipher

35. plant development without sexual organs

36. the opposition of sounds

37. set of three related books or plays

38. process of burning designs on wood or leather

39. containing water; watery

40. instrument for looking inside a bladder

41. the eating of dirt

42. all people born at a given time

43. eldest son's right to inherit his father's estate

44. study of light waves

45. having equal force

46. unit of measure equal to 1/100th meter

47. speech in praise of the dead

48. equality of laws, rights, privileges

49. operated by the force or movement of liquid

50. mob rule

51. dissonance; discordant sound

52. measurement equal to 1000 meters

53. government by the rich or wealthy

54. introduction to a poem or play

55. made up chart of planet and star positions

56. Satan; the chief foe

57. a signature, personally written

58. hermaphroditic

59. deteriorate; a fallen condition

60. a six-pointed star

61. reasoning with two ideas plus a conclusion

62. device for looking at very small objects

63. an abnormal fear of man

64. mirror for signaling using the sun's rays

65. device for measuring angles, esp. of solids

66. native born; produced naturally

67. method for comparing the sizes of zoos

68. a line of verse with six metrical feet

69. producing electricity from water power

70. one who is married to at least two others at once

71. word made from another by rearranging letters

72. the beginning or origin

73. print or copy made from a stone or metal plate

74. one who hates all government

75. scientific study of colors

76. one who hates women

77. chemical decomposition by reaction to water ions

78. a talking together; a conversation

79. angel of the highest rank; the chief angel

80. abnormal fear of women

81. science or method of correct reasoning

82. alike on both sides

83. device for looking at the sun without eye damage

84. having to do with right angles; rectangular

85. spontaneous generation

86. having two or more wives at once

87. study of place names in relation to history

88. record of the heart's action on a graph

89. self-written history of one's own life

90. document written entirely in the author's handwriting

91. living organisms developing other living organisms

92. growing plants in nutrient-rich water instead of soil

93. considered a powerful wizard

94. message sent by wire

95. false prophecy by supposed figures in a handful of earth

96. word with same spelling but different meaning

97. having many sounds

98. not sounded or pronounced

99. of or governed by bishops

100. of psychic origin; caused by mental conflicts

ANSWER SHEET GREEK VOCABULARY TEST 1-9

___ ALTIMETER

___ ANACHRONISM

___ ANAGRAM

___ ANARCHIST

___ ANDROGYNOUS

___ ANDROPHOBIA

___ ANTIPHONY

___ ANTIPYRETIC

___ APHONIC

___ APOGAMY

___ APOLOGUE

___ ARCHANGEL

___ ARCHENEMY

___ ARCHIMAGE

___ AUTOBIOGRAPHY

___ AUTOGENESIS

___ AUTOGRAPH

___ BIGAMIST

___ BIOGENESIS

___ CACOPHONY

___ CHROMATOLOGY

___ CHRONOLOGY

___ CONGENITAL

___ CRYPTOGRAM

___ CYTOLOGY

___ DEGENERATE

___ DIALOGUE

___ DICTAPHONE

___ DOXOLOGY

___ ECOLOGIST

___ ENGENDER

___ EPILOGUE

___ EPISCOPAL

___ EUOGY

___ GENEALOGY

___ GENERATION

___ GENESIS

___ GENRE

___ GEOCENTRIC

___ GEOLOGIST

___ GEOMANCY

___ GEOPHAGY

___ GONIOMETER

___ GYNARCHY

___ GYNOPHOBIA

___ HELIOGRAPH

___ HELIOSCOPE

___ HEXAGON

___ HEXAMETER

___ HOLOGRAPH

___ HOMOGRAPH

___ HOROSCOPE

___ HYDRAULIC

___ HYDROELECTRIC

___ HYDROLYSIS

___ HYDROPONICS

___ HYDROUS

___ INDIGENOUS

___ ISOCRACY

___ ISODYNAMIC

___ ISOTOPE

___ KILOMETER

___ LEXICOGRAPHY

___ LITHOGRAPH

___ LOGARITHM

___ LOGIC

___ LYCANTHROPE

___ MEGAPHONE

___ METRIC

___ MICROGRAPH

___ MICROPHONE

___ MICROSCOPE

___ MISANTHROPE

___ MONOGRAM

___ NECROLOGY

___ OCHLOCRACY

___ ORTHOGONAL

___ PENTAGON

___ PHILANDER

___ PLUTOCRACY

___ POLYGAMIST

___ POLYPHONIC

___ PRIMOGENITURE

___ PROGENY

___ PSYCHOGENIC

___ PYROGRAPHY

___ PYROLYSIS

___ PYROPHOBIA

___ SOTERIOLOGY

___ SPECTROLOGY

___ SPHEROMETER

___ STEREOGRAPHY

___ SYLLOGISM

___ SYMMETRY

___ TECHNOCRACY

___ TELEGRAM

___ THEOCRACY

___ TOPOLOGY

___ TRILOGY

___ ZOOMETRY

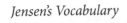
Definitions

DIRECTIONS: Work from this page to the answer sheet. Place each definition number in a correct blank; no # will be used more than once; some will not be used at all. If no # matches a blank, write NONE in the blank. A few words may have two correct numbers in their blanks.

1. government where only a few hold power

2. any of several hymns of praise to God

3. map line connecting equal temperature points

4. offspring; children; descendants

5. a short poem

6. married to one person

7. one who hates people

8. existing since birth

9. government under the immediate direction of God

10. study of word origins and their development

11. an alarm that sounds due to high heat

12. soft, black carbon used for lead in pencils

13. optical device that forms light waves for study

14. to make uniform by blending

15. beautiful handwriting

16. dazzling display, usually of fireworks

17. instrument that measures atmospheric pressure

18. motto or quote at beginning of a book, chapter, etc.

19. study of the nervous system

20. five-pointed star

21. study of the application of the work of redemption

22. list of writings on a subject or of one author

23. small, light motorboat that skims the water

24. slanting line between two corners

25. that which reduces a fever

26. funnel-shaped device to raise voice volume

27. one who has a strong impulse to set fires

28. spiritually born again; give life to again

29. additional comment at the end of a play

30. a triangle with two equal sides

31. not reasonable, based on faulty reasoning

32. rule by experts or engineers

33. one who studies diseases

34. something written in code or cipher

35. having to do with the earth's interior heat

36. the opposition of sounds

37. dry, without water

38. correct spelling

39. excessively well-bred, polite, refined, etc.

40. to make occur at the same time

41. great mental capacity and inventive ability

42. having a pleasant sound

43. clinkstone, igneous rock that rings when struck

44. study of final causes

45. condition established for a given situation

46. unit of measure equal to 1/100th meter

47. extended musical piece for a full orchestra

48. equality of laws, rights, privileges

49. naïve, open, candid, simple, artless

50. measurement of the range and power of vision

51. native; naturally produced in a given region

52. measurement equal to 1000 meters

53. government by the rich or wealthy

54. poison that introduces a fever

55. biblically prohibited belief that stars influence history

56. systematic killing of a people or nation

57. government run by a man or men

58. man of great dignity and age; founder of his line

59. having equal angles

60. government by graded ranks; ranked in order

61. recurring; constant; lasting a long time

62. the study of God and religious doctrines

63. branch of theology that defends the faith

64. outer boundary of a figure; total distance around

65. study of the blood and its diseases

66. harmony of sounds or colors

67. growth in response to earth's gravity

68. a line of verse with five metrical feet

69. information on a body of people

70. cleverness; originality; skill

71. love of learning and literature

72. the beginning or origin

73. a riddle

74. one who hates all government

75. one who habitually doubts and questions

76. state ruled by a king, queen, or emperor

77. inscription on a building, monument, etc.

78. person who is not Jewish

79. measure equal to 1/10th meter

80. similar or comparable is some respects

81. device that beats regular time as for piano practice

82. area of medicine dealing with the skin and its diseases

83. one who writes histories of individual lives

84. exactly alike on both sides

85. science of sound; use of elementary sounds to teach reading

86. having two or more wives at once

87. having equality of measurement

88. record of the heart's action on a graph

89. bad handwriting; incorrect spelling

90. a constant with variables

91. a close friend

92. mother who rules her tribe or family

93. the point farthest from the center of orbit

94. system of rules for speaking or writing a language

95. six friendly or allied states or governments

96. abnormal fear of water

97. set of four related dramas or literary works

98. belief that everyone descended from Adam and Eve

99. nobleman; member of the privileged class

100. of or relating to reproductive organs

ANSWER SHEET GREEK VOCABULARY TEST 1-18

___ ANALOGOUS

___ ANARCHIST

___ ANDROCRACY

___ ANHYDROUS

___ ANTIPHONY

___ APOGEE

___ APOLOGETICS

___ ARISTOCRAT

___ ASTROLOGY

___ ASYMMETRICAL

___ BIBLIOGRAPHY

___ BIOGRAPHER

___ BUREAUCRACY

___ CACOGRAPHY

___ CALLIGRAPHY

___ CARDIOGRAM

___ CENTIMETER

___ CHRONIC

___ CONGENITAL

___ CRONY

___ CRYPTOGRAM

___ DECIMETER

___ DEMOGRAPHY

___ DERMATOLOGY

___ DIAGONAL

___ DOXOLOGY

___ EPIGRAM

___ EPIGRAPH

___ ETYMOLOGY

___ EUPHONIC

___ GAMETE

___ GENESIS

___ GENIAL

___ GENITAL

___ GENIUS

___ GENOCIDE

___ GENTEEL

___ GENTILE

___ GEOTHERMIC

___ GEOTROPISM

___ GRAMMAR

___ GRAPHITE

___ HEMATOLOGY

___ HEXARCHY

___ HIERARCHY

___ HOMOGENIZE

___ HYDROMETER

___ HYDROPHOBIA

___ HYDROPLANE

___ ILLOGICAL

___ INDIGENOUS

___ INGENUITY

___ INGENUOUS

___ ISOMETRIC

___ ISONOMY

___ ISOSCELES

___ ISOTHERM

___ KILOMETER

___ LOGOGRIPH

___ MEGAPHONE

___ METRONOME

___ MISANTHROPE

___ MONARCHY

___ MONOGAMOUS

___ MONOGENISM

___ MONOGYNOUS

___ NEUROLOGY

___ OLIGARCHY

___ OPTOMETRY

___ ORTHOGRAPHY

___ PARAMETER

___ PATHOLOGIST

___ PATRIARCH

___ PENTAGRAM

___ PENTAMETER

___ PERIMETER

___ PERISCOPE

___ PHILOLOGY

___ PHONICS

___ PHONOLITE

___ PHONOMETER

___ PHOTOGENIC

___ PLUTOCRAC

___ POLYGYNY

___ PROGENY

___ PYROMANIAC

___ PYROSTAT

___ PYROTECHNICS

___ PYROTOXIN

___ REGENERATE

___ SKEPTIC

___ SOTERIOLOGY

___ SPECTROSCOPE

___ SYMPHONY

___ SYNCHRONIZE

___ TECHNOCRACY

___ TELEOLOGY

___ TETROLOGY

___ THEOCRACY

___ THEOLOGY

VOCABULARY
APPENDIX

CAD, CAS, CID	to fall, to happen	PON, POS	to place, to put
CRED	to believe	SEC, SEQU	to follow
FER, PHER, PHOR	to carry, to bear	SPEC, SPIC	to look
MIS, MIT	to send	SIST, STA, STIT	to stand
MOB, MOT, MOV	to move	TOR	to twist
NOM, NOMIN, NYM (Gr.)	name	TRACT	to drag, to draw
PEL, PULS	to push	VERS, VERT, VORT	to turn
PEND, PENS	to hang, to weigh, to pay	VID, VIS	to see
PLEX, PLIC, PLY	to fold	VOC, VOKE	to call, voice

****** NOTE: Infrequently used roots and affixes appear below. ******

AERO	air	HEMO	blood	SEMA	sign
AMPHI	both	HOMO	same	SEXT	six
ANIM	spirit	IG	not	SOMNI	sleep
ANN	year	IMEN	something done	STI	coin
ARMI	arms	INTRI/O	inward	THERMO	heat
AU	bird	IR	not	TOPO	place
BEL	beautiful	JUXTA	near	TRI	three
CATA	down	MANU	hand	UNI	one
CLAIR	clear	META	change		
CLAT	to call	MIS	bad		
CRYPT	hidden	MULTI	many		
DEC	ten	OCT	eight		
DU	two	PARA	beyond		
EP	upon	PATR	farther		
EQUI	equal	PHOS	light		
ESCENT	becoming	PSEUDO	false		
GYRO	circle	RETRO	backward		
HELIO	sun	RHEO	current		

BASIC ROOTS FOR GREEK

ANDR, ANTHROP	man, human		GYN	woman
ARCH	first, chief, to rule		HYDR	water
CHRON	time		ISO	equal
CRAT, CRAC	to rule		LOG, LOGUE, -LOGY, -OLOGY	word, discourse, study of, way of speaking
GAM	marriage		METER, METR	measure
GE	earth		PHON	sound
GEN, GENER, GENIT	cause, kind, race		PYR	fire
GON	angle, corner		SCOP	to look
GRAM, GRAPH	to write			

****** NOTE: Infrequently used roots and affixes appear below. ******

A-/AN	not without		CARD	heart	-EME	something done
ACRO	high, extremely		CENT	hundred	EN-	in, into
ALLEL	mutual		CENTR	center	ENDO-	inside
ALT	high		CHOR	to dance	EORA	hovering in the air
ANA-	up, back, again		CHROMA, CHRO	color	EPI-, EP-	year
ANGEA	vessel		-CIDE	to kill, cut	ERG/URG	work, power
ANTI-	against, opposite		COSMOS	universe	-ESIS	state, quality, act
ARISTOS	best		CRYPT	hidden	ETYM	true
ARITHM	number		CYCL	circle	EU-	good, well
ASTER/ ASTR	star		CYT	cell	EXO-	outside
ATM	breath		DEC	ten	GRIPH	fish net
AUL	pipe, flute		DEMO	people	GYR	ring, circle
AUTO-	self		DERM	skin	HELI	sun
BAR	pressure, weight		DI-	two	HEM	blood
BI-	two		DIA-	through	HETERO-	other
BIBLI	book		DICT	to speak	HEX	six
BIO	life		DOX	opinion, praise	HIER	sacred
BUREAU	desk		DYN, DYNAM	power	HOL	whole
CAC	bad		ECO-	house	HOMO-	same
CALLI, KALLI	beautiful		EIDO	form	HOR	hour
					-IA	condition

-ICS	science, system	NOM	law, order	SCEL	leg
IDEO-	idea	OCHLO-	mob	SEISM	to shake
IL-	not	-ODE, -OID	resembling	SOM, SOMAT	body
INDI-	within	OLIGO-	few	SOTER	safety, salvation
-IN, -INE	like, related to	OP	eye, sight	SPEC, SPIC	to look
-ISM	state, quality, act	ORTH-	straight, right	SPHER	ball
-IST	one who	-OSIS, -SIS	condition, act	SPIR	breath, life
-ITE	: having the quality of	PAN-, PANTO-	all	STAT	standing
KILO-	thousand	PAR-, PARA-	beside, variation	STEN	narrow
LEX	word, speech	PATH	feeling, disease	STEREO-	solid, 3-dimensional
-LITE, LITH	stone	PATER, PATR		STETH	chest, breast
LYC	wolf	PED	foot	SYL-, SYM, SYN-	with, together
LYS	to free	PERI-	around	TECHN	art, skill
-MACHY	battle	PENT-	five	TECT	builder
MAN	man, human	PETR	rock	TELE-	from afar
-MANCY	divination	PHAG	to eat	TETRA-	four
MANIA	craving, insanity	PHIL	to love	THE/, THEO	God
MATR, MATER	mother	PHOB	to fear	THEIR (THERION)	beast
MEGA	great, million	PHOT, PHOS	light	THERM	heat
MER	part	PHYSI	nature, natural	TOM, TME	to cut
META-, MET-	beyond, change	PICT	to paint	TOP	place
MICRO-	small	PLAN	flat	TOX	poison
MILLI-	thousand	PLUT	wealth	TRI-	three
MIM	to copy, imitate	POLY	many	TROP	to turn
MIS-	to hate	PONOS	labor	TYP	model
MONO-	one	PORN	prostitute	-Y	state, quality, act
MORPH	form	PRIM	first	zo	animal
NECR-	death, dead	PSYCH	mind		
NEUR	nerve	SAX	made by Aldophe Sax		
NITR	niter				

ALPHABETICAL LIST OF ALL LATIN I WORDS
lesson # - vocabulary word - root

1	abdicate	dict	13	benevolent	bene	2	convoluted	volu
17	abduct	duc	14	benign	bene	15	corporation	corp
17	abject	jac	6	biennial	ann	17	corps	corp
7	abjure	jud	2	biped	ped	18	corpse	corp
15	abscess	cede	1	bisect	sec	9	corpulent	corp
7	abstain	tain	15	bonus	bene	16	corpus	corp
8	abstention	tain	16	boon	bene	13	corpuscle	corp
9	abstinence	tain	16	capable	cap	12	countenance	tain
16	accede	cede	13	capacious	cap	3	curator	cur
17	accept	cap	14	capacity	cap	2	curious	cur
5	accurate	cur	11	capstan	cap	9	decease	cede
2	ddict	dict	12	capsule	cap	2	deceive	cap
18	adduce	duc	9	caption	cap	17	deception	cap
18	adjacent	jac	10	captor	cap	6	dedicate	dict
8	adjudicate	jud/dict	3	centennial	ann	13	deduce	duc
6	aggression	grad	15	centrifugal	fug	14	deduct	duc
4	amanuensis	manu	14	cessation	cede	11	defaced	fac
17	ancestor	cede	15	circumjacent	jac	12	defect	fac
2	animate	anima	2	circumscribe	scribe	13	deficient	fac
8	animism	anima	1	circumvolution	volu	14	deficit	fac
7	animosity	anima	1	claustrophobia	claus	8	degrade	grad
5	annals	ann	2	cloister	claus	9	degree	grad
7	annual	ann	3	closet	claus	13	dejection	jac
2	annuity	ann	18	closure	claus	4	description	scribe
13	antecedent	cede	4	cloture	claus	13	detain	tain
18	anticipate	cap	11	concede	cede	14	detention	tain
15	apperceive	cap	7	conceive	cap	3	devolve	volu
10	appertain	tain	8	concept	cap	13	dictaphone	dict
13	appurtenance	tain	12	concession	cede	7	dictator	dict
15	aqueduct	duc	5	conclave	claus	8	diction	dict
8	artifact	fac	6	conclude	claus	9	dictum	dict
9	artifice	fac	4	condition	dict	10	digression	grad
1	ascribe	scribe	2	conducive	duc	5	disciple	cap
15	assess	sed	16	conduct	duc	14	discipline	cap
17	assiduous	sed	3	conduit	duc	7	disclose	claus
16	assize	sed	10	confection	fac	17	dismal	mal
3	benediction	bene/dict	7	congress	grad	2	dissect	sec
9	benefactor	bene/fac	16	conjecture	jac	14	dissident	sed
10	beneficial	bene/fac	3	conscript	scribe	10	edict	dict
11	beneficiary	bene/fac	11	continent	tain	11	educate	duc
12	benefit	bene/fac	5	contradict	dict	12	educe	duc

ALPHABETICAL LIST OF ALL LATIN I WORDS

lesson # - vocabulary word - root

15	efface	fac	5	inanimate	anima	14	malefactor	mal/fac
16	efficacious	fac	16	inception	cap	11	maleficent	mal/fac
17	efficient	fac	7	incessant	cede	12	malevolent	mal
11	egress	grad	13	include	claus	9	malfeasance	mal/fac
14	ejaculate	jac	10	incorporate	corp	10	malformed	mal
11	eject	jac	11	indict	dict	7	malice	mal
1	emancipate	manu/cap	9	induct	duc	8	malicious	mal
8	enclave	claus	17	infect	fac	5	malign	mal
9	enclose	claus	17	infraction	fract	3	malignant	mal
10	enclosure	claus	12	ingredient	grad	6	malnutrition	mal
14	entertain	tain	13	ingress	grad	4	malodorous	mal
1	equanimity	anima	12	inject	jac	1	malpractice	mal
4	evolution	volu	6	injury	jud	15	manacle	manu
6	exception	cap	5	injustice	jud	16	manciple	manu/cap
10	excess	cede	5	inscription	scribe	11	mandate	manu
11	exclude	claus	3	insect	sec	14	manicure	manu/cur
1	expedient	ped	13	insidious	sed	13	manipulate	manu
4	expedite	ped	8	intercede	cede	12	manufacture	manu/fac
1	facade	fac	1	intercept	cap	6	manuscript	manu/scribe
18	facet	fac	5	intercession	cede			
2	facile	fac	12	interdict	dict	4	millennium	ann
3	facility	fac	9	interject	jac	6	millepede	ped
4	facsimile	fac	4	intersection	sec	12	municipal	cap
5	faction	fac	10	introduce	duc	15	munificence	fac
6	factor	fac	6	involute	volu	6	necessary	cede
7	factual	fac	5	involve	volu	7	nondescript	scribe
18	forceps	cap	7	jetty	jac	10	object	jac
12	foreclose	claus	8	joist	jac	12	obsession	sed
15	fraction	fract	4	judicial	jud/dict	17	obtain	tain
16	fracture	fract	13	judicious	jud/dict	7	obvolute	volu
13	fragile	fract	14	jurisdiction	jud/dict	14	occlusion	claus
14	fragment	fract	3	juror	jud	11	occupation	cap
11	fugue	fug	2	justify	jud	5	octopus	ped
1	gradation	grad	4	magnanimous	anima	16	orifice	fac
5	grade	grad	18	magnificence	fac	4	participate	cap
2	gradient	grad	16	maintain	manu/tain	8	pedal	ped
3	gradual	grad	18	maladjusted	mal/jud	7	pedestal	ped
4	graduate	grad	2	malady	mal	12	pedestrian	ped
3	impede	ped	16	malconduct	mal/duc	6	pedicure	ped/cur
15	imperceptible	cap	13	malcontent	mal/tain	10	pedigree	ped
15	impertinent	tain	15	malediction	mal/dict	3	perception	cap

ALPHABETICAL LIST OF ALL LATIN I WORDS

lesson # - vocabulary word - root

1	perennial	ann	18	refugee	fug	1	supersede	sed
13	perfect	fac	15	regress	grad	4	superjacent	jac
1	perjury	jud	2	reject	jac	10	surface	fac
18	pertain	tain	10	reside	sed	9	susceptible	cap
17	pertinent	tain	7	resident	sed	16	sustain	tain
9	podium	ped	6	residue	sed	1	tenable	tain
11	possess	sed	18	retention	tain	6	tenacity	tain
8	postscript	scribe	15	retinue	tain	5	tenant	tain
3	precede	cede	17	retrocede	cede	4	tenement	tain
1	precept	cap	16	retrograde	grad	3	tenet	tain
15	preclude	claus	17	retrogress	grad	2	tenure	tain
1	predecessor	cede	8	revolve	volu	1	traduce	duc
16	predict	dict	18	scribble	scribe	6	trajectory	jac
14	prefect	fac	10	scribe	scribe	15	transcribe	scribe
9	prescribe	scribe	11	script	scribe	16	transcript	scribe
9	preside	sed	17	scripture	scribe	10	transect	sec
8	president	sed	6	secant	sec	18	transgress	grad
2	principal	cap	16	secede	cede	11	tripod	ped
4	procedure	cede	17	seclusion	claus	11	trisect	sec
2	proceed	cede	14	section	sec	6	unanimous	anima
18	procession	cede	8	sector	sec	17	valediction	dict
7	proctor	cur	9	secure	cur	9	valve	volu
8	procure	cur	18	sedate	sed	10	vault	volu
7	produce	duc	5	sedentary	sed	12	venesection	sec
8	productive	duc	4	sediment	sed	11	veracious	ver
11	proficient	fac	6	seduce	duc	18	verdict	ver/dict
14	progression	grad	7	segment	sec	12	verify	ver
1	project	jac	3	sessile	sed	13	verisimilitude	ver
3	pusillanimous	anima	9	sickle	sec	4	viaduct	duc
18	recede	cede	10	sinecure	cur	5	vivisection	sec
5	receipt	cap	3	subjacent	jac	14	voluble	volu
7	receptacle	cap	5	subject	jac	17	volume	volu
6	reception	cap	12	subscriber	scribe	18	voluminous	volu
4	receptionist	cap	13	subscript	scribe			
8	receptive	cap	2	subsidy	sed			
3	receptor	cap	17	subterfuge	fug			
10	recipe	cap	15	succeed	cede			
16	recluse	claus	9	suffice	fac			
5	reduce	duc	12	sufficient	fac			
18	refractory	fract	8	superficial	fac			
12	refuge	fug	14	superscript	scribe			

ALPHABETICAL LIST OF ALL LATIN II WORDS
lesson # - vocabulary word - root

9	abstract	tract	7	coincide	cad	3	demote	mob
1	accident	cad	18	commissary	mis	18	denomination	nom
5	accomplice	plex	17	commit	mis	17	dependable	pend
14	accredit	cred	2	commotion	mob	2	deploy	plex
18	admission	mis	15	compendium	pend	5	deposit	pon
15	adverse	vers	16	compensate	pend	17	desist	sist
16	adversity	vers	8	complex	plex	5	despicable	spec
17	advertise	vers	15	complicate	plex	6	despite	spec
17	advise	vid	16	complicity	plex	11	destine	sist
15	aerostat	sist	1	component	pon	18	destitute	sist
1	amphora	fer	2	compose	pon	12	detract	tract
18	animadvert	vers	3	compost	pon	16	device	vid
14	anniversary	vers	4	compound	pon	1	devise	vid
14	anonymous	nom	16	compromise	mis	5	differentiate	fer
15	antonym	nom	2	compulsory	pel	12	discredit	cred
16	apostasy	sist	3	confer	fer	14	dismiss	mis
4	appeal	pel	1	consecutive	sec	1	dispel	pel
4	append	pend	2	consequence	sec	18	dispense	pend
6	applicant	plex	18	consistency	sist	3	display	plex
7	appliqué	plex	4	conspicuous	spec	6	dispose	pon
5	armistice	sist	12	constant	sist	17	distant	sist
1	aspect	spec	13	constituent	sist	2	distort	tor
6	assist	sist	1	contort	tor	13	distract	tract
10	attract	tract	11	contract	tract	6	diversify	vers
2	auspice	spec	14	contrast	sist	5	divert	vers
1	automobile	mob	1	controversy	vers	4	diverticulum	vers
11	averse	vers	12	conversant	vers	4	duplex	plex
2	avert	vers	8	converse	vers	5	duplicate	plex
18	avow	voc	7	convert	vers	6	duplicity	plex
17	belvedere	vid	17	convocation	voc	16	ecstatic	sist
2	cadaver	cad	15	credence	cred	13	emit	mis
3	cadence	cad	16	credential	cred	7	employ	plex
4	cadenza	cad	17	credible	cred	14	entreat	tract
5	cascade	cad	18	creditor	cred	2	envisage	vid
6	casualty	cad	13	creed	cred	3	envy	vid
3	catapult	pel	17	cryptonym	nom	15	eponym	nom
2	circumference	fer	8	decadence	cad	16	equivocate	voc
3	circumspect	spec	9	deciduous	cad	4	evidence	vid
7	circumstance	sist	1	decuple	plex	15	evoke	voc
15	clairvoyance	vid	4	deference	fer	3	execute	sec
16	cognomen	nom	15	demise	mis	14	expel	pel

17	expend	pend	5	intrinsic	sec	6	pensive	pend
18	expense	pend	8	introspective	spec	7	penthouse	pend
8	explicate	plex	2	introvert	vers	15	periphery	fer
7	expose	pon	3	inverse	vers	7	permission	mis
8	expound	pon	7	invidious	vid	8	perpendicular	pend
13	expulsion	pel	8	invisible	vid	12	perplex	plex
14	extant	sist	14	invocation	voc	7	persecute	sec
3	extort	tor	13	irrevocable	voc	3	persist	sist
4	extract	tract	14	juxtaposition	pon	9	perspective	spec
4	extrinsic	sec	11	manumit	mis	10	perspicacious	spec
3	extrovert	vers	12	metaphor	fer	5	perversion	vers
6	ferry	fer	6	metastasis	sist	16	phosphorescent	fer
7	fertile	fer	1	metonymy	nom	13	plait	plex
13	gnomen	nom	10	miscreant	cred	14	plexus	plex
13	gyrostatics	sist	2	misnomer	nom	15	pliable	plex
12	heliostat	sist	10	missile	mis	16	plight	plex
11	hemostasis	sist	9	missionary	mis	16	portray	tract
17	homonym	nom	4	mobile	mob	16	positive	pon
18	ignominy	nom	5	motivate	mob	17	posture	pon
12	impel	pel	6	motive	mob	9	preferable	fer
1	impending	pend	10	multiplication	plex	6	premise	mis
9	implicate	plex	7	mutiny	mob	9	preview	vid
9	impose	pon	3	nomenclature	nom	17	proffer	fer
10	impost	pon	4	nominal	nom	5	promise	mis
11	impostor	pon	5	nominate	nom	8	promote	mob
12	impound	pon	6	nominative	nom	10	propel	pel
5	improvise	vid	6	obsequious	sec	10	propensity	pend
11	impulsive	pel	5	obstacle	sist	18	proponent	pon
1	inadvertent	vers	4	obstinate	sist	13	propound	pon
10	incidental	cad	4	obverse	vers	9	propulsion	pel
11	incredible	cred	11	occasion	cad	8	prosecute	sec
2	independent	pend	12	occident	cad	11	prospect	spec
11	inference	fer	11	octuple	plex	12	prospectus	spec
10	insistent	sist	13	offertory	fer	2	prostate	sist
7	inspect	spec	8	omission	mis	1	prostitute	sist
9	instantaneous	sist	15	opponent	pon	17	protract	tract
8	institution	sist	14	paraphernalia	fer	18	protractor	tract
12	intermission	mis	7	patronymic	nom	10	providential	vid
13	interpose	pon	3	penchant	pend	11	provision	vid
7	interstice	sist	4	pendulous	pend	12	provocation	voc
6	interview	vid	5	pension	pend	14	provost	pon

ALPHABETICAL LIST OF ALL LATIN II WORDS
lesson # - vocabulary word - root

8	pseudonym	nom	17	specify	spec	11	tortilla	tor
8	pulsate	pel	18	specimen	spec	12	torture	tor
15	purpose	pon	9	specious	spec	3	trace	tract
9	pursue	sec	10	spectacle	spec	4	tractable	tract
17	quadruple	plex	15	specter	spec	6	tractile	tract
13	recidivist	cad	16	spectrum	spec	5	traction	tract
9	recompense	pend	14	speculate	spec	7	trait	tract
18	reconstitute	sist	17	spite	spec	2	transfer	fer
9	recreant	cred	15	stabilize	sist	1	transmit	mis
18	referee	fer	13	stadium	sist	18	transpose	pon
4	remiss	mis	12	stanchion	sist	9	traverse	vers
9	remote	mob	11	stanza	sist	8	treatise	tract
10	remove	mob	10	static	sist	12	trinomial	nom
9	renown	nom	9	statistic	sist	3	triplex	plex
7	repeal	pel	8	stature	sist	4	triplicate	plex
6	repel	pel	7	staunch	sist	13	trousseau	tor
18	replicate	plex	11	stipend	pend	14	truss	tor
1	reply	plex	3	submissive	mis	10	universe	vers
16	repository	pon	6	subsist	sist	11	versatile	vers
5	repulsive	pel	5	substantiate	sist	12	versus	vers
17	resist	sist	4	substitute	sist	13	vertebra	vers
13	respect	spec	2	subtract	tract	14	vertex	vers
14	respite	spec	8	subversive	vers	15	vertical	vers
16	restitution	sist	8	suffer	fer	16	vertigo	vers
15	restive	sist	3	superstition	sist	14	video	vid
6	retort	tor	13	supervise	vid	15	visage	vid
1	retract	tract	18	supposition	pon	16	visible	vid
15	retrospect	spec	2	surmise	mis	10	vocal	voc
6	retroversion	vers	3	suspect	spec	9	vocation	voc
7	revert	vers	12	suspend	pend	8	vociferous	voc
12	revise	vid	13	suspense	pend	17	vortex	vers
11	revoke	voc	4	suspicious	spec	18	vortical	vers
14	rheostat	sist	10	synonym	nom			
10	sect	sec	2	systemic	sist			
1	semaphore	fer	5	tart	tor			
11	sequel	sec	1	thermostat	sist			
12	sequence	sec	11	toponym	nom			
13	sequester	sec	7	torment	tor			
2	sextuple	plex	8	torque	tor			
10	somniferous	fer	9	torsion	tor			
16	specialize	spec	10	tort	tor			

ALPHABETICAL LIST OF ALL GREEK WORDS
lesson # - vocabulary word - root

10	acrogen	gen
5	acrography	gram
1	altimeter	meter
2	anachronism	chron
6	anagram	gram
14	analogous	log
13	analogue	log
12	analogy	log
1	anarchist	arch
18	androcracy	andr/crat
2	androgen	andr/gen
1	androgynous	andr/gyn
9	androphobia	andr
14	anhydrous	hydr
10	anthropocentric	andr
12	anthropogenesis	andr/gen
11	anthropoid	andr
13	anthropologist	andr/log
14	anthropometry	andr/meter
15	anthropomorhpism	andr
16	anthropopathy	andr
17	anthropophagy	andr
6	antiphon	phon
3	antiphony	phon
2	antipyretic	pyr
4	aphonic	phon
8	apogamy	gam
17	apogee	ge
5	apologue	log
16	apology	log
18	apologetics	log
3	archangel	arch
5	archduke	arch
7	archenemy	arch
9	archimage	arch
11	architect	arch
13	aristocrat	crat
18	astrology	log
11	asymmetrical	meter
14	atmometer	meter

7	autobiography	gram
11	autocratic	crat
6	autogamy	gam
9	autogenesis	gen
8	autograph	gram
13	barometer	meter
10	bibliography	gram
2	bigamist	gam
7	biogenesis	gen
11	biographer	gram
10	biology	log
15	bureaucracy	crat
12	cacography	gram
5	cacophony	phon
13	calligraphy	gram
14	cardiogram	gram
15	centimeter	meter
16	choreography	gram
9	chromatology	log
16	chronic	chron
11	chronicle	chron
4	chronogram	chron/gram
12	chronological	chron/log
8	chronology	chron/log
10	chronometer	chron/meter
6	chronoscope	chron/scop
6	congenital	gen
10	cosmology	log
14	crony	chron
3	cryptogram	gram
17	cyclograph	gram
16	cyclometer	meter
1	cyclonoscope	scop
3	cytology	log
17	decimeter	meter
6	degenerate	gen
11	dehydrate	hydr
17	democratic	crat
18	demography	gram

8	dermatogen	gen
17	dermatology	log
14	diagonal	gon
1	diagram	gram
6	dialogue	log
2	dictaphone	phon
4	digamy	gam
5	doxology	log
4	ecologist	log
10	endogamy	gam
1	engender	gen
10	epigeous	ge
18	epigram	gram
14	epigraph	gram
12	epigraphy	gram
3	epilogue	log
2	episcopal	scop
17	ergograph	gram
10	ergometer	meter
18	etymology	log
2	eulogy	log
12	euphonic	phon
12	exogamy	gam
14	exogen	gen
13	exogenous	gen
14	gamete	gam
3	gender	gen
5	gene gen	
1	genealogy	gen/log
6	generalize	gen
7	generally	gen
8	generate	gen
9	generation	gen
10	generator	gen
11	generic	gen
12	generous	gen
4	genesis	gen
14	genetics	gen
15	genial	gen
16	genital	gen
17	genius	gen

ALPHABETICAL LIST OF ALL GREEK WORDS

lesson # - vocabulary word - root

18	genocide	gen	7	holograph	gram	13	isomorphic	iso	
9	genre	gen	11	homogeneous	gen	15	isonomy	iso	
11	genteel	gen	14	homogenize	gen	3	isopyre	iso/pyr	
12	gentile	gen	6	homograph	gram	17	isosceles	iso	
13	gentle	gen	14	horology	log	18	isotherm	iso	
2	gentleman	gen	7	horoscope	scop	2	isotope	iso	
15	genuine	gen	1	hydrangea	hydr	4	isotropic	iso	
16	genus	gen	2	hydrant	hydr	8	kaleidoscope	scop	
1	geocentric	ge	3	hydraulic	hydr	5	kilometer	meter	
3	geode	ge	4	hydrodynamics	hydr	4	lexicography	gram	
5	geodetic	ge	5	hydroelectric	hydr	3	lithograph	gram	
4	geographer	ge/gram	10	hydrogen	hydr/gen	8	logarithm	log	
6	geologist	ge/log	11	hydrography	hydr/gram	9	logic	log	
7	geomancy	ge	12	hydrology	hydr/log	7	logogram	log/gram	
8	geometric	ge/meter	6	hydrolysis	hydr	18	logogriph	log	
9	geophagy	ge	13	hydrometer	hydr/meter	17	logomachy	log	
11	geophysics	ge	15	hydropathy	hydr	7	lycanthrope	andr	
13	geothermic	ge	16	hydrophobia	hydr	14	matriarch	arch	
15	geotropism	ge	17	hydrophone	hydr/phon	2	megaphone	phon	
4	goniometer	gon/meter	18	hydroplane	hydr	4	meteorology	log	
16	grammar	gram	7	hydroponics	hydr	7	meter	meter	
13	graphics	gram	14	hydroscope	hydr/scop	9	metric	meter	
15	graphite	gram	8	hydrotropism	hydr	12	metronome	meter	
2	graphology	gram/log	9	hydrous	hydr	2	micrograph	gram	
2	gynarchy	gyn/arch	15	ideograph	gram	3	micrometer	meter	
8	gynecology	gyn/log	11	ideology	log	8	microphone	phon	
3	gynophobia	gyn	15	illogical	log	9	microscope	scop	
4	gyroscope	scop	4	indigenous	gen	2	millimeter	meter	
9	heliograph	gram	18	ingenious	gen	1	mimeograph	gram	
8	heliometer	meter	15	ingenue	gen	8	misanthrope	andr	
5	helioscope	scop	17	ingenuity	gen	12	misogynist	gyn	
1	hematology	log	16	ingenuous	gen	17	monarchy	arch	
16	heterogamy	gam	1	isobar	iso	18	monogamous	gam	
18	heterogeneous	gen	5	isochromatic	iso	13	monogenism	gen	
10	heterography	gram	9	isocracy	iso/crat	5	monogram	gram	
1	hexagon	gon	7	isodynamic	iso	4	monograph	gram	
8	hexagram	gram	6	isogenous	iso/gen	16	monogynous	gyn	
6	hexameter	meter	16	isogonal	iso/gon	11	monologue	log	
13	hexarchy	arch	11	isomer	iso	9	monophonic	phon	
15	hierarchy	arch	10	isometric	iso/meter	12	morphogenesis	gen	

ALPHABETICAL LIST OF ALL GREEK WORDS
lesson # - vocabulary word - root

Lesson	Word	Root
5	morphology	log
8	necrology	log
15	neurology	log
5	nitrogen	gen
12	nomography	gram
10	nomology	log
13	oceanography	gram
7	ochlocracy	crat
18	oligarchy	arch
17	optometry	meter
1	orthogamy	gam
6	orthogonal	gon
14	orthography	gram
13	orthoscopic	scop
15	pantograph	gram
16	paragraph	gram
17	parallelogram	gram
18	parameter	meter
12	parapsychology	log
17	pathologist	log
16	patriarch	arch
6	pedometer	meter
8	pentagon	gon
18	pentagram	gram
16	pentameter	meter
2	perigee	ge
15	perimeter	meter
12	periscope	scop
7	petrology	log
3	philander	andr
4	philanthropy	andr
5	philogynist	gyn
14	philology	log
10	phoneme	phon
7	phonetic	phon
13	phonics	phon
15	phonograph	phon/gram
14	phonolite	phon
16	phonology	phon/log
18	phonometer	phon/meter
11	phonoscope	phon/scop
12	phonotype	phon
7	photogenic	gen
13	photograph	gram
11	photometry	meter
14	pictograph	gram
5	plutocracy	crat
5	polyandry	andr
9	polygamist	gam
8	polygenesis	gen
10	polygon	gon
3	polygraph	gram
14	polygyny	gyn
4	polyphonic	phon
11	pornography	gram
2	primogenitor	gen
3	primogeniture	gen
4	progenitor	gen
5	progeny	gen
2	program	gram
3	prologue	log
3	psychogenic	gen
5	psychograph	gram
6	psychologist	log
10	psychometry	meter
8	pyre	pyr
10	pyrite	pyr
13	pyrogenic	pyr/gen
9	pyrography	pyr/gram
1	pyrolysis	pyr
12	pyromancy	pyr
15	pyromaniac	pyr
7	pyrometer	pyr/meter
6	pyrophobia	pyr
4	pyrosis	pyr
16	pyrostat	pyr
17	pyrotechnics	pyr
18	pyrotoxin	pyr
17	regenerate	gen
1	saxophone	phon
16	scope	scop
6	seismograph	gram
17	skeptic	scop
7	somatology	log
8	soteriology	log
9	spectrology	log
18	spectroscope	scop
9	spherometer	meter
6	spirometer	meter
7	stenographer	gram
8	stereography	gram
2	stereometry	meter
13	stereophonic	phon
1	stethometer	meter
10	stethoscope	scop
9	syllogism	log
3	symmetry	meter
17	symphony	phon
18	synchronize	chron
3	technocracy	crat
11	technology	log
9	telegram	gram
10	telegraph	gram
12	teleology	log
7	telephone	phon
15	telescope	scop
13	tetrology	log
1	theocracy	crat
16	theologian	log
15	theology	log
6	therianthropic	andr
5	thermometer	meter
11	tomography	gram
1	topographer	gram
4	topology	log
3	travelogue	log
12	trigonometry	gon/meter
2	trilogy	log
1	zoology	log
4	zoometry	meter

WORD PARTS LIST LATIN I
lesson # - word - parts

1 abdicate — ab/away, from dict/to speak ate/to do

17 abduct — ab/away, from duc/to lead

● 17 abject — ab/away, from jac/to throw

7 abjure — ab/away, from jud/law, right

15 abscess — ab/away, from cede/go, yield

7 abstain — ab/away, from tain/to hold

8 abstention — ab/away, from tain/to hold ion/state, quality

9 abstinence — ab/away, from tain/to hold ence/state, quality

16 accede — ac/to, at cede/go, yield

17 accept — ac/to, at cap/to take

5 accurate — ac/to, at cur/care ate/having the quality of

2 addict — ad/to, at dict/to speak

18 adduce — ad/to, at duc/to lead

18 adjacent — ad/to, at jac/to throw ent/like, related to

8 adjudicate — ad/to, at jud/law, right dict/to speak ate/to make

6 aggression — ag/to, at grad/to step ion/state, quality, act

● 4 amanuensis — a/from manu/hand ensis/like, relating to

17 ancestor — an(te)/before cede/go, yield or/one who

2 animate — anima/spirit ate/to make, do

8 animism — anima/spirit ism/belief

7 animosity — anima/spirit ity/state, quality, act

5 annals — ann/year al/like, related to s/plural

7 annual — ann/year al/like, related to

2 annuity — ann/year ity/state, quality, act

13 antecedent — ante/before cede/go, yield ent/one who, that which

18 anticipate — ante/before cap/to take ate/to make, do

15 apperceive — ap/to, at per/through cap/to take

10 appertain — ap/to, at per/through tain/to hold

13 appurtenance — ap/to, at per/through tain/to hold ance/quality

15 aqueduct — aqua/water duc/to lead

● 8 artifact — art/skill fac/to make, do

9 artifice — art/skill fac/to make, do

1 ascribe — a(d)/to, at scribe/to write

15 assess — a(d)/to, at sed/to sit

17 assiduous — a(d)/to, at sed/to sit ous/having the quality of

16 assize — a(d)/to sed/to sit

3 benediction — bene/good dict/to speak ion/state, quality, act

9 benefactor — bene/good fac/to make, do or/one who

10 beneficial — bene/good fac/to make, do al/like, related to

11 beneficiary — bene/good fac/to make, do ary/related to

12 benefit — bene/good fac/to make, do

13 benevolent — bene/good vol/will, wish ent/like, related to

14 benign — bene/good gn/birth, race, kind

6 biennial — bi/two ann/year al/like, related to

2 biped — bi/two ped/foot

1 bisect — bi/two sec/to cut

15 bonus — bene/good

16 boon — bene/good

16 capable — cap/to take able/able to be

13 capacious — cap/to take ous/having the quality of

14 capacity — cap/to take ity/state, quality, act

11 capstan — cap/to take

12 capsule — cap/to take cule/small

9 caption — cap/to take ion/state, quality, act

10 captor — cap/to take or/one who

3 centennial — cent/hundred ann/year al/like, related to

15 centrifugal — centri/center fug/to flee al/like, related to

14 cessation — cede/go, yield ion/state, quality, act

15 circumjacent — circum/around jac/to throw ent/like, related to

2 circumscribe — circum/around scribe/to write

1 circumvolution — circum/around volu/to roll ion/state, quality, act

1 claustrophobia — claus/shut, close phobe/fear ia/condition

2 cloister — claus/shut, close er/that which

3	closet	claus/shut, close et/small	
18	closure	claus/shut, close ure/that which	
4	cloture	claus/shut, close ure/that which	
11	concede	con/with, together cede/go, yield	
7	conceive	con/with, together cap/to take	
8	concept	con/with, together cap/to take	
12	concession	con/with, together cede/go, yield ion/state, quality	
5	conclave	con/with, together claus/shut, close	
6	conclude	con/with, together claus/shut, close	
4	condition	con/with, together dict/to speak ion/state, quality	
2	conducive	con/with, together duc/to lead ive/having the power	
16	conduct	con/with, together duc/to lead	
3	conduit	con/with, together duc/to lead	
10	confection	con/with, together fac/to make, do ion/state	
7	congress	con/with, together grad/to step	
16	conjecture	con/with, together jac/to throw ure/state, quality	
3	conscript	con/with, together scribe/to write	
11	continent	con/with, together tain/to hold ent/that which	
5	contradict	contra/against dict/to speak	
2	convoluted	con/with, together volu/to roll ed/past action	
15	corporation	corp/body ate/to make, do ion/state, quality, act	
17	corps	corp/body	
18	corpse	corp/body	
9	corpulent	corp/body ent/like, related to	
16	corpus	corp/body us/Latin ending	
13	corpuscle	corp/body cle/small	
12	countenance		
		con/with, together tain/to hold ance/state, quality	
3	curator	cur/care or/one who	
2	curious	cur/care ous/having the quality of	
9	decease	de/down, away cede/go, yield	
2	deceive	de/down, away cap/to take	
17	deception	de/down, away cap/to take ion/state, quality, act	
6	dedicate	de/down, away dict/to speak ate/to	

		make, do
13	deduce	de/down, away duc/to lead
14	deduct	de/down, away duc/to lead
11	defaced	de/down, away fac/face ed/past action
12	defect	de/down, away fac/to make, do
13	deficient	de/down, away fac/to make, do ent/like, related to
14	deficit	de/down, away fac/to make, do
8	degrade	de/down, away grad/to step
9	degree	de/down, away grad/to step
13	dejection	de/down, away jac/to throw ion/state, quality
4	description	de/down, away scribe/to write ion/state, quality
13	detain	de/down, away tain/to hold
14	detention	de/down, away tain/to hold ion/state, quality
3	devolve	de/down, away volu/to roll
13	dictaphone	dict/to speak phon/sound
7	dictator	dict/to speak ate/to make, do or/one who
8	diction	dict/to speak ion/state, quality
9	dictum	dict/to speak um/Latin ending
10	digression	di/apart, not grad/to step ion/state, quality
5	disciple	di/apart, not cap/to take le/one who
14	discipline	di/apart, not cap/to take ine/having nature of
7	disclose	di/apart, not claus/shut, close
17	dismal	di/apart, not mal/bad
2	dissect	di/apart, not sec/to cut
14	dissident	di/apart, not sed/to sit ent/one who
10	edict	e/out, away dict/to speak
11	educate	e/out, away duc/to lead ate/to make, do
12	educe	e/out, away duc/to lead
15	efface	e/out, away fac/face
16	efficacious	e/out, away fac/to make, do ous/having the quality
17	efficient	e/out, away fac/to make, do ent/like, related to
11	egress	e/out, away grad/to step
14	ejaculate	e/out, away jac/to throw ate/to make, do

11	eject	e/out, away jac/to throw
1	emancipate	e/out, away manu/hand cap/to take ate/to make, do
8	enclave	en/in, into claus/shut, close
9	enclose	en/in, into claus/shut, close
10	enclosure	en/in, into claus/shut, close ure/that which
14	entertain	inter/between tain/to hold
1	equanimity	equ/equal anima/spirit ity/state, quality
4	evolution	e/out, away volu/to roll ion/state, quality
6	exception	ex/out, away cap/to take ion/state, quality
10	excess	ex/out, away cede/go, yield
11	exclude	ex/out, away claus/shut, close
1	expedient	ex/out, away ped/foot ent/like, related to
4	expedite	ex/out, away ped/foot ite/to make, do
1	facade	fac/face
18	facet	fac/face et/small?
2	facile	fac/to make, do ile/like, related to
3	facility	fac/to make, do ile/like, related to ity/state
4	facsimile	fac/to make, do simil/like
5	faction	fac/to make, do ion/state, quality
6	factor	fac/to make, do or/one who, that which
7	factual	fac/to make, do al/like, related to
18	forceps	formus/hot cap/to take s/plural
12	foreclose	fore/before claus/shut, close
15	fraction	fract/to break ion/state, quality
16	fracture	fract/to break ure/state, quality, that which
13	fragile	fract/to break ile/like, related to
14	fragment	fract/to break ment/state, quality, that which
11	fugue	fug/to flee
1	gradation	grad/to step ate/to make, do ion/state, quality
5	grade	grad/to step
2	gradient	grad/to step ent/like, related to, that which
3	gradual	grad/to step al/like, related to

4	graduate	grad/to step ate/to make, do
3	impede	im/not ped/foot
15	imperceptible	im/not per/through cap/to take able/able to be
15	impertinent	im/not per/through tain/to hold ent/like, related
5	inanimate	in/in, not anima/spirit ate/to make, do
16	inception	in/in, not cap/to take ion/state, quality
7	incessant	in/in, not cede/go, yield ant/like, related to
13	include	in/in, not claus/shut, close
10	incorporate	in/in, not corp/body ate/to make, do
11	indict	in/in, not dict/to speak
9	induct	in/in, not duc/to lead
17	infect	in/in, not fac/to make, do
17	infraction	in/in, not fract/to break ion/state, quality
12	ingredient	in/in, not grad/to step ent/that which
13	ingress	in/in, not grad/to step
12	inject	in/in, not jac/to throw
6	injury	in/in, not jud/law, right y/quality, condtion
5	injustice	in/in, not jud/law, right ice/act of
5	inscription	in/in, not scribe/to write ion/state, quality
3	insect	in/in, not sec/to cut
13	insidious	in/in, not sed/to sit ous/having the quality of
8	intercede	inter/between cede/go, yield
1	intercept	inter/between cap/to take
5	intercession	inter/between cede/go, yield ion/state, quality
12	interdict	inter/between dict/to speak
9	interject	inter/between jac/to throw
4	intersection	inter/between sec/to cut ion/state, quality
10	introduce	intro/inside duc/to lead
6	involute	in/in, not volu/to roll
5	involve	in/in, not volu/to roll
7	jetty	jac/to throw
8	joist	jac/to throw

4 judicial   jud/law, right dict/to speak al/like, related to

13 judicious   jud/law, right dict/to speak ous/having the quality

14 jurisdiction jud/law, right dict/to speak ion/state, quality

3 juror   jud/law, right or/one who

2 justify   jud/law, right fy/to do, to make

4 magnanimous
    magn/great anima/spirit ous/having the quality

18 magnificence
    magn/great fac/to make, do ence/state, quality

16 maintain   manu/hand tain/to hold

18 maladjusted
    mal/bad ad/to, at jud/law, right

2 malady   mal/bad ady/French-Latin derivative

16 malconduct
    mal/bad con/with, together duc/to lead

13 malcontent mal/bad con/with, together tain/to hold

15 malediction mal/bad dict/to speak ion/state, quality

14 malefactor mal/bad fac/to make, do or/one who

11 maleficent mal/bad fac/to make, do ent/like, related to

12 malevolent mal/bad vol/will, wish ent/like, related to

9 malfeasance
    mal/bad fac/to make, do ance/state, quality

10 malformed mal/bad form/form, shape ed/past action

7 malice   mal/bad ice/quality of

8 malicious   mal/bad ice/quality of ous/having the quality

5 malign   mal/bad gn/birth, race, kind

3 malignant mal/bad gn/birth, race, kind ant/like, related to

6 malnutrition
    mal/bad nutri/nourish ion/state, quality

4 malodorous
    mal/bad odor/odor, smell ous/having the quality

1 malpractice
    mal/bad pract/to do ice/act or quality of

15 manacle   manu/hand cle/small

16 manciple   manu/hand cap/to take le/one who

11 mandate   manu/hand dare/to give

14 manicure   manu/hand cur/care

13 manipulate manu/hand plere/to fill ate/to make, do

12 manufacture
    manu/hand fac/to make, do ure/that which, state

6 manuscript manu/hand scribe/to write

4 millennium
    milli/thousand ann/year um/Latin ending

6 millepede   milli/thousand ped/foot

12 municipal   muni/gift, service cap/to take al/like, related to

15 munificence
    muni/gift, service fac/to make, do ence/state

6 necessary   non/not cede/go, yield ary/like, related to

7 nondescript non/not de/down, away scribe/to write

10 object   ob/to, against jac/to throw

12 obsession   ob/to, against sed/to sit ion/state, quality

17 obtain   ob/to, against tain/to hold

7 obvolute   ob/to, against volu/to roll

14 occlusion   oc/to, against claus/shut, close ion/state, quality

11 occupation oc/to, against cap/to take ion/state, quality

5 octopus   oct/eight ped/foot

16 orifice   or/mouth fac/to make, do

4 participate part/part cap/to take ate/to make, do

8 pedal   ped/foot al/like, related to

7 pedestal   ped/foot stal/place, a rest

12 pedestrian ped/foot ian/one who

6 pedicure   ped/foot cur/care

10 pedigree   ped/foot grad/to step

3 perception per/through cap/to take ion/state, quality

WORD PARTS LIST LATIN I
lesson # - word - parts

1 perennial — per/through ann/year al/like, related to

13 perfect — per/through fac/to make, do

1 perjury — per/through jud/law, right y/quality, condition

18 pertain — per/through tain/to hold

17 pertinent — per/through tain/to hold ent/like, related to

9 podium — ped/foot um/Latin ending

11 possess — pos/?after? sed/to sit

8 postscript — post/after scribe/to write

3 precede — pre/before cede/go, yield

1 precept — pre/before cap/to take

15 preclude — pre/before claus/shut, close

1 predecessor — pre/before cede/go, yield or/one who

6 predict — pre/before dict/to speak

14 prefect — pre/before fac/to make, do

9 prescribe — pre/before scribe/to write

9 preside — pre/before sed/to sit

8 president — pre/before sed/to sit ent/one who

2 principal — prin/first cap/to take al/like, related to

4 procedure — pro/for, forward cede/go, yield ure/state, quality

2 proceed — pro/for, forward cede/go, yield

18 procession — pro/for, forward cede/go, yield ion/state, quality

7 proctor — pro/for, forward cur/care or/one who

8 procure — pro/for, forward cur/care

7 produce — pro/for, forward duc/to lead

8 productive — pro/for, forward duc/to lead ive/having the power

11 proficient — pro/for, forward fac/to make, do ent/like, related

14 progression — pro/for, forward grad/to step ion/state, quality

1 project — pro/for, forward jac/to throw

3 pusillanimous — pusil/tiny anima/spirit ous/having the quality

18 recede — re/back, again cede/go, yield

5 receipt — re/back, again cap/to take

7 receptacle — re/back, again cap/to take cle/small

6 reception — re/back, again cap/to take ion/state, quality

4 receptionist — re/back, again cap/to take ion/state ist/one who

8 receptive — re/back, again cap/to take ive/having the power

3 receptor — re/back, again cap/to take or/one who, that which

10 recipe — re/back, again cap/to take

16 recluse — re/back, again claus/shut, close

5 reduce — re/back, again duc/to lead

18 refractory — re/back, again fract/to break ary/like, related to

12 refuge — re/back, again fug/to flee

18 refugee — re/back, again fug/to flee ee/one who

15 regress — re/back, again grad/to step

2 reject — re/back, again jac/to throw

10 reside — re/back, again sed/to sit

7 resident — re/back, again sed/to sit ent/one who

6 residue — re/back, again sed/to sit

18 retention — re/back, again tain/to hold ion/state, quality

15 retinue — re/back, again tain/to hold

17 retrocede — retro/backwards cede/go, yield

16 retrograde — retro/backwards grad/to step

17 retrogress — retro/backwards grad/to step

8 revolve — re/back, again volu/to roll

18 scribble — scribe/to write le/?small?

10 scribe — scribe/to write

11 script — scribe/to write

17 scripture — scribe/to write ure/that which, state, quality

6 secant — sec/to cut ant/like, related to

16 secede — se/apart cede/go, yield

17 seclusion — se/apart claus/shut, close ion/state, quality

14 section — sec/to cut ion/state, quality, act

8 sector — sec/to cut or/that which

9 secure — se/apart cur/care

18 sedate — sed/to sit ate/to make, do

5 sedentary — sed/to sit ent/that which ary/like, related

4 sediment — sed/to sit ment/that which, state, quality

6 seduce — se/apart duc/to lead

7 segment — sec/to cut ment/that which, state, quality

3 sessile — sed/to sit ile/like, related to

9 sickle — sec/to cut le/a thing used

10 sinecure — sine/without cur/care

3 subjacent — sub/under jac/to throw ent/like, related to

5 subject — sub/under jac/to throw

12 subscriber — sub/under scribe/to write er/one who

13 subscript — sub/under scribe/to write

2 subsidy — sub/under sed/to sit y/quality, condition

17 subterfuge — sub/under fug/to flee

15 succeed — sub/under cede/go, yield

9 suffice — sub/under fac/to make, do

12 sufficient — sub/under fac/to make, do ent/like, related to

8 superficial — super/over, above fac/to make, do al/like, related

14 superscript — super/over, above scribe/to write

1 supersede — super/over, above sed/to sit

4 superjacent — super/over, above jac/to throw ent/like, related

10 surface — sub/under fac/face

9 susceptible — sub/under cap/to take ible/able to be

16 sustain — sub/under tain/to hold

1 tenable — tain/to hold able/able to be

6 tenacity — tain/to hold aci(ous)/having quality ity/state

5 tenant — tain/to hold ant/one who

4 tenement — tain/to hold ment/that which, state, quality

3 tenet — tain/to hold

2 tenure — tain/to hold ure/that which

1 traduce — tra/across duc/to lead

6 trajectory — tra/across jac/to throw ary/like, related to

15 transcribe — trans/across scribe/to write

16 transcript — trans/across scribe/to write

10 transect — trans/across sec/to cut

18 transgress — trans/across grad/to step

11 tripod — tri/three ped/foot

11 trisect — tri/three sec/to cut

6 unanimous — uni/one anima/spirit ous/having the quality

17 valediction — vale/farewell dict/to speak ion/state, quality

9 valve — volu/to roll

10 vault — volu/to roll

12 venesection — vene/vein sec/to cut ion/state, quality

11 veracious — ver/true acious/having the quality of

18 verdict — ver/true dict/to speak

12 verify — ver/true ify/to make, do

13 verisimilitude — ver/true simil/like tude/state, quality

4 viaduct — via/way, road duc/to lead

5 vivisection — vivi/to live sec/to cut ion/state, quality

14 voluble — volu/to roll able/able to be

17 volume — volu/to roll um/Latin ending

18 voluminous — volu/to roll um/Latin ending ous/having the quality

9	abstract	ab(s)/from tract/to draw
1	accident	ac/to cid/to fall ent/like, related to
5	accomplice	(a)ccom/with plex/to fold
14	accredit	ac/to cred/to believe
18	admission	ad/to mis/to send ion/state, quality, act
15	adverse	ad/to verse/to turn
16	adversity	ad/to vers/to turn ity/state, quality, act
17	advertise	ad/to vert/to turn ise/to make, act
17	advise	ad/to vid/to see
15	aerostat	aero/air stat/to stand
13	agnomen	ag/to gnom/name en/having the quality of
1	amphora	amph/both phora/to carry
18	animadvert	anim/spirit ad/to vert/to turn
14	anniversary	ann(i)/year vers/to turn ary/like, related to
14	anonymous	an/without onym/name ous/has quality of
15	antonym	ant/opposite onym/name
16	apostasy	apo/away sta/to stand sy/state, quality, act
4	appeal	ap/to peal/to push
14	append	ap/to pend/to hang
6	applicant	ap/to plic/to fold ant/one who
7	appliqué	ap/to plique/to fold
5	armistice	armi/arms stice/to stand
1	aspect	a/to spect/to look
6	assist	as/to sist/to stand
10	attract	at/to tract/to draw
2	auspice	au/bird spice/to look
1	automobile	auto/self mob/to move ile/like, related to
11	averse	a/from verse/to turn
2	avert	a/from vert/to turn
18	avow	a/to vow/to call
17	belvedere	bel/beautiful, fine vedere/to see
2	cadaver	cad/to fall aver/?
3	cadence	cad/to fall ence/state, quality, act
4	cadenza	cad/to fall enza/Italian derivative

5	cascade	cascade/to fall
6	casualty	cas/to fall ual/related to ty/state, quality
3	catapult	cata/down pult/to push
2	circumference	circum/around fer/to carry ence/state
3	circumspect	circum/around spec/to look
7	circumstance	circum/around sta/to stand nce/state
15	clairvoyance	clair/clear voy/to see ance/state, quality
16	cognomen	co/with gnom/name en/having quality of
7	coincide	co/with in/upon cide/to fall
18	commissary	com/with miss/to send ary/like, related to
17	commit	com/with mit/to send
2	commotion	com/with mot/to move ion/state, quality
15	compendium	com/with pend/to hang ium/Latin ending
16	compensate	com/with pens/to hang ate/to do, make
8	complex	com/with plex/to fold
15	complicate	com/with plic/to fold ate/to do, make
16	complicity	com/with plic/to fold ity/state, quality, act
1	component	com/with pon/to place ent/that which
2	compose	com/with pose/to place
3	compost	com/with post/to place
4	compound	com/with pound/to place
16	compromise	com/with pro/forth mise/to send
2	compulsory	com/with puls/to push ory/like
3	confer	con/with fer/to carry
1	consecutive	con/with secu/to follow (t)ive/that which
2	consequence	con/with sequ/to follow ence/state

18 consistency con/with sist/to stand ency/state, quality

4 conspicuous
con/with spic/to look uous/has quality of

12 constant con/with sta/to stand ant/that which

13 constituent con/with stit/to stand uent/that which

1 contort con/with tort/to twist

11 contract con/with tract/to draw

14 contrast contra/against st/to stand

1 controversy
contro/against vers/to turn y/state

12 conversant con/with vers/to turn ant/like, related to

8 converse con/with verse/to turn

7 convert con/with vert/to turn

17 convocation
con/with voc/to call ation/state, quality

15 credence cred/to believe ence/state, quality, act

16 credential cred/to believe enti/state al/like

17 credible cred/to believe ible/able to be

18 creditor cred/to believe it/Latin or/one who

13 creed creed/to believe

17 cryptonym crypt/hidden onym/name

8 decadence de/down cad/to fall ence/state, quality

9 deciduous de/down cid/to fall uous/having quality of

1 decuple decu/ten ple/to fold

4 deference de/down fer/to carry ence/state, quality

15 demise de/down mise/to send

3 demote de/down mote/to move

18 denomination
de/down nomin/name at/to do ion/state

17 dependable
de/down pend/to hang able/able to be

2 deploy de/down ploy/to fold

5 deposit de/down pos/to place it/Latin

17 desist de/down sist/to stand

5 despicable de/down spic/to look able/able to be

6 despite de/down spite/to look

11 destine de/down stine/to stand

18 destitute de/down stit/to stand ute/

12 detract de/down tract/to draw

16 device de/down vice/to see

1 devise de/down vise/to see

5 differentiate
dif/apart fer/to carry ent/like ate/to do

12 discredit dis/away cred/to believe it/Latin

14 dismiss dis/away miss/to send

1 dispel dis/away pel/to push

18 dispense dis/away pense/to hang

3 display dis/away play/to fold

6 dispose dis/away pose/to place

17 distant dis/away sta/to stand ant/like, related to

2 distort dis/away tort/to twist

13 distract dis/away tract/to draw

6 diversify di/away vers/to turn ify/to do

5 divert di/away vert/to turn

4 diverticulum
di/away vert/to turn iculum/Latin

4 duplex du/two plex/to fold

5 duplicate du/two plic/to fold ate/to do

6 duplicity du/two plic/to fold ity/state, quality

16 ecstatic ec/out stat/to stand ic/like, related to

13 emit e/out mit/to send

7 employ em/in ploy/to fold

14 entreat en/in treat/to draw

2 envisage en/in vis/to see age/state, quality, act

3 envy en/in vy/to see

15 eponym epo/upon nym/name

16 equivocate equi/equal voc/to call ate/to do

4 evidence e/out vid/to see ence/state, quality

15 evoke e/out voke/to call

3 execute exe/out cute/to follow

14 expel ex/out pel/to push

17 expend ex/out pend/to hang

18 expense ex/out pense/to hang

8 explicate ex/out plic/to fold ate/to do

7 expose ex/out pose/to place

8 expound ex/out pound/to place

WORD PARTS LIST LATIN II
lesson # - word - root

13 expulsion ex/out puls/to push ion/state, quality

14 extant ex/out tant/to stand

3 extort ex/out tort/to turn

4 extract ex/out tract/to draw

4 extrinsic extri/outside (n)sic/to follow

3 extrovert extro/outside vert/to turn

6 ferry fer/to carry ry/quality

7 fertile fert/to carry ile/able to

13 gyrostatics gyro/circle stat/to stand ics/like, related to

12 heliostat helio/sun stat/to stand

11 hemostasis hemo/blood stasis/standing

17 homonym homo/same nym/name

18 ignominy ig/not, without nomin/name y/state

12 impel im/in pel/to push

1 impending im/in pend/to hang ing/pres part ending

9 implicate im/in plic/to fold ate/to do

9 impose im/in pose/to place

10 impost im/in post/to place

11 impostor im/in post/to place or/one who

12 impound im/in pound/to place

5 improvise im/in pro/before vise/to see

11 impulsive im/in puls/to push ive/having the power of

1 inadvertent in/not ad/to vert/to turn ent/like

10 incidental in/on cid/to fall ent/that which al/like

11 incredible in/not cred to believe ible/able to

2 independent in/not de/down pend/to hang ent/like

11 inference in/in fer/to carry ence/state, quality

10 insistent in/in sist/to stand ent/like, related to

7 inspect in/in spect/to look

9 instantaneous in/in stant/to stand aneous/has quality of

8 institution in/in stit/to stand ution/state, quality

12 intermission nter/between mis/to send sion/state

13 interpose inter/between pos/to place

7 interstice inter/between stice/to stand, set

6 interview inter/between view/to see

5 intrinsic intrin/inward sic/to follow

8 introspective intro/inward spect/to look ive/has power of

2 introvert intro/inward vert/to turn

3 inverse in/in verse/to turn

7 invidious in/in vid/to see ious/having quality of

8 invisible in/in vis/to see ible/able to

14 invocation in/in voc/to call ation/state, quality

13 irrevocable ir/not re/back voc/to call able/able to

14 juxtaposition juxta/near to pos/to place ition/state

11 manumit manu/hand mit/to send

12 metaphor meta/change phor/to carry

6 metastasis meta/change stasis/standing

1 metonymy met/change onym/name y/state, quality

10 miscreant mis/bad cre/to believe ant/one who, like

2 misnomer mis/bad nom/name er/that which

10 missile miss/to send ile/like, related to

9 missionary miss/to send ion/state ary/one who

4 mobile mob/to move ile/like

5 motivate mot/to move ive/that which ate/to do

6 motive mot/to move ive/that which

10 multiplicity multi/many plic/to fold ity/state

7 mutiny mut/to move iny/French

3 nomenclature nomen/name clat/to call ure/that which

4 nominal nomin/name al/like, related to

5 nominate nomin/name ate/to do

6 nominative nomin/name at/to do ive/that which

6 obsequious ob/to seq/to follow uious/having quality of

5 obstacle ob/to sta/to stand cle/small

4 obstinate ob/to stin/to stand ate/having quality of

4 obverse ob/to verse/to turn

11 occasion oc/to cas/to fall ion/state, quality

12 occident oc/to cid/to fall ent/that which

11 octuple octu/eight ple/to fold

WORD PARTS LIST LATIN II

lesson # - word - parts

13 offertory — of/to fer/to carry tory/having quality of

8 omission — o/to miss/to send ion/state, quality

15 opponent — op/to pon/to place ent/one who

14 paraphernalia — para/beyond pher/to carry nalia/?

7 patronymic — patr/father onym/name ic/like, related to

3 penchant — pench/to hang ant/that which

4 pendulous — pend/to hang ulous/having the quality of

5 pension — pens/to hang ion/state, quality, act

6 pensive — pens/to hang ive/having the quality of

7 penthouse — pent/to hang house/house

15 periphery — peri/around pher/to carry y/state, quality

7 permission — per/through miss/to send ion/state, quality

8 perpendicular — per/through pend/to hand icul/? ar/like

12 perplex — per/through plex/to fold

7 persecute — per/through sec/to follow ute/?

3 persist — per/through sist/to stand

9 perspective — per/through spect/to look ive/has power of

10 perspicacious — per/through spic/to look acious/quality of

5 perversion — per/through vers/to turn ion/state, quality

16 phosphorescent — phos/light pher/to carry escent/becoming

13 plait — plait/to fold

14 plexus — plex/to fold us/Latin ending

15 pliable — pli/to fold able/able to be

16 plight — plight/to fold

16 portray — por/forth tray/to draw

16 positive — pos/to place it/Latin ive/has the power of

17 posture — post/to place ure/that which, state

9 preferable — pre/before fer/to carry able/able to be

6 premise — pre/before mise/to send

9 preview — pre/before view/to see

17 proffer — pro/forth fer/to carry

5 promise — pro/forth mise/to send

8 promote — pro/forth mote/to move

10 propel — pro/forth pel/to push

10 propensity — pro/forth pens/to hang ity/state, quality, act

18 proponent — pro/forth pon/to push ent/one who

13 propound — pro/forth pound/to place

9 propulsion — pro/forth puls/to push ion/state, quality, act

8 prosecute — pro/forth sec/to follow ute/

11 prospect — pro/forth spect/to look

12 prospectus — pro/forth spect/to look us/Latin

2 prostate — pro/forth state/to stand

1 prostitute — pro/forth stit/to stand ute/

17 protract — pro/forth tract/to draw

18 protractor — pro/forth tract/to draw or/that which

10 providential — pro/forth vid/to see ent/that which al/like

11 provision — pro/forth vis/to see ion/state, quality, act

12 provocation — pro/forth voc/to call at/to do ion/state

14 provost — pro/forth vost/to place

8 pseudonym — pseudo/false nym/name

8 pulsate — puls/to push ate/to do

15 purpose — pur/forth pose/to place

9 pursue — pur/forth sue/to follow

17 quadruple — quadr/four uple/to fold

13 recidivist — re/back cid/to fall ivist/one who

9 recompense — re/back com/with pense/to hang

18 reconstitute — re/back con/with stit/to stand ute/

9 recreant — re/back cre/to believe ant/one who

18 referee — re/back fer/to carry ee/one who

4 remiss — re/back miss/to send

9 remote — re/back mote/to move

10 remove — re/back move/to move

9 renown — re/back nown/name

7	repeal	re/back peal/to push
6	repel	re/back pel/to push
● 18	replicate	re/back plic/to fold ate/to do
1	reply	re/back ply/to fold
16	repository	re/back pos/to place it/Lt. ory/place where
5	repulsive	re/back puls/to push ive/that which
17	resist	re/back sist/to stand
13	respect	re/back spect/to look
14	respite	re/back spite/to look
16	restitution	re/back stit/to stand ution/state, quality
15	restive	re/back st/to stand ive/that which
6	retort	re/back tort/to twist
1	retract	re/back tract/to draw
15	retrospect	retro/backward spect/to look
6	retroversion	retro/backward vers/to turn ion/state
7	revert	re/back vert/to turn
12	revise	re/back vise/to see
11	revoke	re/back voke/to call
● 14	rheostat	rheo/current stat/to stand
● 10	sect	sect/to follow
1	semaphore	sema/a sign phore/to carry
11	sequel	sequel/to follow
12	sequence	sequ/to follow ence/state, quality
13	sequester	sequ/to follow ester/?
2	sextuple	sextu/six ple/to fold
10	somniferous	somni/sleep fer/to carry ous/quality of
16	specialize	spec/to look ial/like ize/to do
17	specify	spec/to look ify/to do
18	specimen	spec/to look imen/something done
9	specious	spec/to look ious/having quality of
10	spectacle	spect/to look acle/that which
15	specter	spect/to look er/that which
16	spectrum	spectr/to look um/Latin ending
14	speculate	spec/to look ate/to do
17	spite	spite/to look
● 15	stabilize	sta/to stand bil/able ize/to do
● 13	stadium	sta/to stand dium/Latin ending
12	stanchion	stan/to stand chion/French derivative

11	stanza	stan/to stand za/Italian derivative
10	static	stat/to stand ic/like, related to
9	statistic	stat/to stand ic/like, related to
8	stature	stat/to stand ure/state, quality
7	staunch	sta/to stand unch/
11	stipend	sti/coin pend/to hang, pay
3	submissive	sub/under miss/to send ive/that which
6	subsist	sub/under sist/to stand
5	substantiate	sub/under sta/to stand ant/that which ate/to do
4	substitute	sub/under stit/to stand ute/
2	subtract	sub/under tract/to draw
8	subversive	sub/under vers/to turn ive/one who
8	suffer	suf/under fer to carry
3	superstition	super/above stit/ to stand ion/state, quality
13	supervise	super/above vise/to see
18	supposition	sup/under pos/to place it/Latin ion/state
2	surmise	sur/above mise/to send
3	suspect	su/under spect/to look
12	suspend	sus/under pend/to hang
13	suspense	sus/under pense/to hang
4	suspicious	su/under spic/to look ious/quality of
10	synonym	syn/with onym/name
2	systemic	sy/with stem/to stand ic/like, related to
5	tart	tart/to twist
1	thermostat	thermo/heat stat/to stand
11	toponym	topo/place nym/name
7	torment	tor/to twist ment/state, act
8	torque	torque/to twist
9	torsion	tor/to twist sion/state, quality
10	tort	tort/to twist
11	tortilla	tort/to twist illa/Spanish
12	torture	tort/to twist ure/state, quality
3	trace	trace/to draw
4	tractable	tract/to draw able/able to
6	tractile	tract/to draw ile/like, able to be
5	traction	tract/to draw ion/state, quality

7	trait	trait/to draw
2	transfer	trans/across fer/to carry
1	transmit	trans/across mit/to sent
18	transpose	trans/across pose/to place
9	traverse	tra/across verse/to turn
8	treatise	treat/to draw ise/to make, to act
12	trinomial	tri/three nom/name ial/like, related to
3	triplex	tri/three plex/to fold
4	triplicate	tri/three plic/to fold ate/having quality of
13	trousseau	trousseau/to twist (French)
14	truss	truss/to twist (French)
10	universe	uni/one verse/to turn
11	versatile	versa/to turn ile/able to
12	versus	versus/to turn
13	vertebra	verte/to turn bra/
14	vertex	vertex/to turn
15	vertical	verti/to turn cal/like, related to
16	vertigo	vert/to turn igo/
14	video	video/to see
15	visage	vis/to see age/state, quality
16	visible	vis/to see ible/able to
10	vocal	voc/to call al/like, related to
9	vocation	voc/to call at/to do ion/state, quality
8	vociferous	voc/to call ifer/to carry ous/has quality of
17	vortex	vortex/to turn
18	vortical	vorti/to turn ical/like, related to

10 acrogen   acro/high gen/cause

5 acrography acro/high gram/to write y/state, quality

1 altimeter   alt/high meter/measure

2 anachronism
       ana/back, again chron/time ism/state

6 anagram   ana/back, again gram/to write

14 analogous ana/back, again log/word ous/quality of

13 analogue   ana/back, again logue/word

12 analogy   ana/back, again logy/word

1 anarchist   an/not, without arch/to rule ist/one who

18 androcracy andr/man crat/to rule y/state, quality, act

2 androgen   andr/man gen/cause

1 androgynous
       andr/man gyn/woman ous/quality of

9 androphobia
       andr/man phob/to fear ia/condition

14 anhydrous an/not, withou hydr/water ous/quality of

10 anthropocentric
       andr/man centr/center ic/like, related to

12 anthropogenesis
       andr/man gen/cause esis/state, quality

11 anthropoid andr/man oid/resembling

13 anthropologist
       andr/man logy/study of ist/one who

14 anthropometry
       andr/man meter/measure

15 anthropomorhpism
       andr/man morph/form ism/state

16 anthropopathy
       andr/man path/feeling, disease y/state

17 anthropophagy
       andr/man phag/to eat y/state, quality, act

6 antiphon   anti/against, oppositie phon/sound

3 antiphony   anti/against phon/sound y/state, quality

2 antipyretic anti/against pyr/fire ic/like, related to

4 aphonic   a/not, without phon/sounc ic/like, related

8 apogamy   apo/from, away gam/marriage y/state

17 apogee   apo/from, away ge/earth

5 apologue   apo/from, away logue/word

16 apology   apo/from, away logy/way of speaking

18 apologetics apo/from, away log/word ics/science

3 archangel   arch/first, chief, to rule angel/angel

5 archduke   arch/first, chief, to rule duke/duke

7 archenemy arch/first, chief, to rule enemy/enemy

9 archimage   arch/first, chief, to rule mage/magician

11 architect   arch/first, chief, to rule tect/builder

13 aristocrat   aristo/best crat/to rule

18 astrology   astr/ star logy/study of

11 asymmetrical
       a/not sym/with meter/measure ical/like

14 atmometer atm/breath meter/measure

7 autobiography
       auto/self bio/life gram/to write y/state

11 autocratic auto/self crat/to rule ic/like, related to

6 autogamy   auto/self gam/marriage y/state, quality

9 autogenesis auto/self gen/cause esis/state, quality, act

8 autograph auto/self gram/to write

13 barometer   bar/pressure, weight meter/measure

10 bibliography
       bibli/book gram/to write y/state, act

2 bigamist   bi/two gam/marriage ist/one who

7 biogenesis bio/life gen/cause esis/state, quality, act

11 biographer bio/life gram/to write er/one who

10 biology   bio/life logy/study of

15 bureaucracy
       bureau/desk crat/to rule y/state

12 cacography cac/bad gram/to write y/state, quality, act

5 cacophony cac/bad phon/sound y/state, quality, act

13 calligraphy calli/beautiful gram/to write y/state, quality

14 cardiogram card/heart gram/to write

15 centimeter cent/hundred meter/measure

16 choreography
  chor/to dance gram/to write y/state, quality

9 chromatology   chroma/color logy/study of

16 chronic   chron/time ic/like, related to

11 chronicle   chron/time icle/like, related to

4 chronogram
  chron/time gram/to write

12 chronological
  chron/time log/word ical/like, related to

8 chronology chron/time logy/study of

10 chronometer
  chron/time meter/measure

6 chronoscope
  chron/time scop/to look

6 congenital   con/with, together gen/cause al/like

10 cosmology cosmo/universe logy/study of

14 crony   chron/time y/state, quality, act

3 cryptogram
  crypt/hidden gram/to write

17 cyclograph cycl/circle gram/to write

16 cyclometer cycl/circle meter/measure

1 cyclonoscope
  cycl/circle scop/to look

3 cytology   cyt/cell logy/study of

17 decimeter   dec/ten meter/measure

6 degenerate   de/down, away gen/cause ate/to make

11 dehydrate   de/down, away hydr/water ate/to make

17 democratic demo/people crat/to rule ic/like, related to

18 demography
  demo/people gram/to write y/state, quality

8 dermatogen
  derm/skin gen/cause

17 dermatology
  derm/skin logy/study of

14 diagonal   dia/through gon/angle al/like, related to

1 diagram   dia/through gram/to write

6 dialogue   dia/through logue/discourse

2 dictaphone dict/to speak phon/sound

4 digamy   di/two gam/marriage y/state, quality, act

5 doxology   dox/opinion, praise logy/way of speaking

4 ecologist   eco/house log/word ist/one who

10 endogamy   endo/inside gam/marriage y/state, quality

1 engender   en/in, into gen/cause er/that which

10 epigeous   epi/on, outside ge/earth ous/quality of

18 epigram   epi/on, outside gram/to write

14 epigraph   epi/on, outside gram/to write

12 epigraphy   epi/on, outside gram/to write y/state

3 epilogue   epi/on, outside logue/discourse

2 episcopal   epi/on, outside scop/to look al/ like

17 ergograph   erg/work, power gram/to write

10 ergometer   erg/work, power meter/measure

18 etymology   etym/true logy/study of

2 eulogy   eu/good logy/way of speaking

12 euphonic   eu/good phon/sound ic/like, related to

12 exogamy   exo/outside gam/marriage y/state, quality

14 exogen   exo/outside gen/cause

13 exogenous exo/outside gen/cause ous/quality of

14 gamete   gam/marriage ete/little(?)

3 gender   gen/kind er/that which

5 gene   gen/kind

1 genealogy   gen/kind logy/study of

6 generalize   gen/kind al/like ize/to make, to do

7 generally   gen/kind al/like ly/in the manner of

8 generate   gen/cause ate/to make, to do

9 generation gen/cause ate/to make ion/state, quality

10 generator   gen/cause ate/to do or/that which

11 generic   gen/kind ic/like, related to

12 generous   gen/kind ous/having the quality of

4 genesis   gen/cause esis/state, quality, act

14 genetics   gen/kind ics/science, system

15 genial   gen/kind al/like, related to

16 genital   gen/cause al/like, related to

17 genius   gen/kind us/Latin form

18 genocide   gen/kind cide/to kill

9 genre   gen/kind re/French spelling

11 genteel   gen/kind teel/French spelling

⚫ 12 gentile   gen/kind ile/like, related to

13 gentle   gen/kind tle/(Fr) like, related to

2 gentleman gen/kind tle/(Fr)like man/man

15 genuine   gen/kind ine/like, related to

16 genus   gen/kind us/Latin form

1 geocentric ge/earth centr/center ic/like, related to

3 geode   ge/earth ode/resembling

5 geodetic   ge/earth ode/resembling ic/like, related to

4 geographer ge/earth gram/to write er/one who

6 geologist ge/earth log/study of ist/one who

7 geomancy   ge/earth mancy/divination

8 geometric ge/earth meter/measure ic/like, related to

9 geophagy   ge/earth phag/to eat y/state, quality, act

11 geophysics ge/earth physi/nature ics/science, system

13 geothermic ge/earth therm/heat ic/like, related to

⚫ 15 geotropism ge/earth trop/to turn ism/state, quality, act

4 goniometer gon/angle meter/measure

16 grammar   gram/to write ar/like, related to

13 graphics   gram/to write ics/science, system

15 graphite   gram/to write ite/having the quality of

2 graphology gram/to write logy/study of

2 gynarchy   gyn/woman arch/to rule y/state, quality

8 gynecology gyn/woman logy/study of

3 gynophobia gyn/woman phob/to fear ia/condition

4 gyroscope gyr/ring, circle scop/to look

9 heliograph heli/sun gram/to write

8 heliometer heli/sun meter/measure

5 helioscope heli/sun scop/to look

1 hematology hem/blood logy/study of

⚫ 16 heterogamy hetero/other gam/marriage y/state, quality

18 heterogeneous hetero/other gen/kind ous/having quality of

10 heterography hetero/other gram/to write y/state, quality

1 hexagon   hex/six gon/angle

8 hexagram   hex/six gram/to write

6 hexameter hex/six meter/measure

13 hexarchy   hex/six arch/to rule y/state, quality, act

15 hierarchy hier/sacred arch/to rule y/state, quality, act

7 holograph hol/whole gram/to write

11 homogeneous homo/same gen/kind ous/having quality of

14 homogenize homo/same gen/kind ize/to make, to act

6 homograph homo/same gram/to write

14 horology   hor/hour logy/study of

7 horoscope hor/hour scop/to look

1 hydrangea hydr/water angea/vessel

2 hydrant   hydr/water ant/that which

3 hydraulic hydr/water aul/pipe ic/like, related to

4 hydrodynamics hydr/water dynam/power ics/science

5 hydroelectric hydr/water electric/electricity

10 hydrogen   hydr/water gen/cause

11 hydrography hydr/water gram/to write y/state, quality

12 hydrology hydr/water logy/study of

6 hydrolysis hydr/water lys/to free

13 hydrometer hydr/water meter/measure

15 hydropathy hydr/water path/feeling, disease y/state

16 hydrophobia hydrwater phob/to fear ia/condition

17 hydrophone hydr/water phon/sound

18 hydroplane hydr/water plan/flat

7 hydroponics
hydr/water pon/labor ics/science, system

14 hydroscope
hydr/water scop/to look

8 hydrotropism
hydr/water trop/to turn ism/state, quality

9 hydrous   hydr/water ous/having the quality of

15 ideograph ideo/idea gram/to write

11 ideology   ideo/idea logy/word, study of

15 illogical   il/not log/word ical/like, related to

4 indigenous indi/within gen/kind ous/having quality of

18 ingenious in/in, into gen/cause ous/having quality of

15 ingenue   in/in, into gen/cause ue/French spelling

17 ingenuity in/in, into gen/cause ity/state, quality, act

16 ingenuous in/in, into gen/cause ous/having quality of

1 isobar   iso/equal bar/pressure, weight

5 isochromatic
iso/equal chroma/color ic/like, related to

9 isocracy   iso/equal crat/to rule y/state, quality, act

7 isodynamic iso/equal dynam/power ic/like, related to

6 isogenous iso/equal gen/kind ous/having quality of

16 isogonal   iso/equal gon/angle al/like, related to

11 isomer   iso/equal mer/part

10 isometric iso/equal meter/measure ic/like, related to

13 isomorphic iso/equal morph/form ic/like, related to

15 isonomy   iso/equal nom/law, order y/state, quality

3 isopyre   iso/equal pyr/fire

17 isosceles iso/equal scel/leg

18 isotherm   iso/equal therm/heat

2 isotope   iso/equal top/place

4 isotropic iso/equal trop/to turn ic/like, related to

8 kaleidoscope
kal/beautiful eido/form scop/to look

5 kilometer   kilo/thousand meter/measure

4 lexicography
lexico/word gram/to write y/state, quality

3 lithograph lith/stone gram/to write

8 logarithm   log/word arithm/number

9 logic   log/word ic/like, related to

7 logogram   log/word gram/to write

18 logogriph   log/word griph/fish net

17 logomachy   log/word machy/battle

7 lycanthrope
lyc/wolf andr/man

14 matriarch   matr/mother arch/to rule

2 megaphone
mega/great phon/sound

4 meteorology
met/beyond eora/hovering in air logy/study

7 meter   meter/measure

9 metric meter/measure ic/like, related to

12 metronome
meter/measure nom/law, order

2 micrograph
micro/small gram/to write

3 micrometer
micro/small meter/measure

8 microphone
micro/small phon/sound

9 microscope micro/small scop/to look

2 millimeter milli/thousand meter/measure

1 mimeograph
mim/to copy, imitate gram/to write

8 misanthrope
mis/to hate andr/man

12 misogynist mis/to hate gyn/woman ist/one who

17 monarchy   mono/one arch/to rule y/state, quality, act

18 monogamous
mono/one gam/marriage ous/quality of

13 monogenism
mono/one gen/cause ism/state, quality

5 monogram mono/one gram/to write

4 monograph
    mono/one gram/to write

16 monogynous
    mono/one gyn/woman ous/quality of

11 monologue
    mono/one logue/way of speaking

9 monophonic
    mono/one phon/sound

12 morphogenesis
    morph/form gen/cause esis/state, quality

5 morphology
    morph/form logy/study of

8 necrology   necr/death, dead logy/study of

15 neurology   neur/nerve logy/study of

5 nitrogen   nitr/niter gen/cause

12 nomography
    nom/law, order gram/to write y/state

10 nomology   nom/law, order logy/study of

13 oceanography
    ocean/ocean gram/to write y/state, quality

7 ochlocracy ochlo/mob crat/to rule y/state, quality, act

18 oligarchy   olig/few arch/to rule y/state, quality, act

17 optometry op/eye meter/measure y/state, quality, act

1 orthogamy orth/straight, right gam/marriage y/state

6 orthogonal orth/straight, right gon/angle al/like

14 orthography
    orth/straight, right gram/to write y/state

13 orthoscopic
    orth/straight, right scop/to look ic/like

15 pantograph
    panto/all gram/to write

16 paragraph para/beside gram/to write

17 parallelogram
    para/beside allel/mutual/ gram/to write

18 parameter para/beside meter/measure

12 parapsychology
    para/beside psych/mind logy/study of

17 pathologist path/disease log/study of ist/one who

16 patriarch   patr/father arch/to rule

6 pedometer ped/foot meter/measure

8 pentagon   pent/five gon/angle

18 pentagram pent/five gram/to write

16 pentameter pent/five meter/measure

2 perigee   peri/around ge/earth

15 perimeter   peri/around meter/measure

12 periscope   peri/around scop/to look

7 petrology   petr/rock logy/study of

3 philander   phil/to love andr/man

4 philanthropy
    phil/to love andr/man y/state, quality, act

5 philogynist phil/to love gyn/woman ist/one who

14 philology   phil/to love logy/study of

10 phoneme   phon/sound eme/something done

7 phonetic   phon/sound ic/like, related to

13 phonics   phon/sound ics/science, system

15 phonograph
    phon/sound gram/to write

14 phonolite   phon/sound lite/stone

16 phonology phon/sound logy/study of

18 phonometer
    phon/sound meter/measure

11 phonoscope
    phon/sound scop/to look

12 phonotype phon/sound typ/model

7 photogenic phot/light genkind ic/like, related to

13 photograph
    phot/light gram/to write

11 photometry
    phot/light meter/measure

14 pictograph pict/to paint gram/to write

5 plutocracy plut/wealth crat/to rule y/state, quality, act

5 polyandry poly/many andr/man y/state, quality, act

9 polygamist poly/many gam/marriage ist/one who

8 polygenesis poly/many gen/cause esis/state, quality

10 polygon   poly/many gon/angle

3 polygraph poly/many gram/to write

14 polygyny   poly/many gyn/woman y/state, quality, act

4 polyphonic
poly/many phon/sound ic/like, related to

11 pornography
porn/prostitute gram/to write y/state

2 primogenitor
prim/first gen/cause or/one who

3 primogeniture
prim/first gen/cause ure/state, quality, act

4 progenitor   pro/before gen/cause or/one who

5 progeny   pro/before gen/cause y/state, quality, act

2 program   pro/before gram/to write

3 prologue   pro/beofre logue/discourse

3 psychogenic
psych/mind gen/cause ic/like, related to

5 psychograph
psych/mind gram/to write

6 psychologist
psych/mind logy/study of ist/one who

10 psychometry
psych/mind meter/measure y/state, quality

8 pyre   pyr/fire

10 pyrite   pyr/fire ite/having the quality of

13 pyrogenic   pyr/fire gen/cause ic/like, related to

9 pyrography
pyr/fire gram/to write y/state quality, act

1 pyrolysis   pyr/fire lys/to free

12 pyromancy
pyr/fire mancy/divination

15 pyromaniac
pyr/fire mania/craving ac/related to

7 pyrometer   pyr/fire meter/measure

6 pyrophobia
pyr/fire phob/to fear ia/condition

4 pyrosis   pyr/fire osis/condition, act

16 pyrostat   pyr/fire stat/standing

17 pyrotechnics
pyr/fire techn/art, skill ics/science, system

18 pyrotoxin   pyr/fire tox/poison in/like, related to

17 regenerate   re/back, again gen/cause ate/to make

1 saxophone   sax/made by Adolph Sax phon/sound

16 scope   scop/to look

6 seismograph
seism/to shake gram/to write

17 skeptic   scop/to look ic/like, related to

7 somatology
somat/body logy/study of

8 soteriology   soter/safety, salvation logy/study of

9 spectrology
spec/to look logy/study of

18 spectroscope
spec/to look scop/to look

9 spherometer
spher/ball meter/measure

6 spirometer   spir/breath, life meter/measure

7 stenographer
sten/narrow gram/to write er/one who

8 stereography
stereo/solid, 3-D gram/to write y/state

2 stereometry
stereo/solid, 3-D meter/measure y/state

13 stereophonic
stereo/solid, 3-D phon/sound ic/like

1 stethometer
steth/chest, breath meter/measure

10 stethoscope
steth/chest, breath scop/to look

9 syllogism   syl/with, together log/word ism/state

3 symmetry   sym/with, together meter/measure y/state

17 symphony   sym/with, together phon/sound y/state

18 synchronize
syn/with, together chron/time ize/to make

3 technocracy
techn/art, skill crat/to rule y/state, quality

11 technology   techn/art, skill logy/study of

9 telegram   tele/from afar gram/to write

10 telegraph   tele/from afar gram/to write

12 teleology   tele/from afar logy/study

7 telephone   tele/from afar phon/sound

15 telescope   tele/from afar scop/to look

13	tetrology	tetra/four logy/word, discourse
1	theocracy	theo/God crat/to rule y/state, quality, act
16	theologian	theo/God log/study of ian/one who
15	theology	theo/God logy/study of
6	therianthropic	theri/beast andr/man ic/like, related to
5	thermometer	therm/heat meter/measure
11	tomography	tom/to cut gram/to write y/state, quality
1	topographer	top/place gram/to write er/one who
4	topology	top/place logy/study of
3	travelogue	travel/travel logue/discourse
12	trigonometry	tri/three gon/angle meter/measure y/state
2	trilogy	tri/three logy/word, discourse
1	zoology	zo/animal logy/study of
4	zoometry	zo/animal meter/measure y/state, quality

NOTE #1: not all letters of every word are given since some letters are used as combining forms. CARDIOGRAM is really CARD + GRAM with the IO put in so that the word flows and is more easily pronounced.

NOTE #2: in most cases only one spelling is given for each root even though variations occur. For instance, ANDR stands for both ANDR and ANTHROP. For LOG, LOGUE, and LOGY, however, differentiation is made.

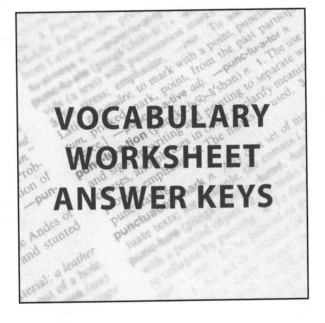

VOCABULARY
WORKSHEET
ANSWER KEYS

LATIN I ANSWERS

1A ✔	1B	1C	1D
3. abdicate	dict	1. project	1. intercept
6. ascribe	scribe	2. perennial	2. malpractice
20. bisect	sec	3. intercept	3. circumvolution
9. circumvolution	volu	4. malpractice	4. bisect
18. claustrophobia	claus	5. supersede	5. precept
1. emancipate	manu/cap	6. perjury	6. traduce
4. equanimity	anima	7. claustrophobia	7. tenable
5. expedient	ped	8. bisect	8. equanimity
13. facade	fac	9. facade	9. abdicate
17. gradation	grad	10. emancipate	10. perennial
7. intercept	cap	11. precept	11. perjury
15. malpractice	mal/pract	12. ascribe	12. predecessor
2. perennial	ann	13. predecessor	13. facade
12. perjury	jud	14. abdicate	14. ascribe
10. precept	cap	15. gradation	15. supersede
11. predecessor	cede	16. traduce	16. gradation
8. project	jac	17. circumvolution	17. emancipate
19. supersede	sed	18. expedient	18. claustrophobia
16. tenable	tain	19. tenable	19. project
14. traduce	duc	20. equanimity	20. expedient

2A	2B	2C	2D
4. addict	dict	1. circumscribe	1. dissect
8. animate	anima	2. dissect	2. annuity
1. annuity	ann	3. convoluted	3. curious
16. biped	ped	4. cloister	4. addict
9. circumscribe	scribe	5. conducive	5. tenure
2. cloister	claus	6. biped	6. gradient
11. conducive	duc	7. gradient	7. deceive
10. convoluted	volu	8. malady	8. principal
7. curious	cur	9. curious	9. subsidy
6. deceive	cap	10. annuity	10. conducive
19. dissect	sec	11. reject	11. biped
13. facile	fac	12. tenure	12. malady
17. gradient	grad	13. facile	13. convoluted
15. justify	jud	14. addict	14. animate
20. malady	mal	15. proceed	15. proceed
3. principal	cap	16. justify	16. circumscribe
18. proceed	cede	17. animate	17. reject
12. reject	jac	18. principal	18. cloister
14. subsidy	sed	19. subsidy	19. facile
5. tenure	tain	20. deceive	20. justify

LATIN I ANSWERS

3A

16. benediction
10. centennial
8. closet
6. conduit
19. conscript
20. curator
14. devolve
9. facility
15. gradual
7. impede
13. insect
17. juror
5. malignant
3. perception
18. precede
11. pusillanimous

1. receptor
4. sessile
2. subjacent
12. tenet

3B

bene/dict
ann
claus
duc
scribe
cur
volu
fac
grad
ped
sec
jud
mal
cap
cede
anima

cap
sed
jac
tain

3C

1. curator
2. conscript
3. impede
4. tenet
5. devolve
6. insect
7. gradual
8. malignant
9. receptor
10. pusillanimous
11. conduit
12. centennial
13. subjacent
14. juror
15. precede
16. closet
17. benediction
18. sessile
19. perception
20. facility

3D

1. devolve
2. malignant
3. facility
4. benediction
5. tenet
6. conduit
7. sessile
8. precede
9. impede
10. pusillanimous
11. centennial
12. juror
13. curator
14. receptor
15. closet
16. subjacent
17. insect
18. conscript
19. perception
20. gradual

4A

14. amanuensis
16. cloture
7. condition
2. description
11. evolution
15. expedite
12. facsimile
1. graduate
9. intersection
13. judicial
17. magnanimous
18. malodorous
19. millennium
20. participate
8. procedure
4. receptionist
10. sediment
5. superjacent
6. tenement
3. viaduct

4B

manu
claus
dict
scribe
volu
ped
fac
grad
sec
jud/dict
anima
mal
ann
cap
cede
cap
sed
jac
tain
duc

4C

1. malodorous
2. tenement
3. millennium
4. superjacent
5. facsimile
6. condition
7. magnanimous
8. receptionist
9. viaduct
10. sediment
11. expedite
12. cloture
13. participate
14. judicial
15. evolution
16. graduate
17. amanuensis
18. procedure
19. intersection
20. description

4D

1. participate
2. expedite
3. graduate
4. procedure
5. viaduct
6. magnanimous
7. amanuensis
8. receptionist
9. cloture
10. superjacent
11. facsimile
12. malodorous
13. description
14. condition
15. tenement
16. evolution
17. judicial
18. sediment
19. millennium
20. intersection

LATIN I ANSWERS

5A	5B	5C	5D
13. accurate	cur	1. involve	1. octopus
11. annals	ann	2. faction	2. inscription
12. conclave	claus	3. injustice	3. sedentary
9. contradict	dict	4. tenant	4. malign
3. disciple	cap	5. malign	5. annals
8. faction	fac	6. grade	6. receipt
14. grade	grad	7. subject	7. conclave
10. inanimate	anima	8. disciple	8. accurate
16. injustice	jud	9. octopus	9. faction
15. inscription	scribe	10. annals	10. subject
17. intercession	cede	11. inanimate	11. grade
18. involve	volu	12. sedentary	12. reduce
19. malign	mal	13. contradict	13. tenant
20. octopus	ped	14. receipt	14. inanimate
2. receipt	cap	15. intercession	15. involve
1. reduce	duc	16. accurate	16. disciple
5. sedentary	sed	17. inscription	17. intercession
7. subject	jac	18. vivisection	18. contradict
4. tenant	tain	19. conclave	19. injustice
6. vivisection	sec	20. reduce	20. vivisection

6A	6B	6C	6D
10. aggression	grad	1. tenacity	1. dedicate
18. biennial	ann	2. malnutrition	2. involute
9. conclude	claus	3. trajectory	3. conclude
3. dedicate	dict	4. millepede	4. residue
14. exception	cap	5. reception	5. seduce
8. factor	fac	6. injury	6. millepede
15. injury	jud	7. seduce	7. unanimous
19. involute	volu	8. manuscript	8. factor
17. malnutrition	mal	9. residue	9. biennial
13. manuscript	manu/scribe	10. biennial	10. injury
2. millepede	ped	11. dedicate	11. necessary
16. necessary	cede	12. factor	12. malnutrition
20. pedicure	ped/cur	13. secant	13. secant
7. reception	cap	14. involute	14. trajectory
1. residue	sed	15. pedicure	15. pedicure
11. secant	sec	16. aggression	16. aggression
5. seduce	duc	17. conclude	17. tenacity
4. tenacity	tain	18. exception	18. exception
6. trajectory	jac	19. unanimous	19. reception
12. unanimous	anima	20. necessary	20. manuscript

LATIN I ANSWERS

7A
4. abjure
16. abstain
10. animosity
17. annual
15. conceive
7. congress
19. dictator
13. disclose
18. factual
8. incessant
5. jetty
1. malice
9. nondescript
6. obvolute
3. pedestal
20. proctor
11. produce
12. receptacle
2. resident
14. segment

7B
jud
tain
anima
ann
cap
grad
dict
claus
fac
cede
jac
mal
scribe
volu
ped
cur
duc
cap
sed
sec

7C
1. segment
2. jetty
3. resident
4. disclose
5. annual
6. factual
7. obvolute
8. pedestal
9. dictator
10. abjure
11. incessant
12. nondescript
13. receptacle
14. conceive
15. abstain
16. malice
17. produce
18. animosity
19. congress
20. proctor

7D
1. pedestal
2. incessant
3. segment
4. annual
5. dictator
6. jetty
7. resident
8. congress
9. abstain
10. disclose
11. nondescript
12. receptacle
13. proctor
14. factual
15. animosity
16. produce
17. malice
18. abjure
19. conceive
20. obvolute

8A
18. abstention
16. adjudicate
9. animism
10. artifact
15. concept
3. degrade
19. diction
17. enclave
13. intercede
12. joist
14. malicious
2. pedal
20. postscript
4. president
1. procure
8. productive
7. receptive
6. revolve
11. sector
5. superficial

8B
tain
jud/dict
anima
fac
cap
grad
dict
claus
cede
jac
mal
ped
scribe
sed
cur
duc
cap
volu
sec
fac

8C
1. malicious
2. enclave
3. sector
4. concept
5. adjudicate
6. president
7. revolve
8. pedal
9. superficial
10. diction
11. abstention
12. postscript
13. joist
14. receptive
15. animism
16. procure
17. intercede
18. degrade
19. productive
20. artifact

8D
1. president
2. joist
3. revolve
4. diction
5. pedal
6. sector
7. degrade
8. artifact
9. adjudicate
10. postscript
11. abstention
12. concept
13. receptive
14. enclave
15. superficial
16. procure
17. malicious
18. productive
19. intercede
20. animism

LATIN I ANSWERS

9A

7. abstinence
14. artifice
13. benefactor
15. caption
18. corpulent
4. decease
20. degree
3. dictum
19. enclose
6. induct
9. interject
8. malfeasance
5. podium
1. prescribe
17. preside
10. secure
11. sickle
2. suffice
12. susceptible
16. valve

9B

tain
fac
bene/fac
cap
corp
cede
grad
dict
claus
duc
jac
mal
ped
scribe
sed
cur
sec
fac
cap
volu

9C

1. podium
2. secure
3. abstinence
4. induct
5. dictum
6. malfeasance
7. interject
8. preside
9. suffice
10. valve
11. benefactor
12. enclose
13. corpulent
14. degree
15. caption
16. susceptible
17. sickle
18. decease
19. artifice
20. prescribe

9D

1. prescribe
2. degree
3. secure
4. suffice
5. enclose
6. interject
7. corpulent
8. dictum
9. susceptible
10. preside
11. malfeasance
12. decease
13. sickle
14. abstinence
15. valve
16. benefactor
17. induct
18. caption
19. artifice
20. podium

10A

7. appertain
13. beneficial
1. captor
15. confection
17. digression
14. edict
16. enclosure
20. excess
3. incorporate
12. introduce
5. malformed
8. object
4. pedigree
19. recipe
18. reside
11. scribe
9. sinecure
10. surface
2. transect
6. vault

10B

tain
bene/fac
cap
fac
grad
dict
claus
cede
corp
duc
mal
jac
ped
cap
sed
scribe
cur
fac
sec
volu

10C

1. confection
2. sinecure
3. enclosure
4. beneficial
5. pedigree
6. malformed
7. digression
8. vault
9. incorporate
10. edict
11. appertain
12. recipe
13. surface
14. excess
15. object
16. scribe
17. captor
18. transect
19. reside
20. introduce

10D

1. introduce
2. recipe
3. edict
4. beneficial
5. excess
6. transect
7. surface
8. digression
9. malformed
10. sinecure
11. captor
12. reside
13. pedigree
14. enclosure
15. appertain
16. object
17. vault
18. scribe
19. incorporate
20. confection

LATIN I ANSWERS

11A	11B	11C	11D
9. beneficiary	bene/fac	1. occupation	1. eject
13. capstan	cap	2. capstan	2. occupation
5. concede	cede	3. beneficiary	3. tripod
15. continent	tain	4. concede	4. maleficent
2. defaced	fac	5. maleficent	5. capstan
11. educate	duc	6. fugue	6. exclude
1. egress	grad	7. educate	7. script
20. eject	jac	8. trisect	8. beneficiary
18. exclude	claus	9. indict	9. mandate
3. fugue	fug	10. mandate	10. continent
14. indict	dict	11. continent	11. veracious
7. maleficent	mal/fac	12. egress	12. trisect
17. mandate	manu	13. defaced	13. egress
12. occupation	cap	14. tripod	14. defaced
19. possess	sed	15. proficient	15. indict
4. proficient	fac	16. script	16. possess
16. script	scribe	17. eject	17. educate
6. tripod	ped	18. veracious	18. fugue
10. trisect	sec	19. exclude	19. proficient
8. veracious	ver	20. possess	20. concede

12A	12B	12C	12D
6. benefit	bene/fac	1. concession	1. municipal
17. capsule	cap	2. malevolent	2. foreclose
9. concession	cede	3. refuge	3. refuge
20. countenance	tain	4. educe	4. defect
13. defect	fac	5. verify	5. verify
4. educe	duc	6. subscriber	6. interdict
14. foreclose	claus	7. benefit	7. benefit
10. ingredient	grad	8. ingredient	8. venesection
2. inject	jac	9. municipal	9. educe
12. interdict	dict	10. venesection	10. ingredient
15. malevolent	mal	11. defect	11. subscriber
19. manufacture	manu/fac	12. capsule	12. sufficient
18. municipal	cap	13. inject	13. malevolent
3. obsession	sed	14. foreclose	14. capsule
11. pedestrian	ped	15. sufficient	15. pedestrian
1. refuge	fug	16. interdict	16. manufacture
8. subscriber	scribe	17. obsession	17. inject
7. sufficient	fac	18. countenance	18. concession
5. venesection	sec	19. manufacture	19. obsession
16. verify	ver	20. pedestrian	20. countenance

LATIN I ANSWERS

13A
11. antecedent
6. appurtenance
15. benevolent
9. capacious
20. corpuscle
1. deduce
12. deficient
4. dejection
14. detain
5. dictaphone
19. fragile
13. include
17. ingress
2. insidious
10. judicious
7. malcontent
18. manipulate
3. perfect
8. subscript
16. verisimilitude

13B
cede
tain
bene
cap
corp
duc
fac
jac
tain
dict
fract
claus
grad
sed
jud/dict
mal/tain
manu
fac
scribe
ver

13C
1. corpuscle
2. ingress
3. subscript
4. deduce
5. fragile
6. manipulate
7. detain
8. dictaphone
9. benevolent
10. malcontent
11. antecedent
12. judicious
13. insidious
14. deficient
15. appurtenance
16. verisimilitude
17. perfect
18. include
19. capacious
20. dejection

13D
1. benevolent
2. malcontent
3. insidious
4. detain
5. verisimilitude
6. antecedent
7. perfect
8. judicious
9. deduce
10. capacious
11. manipulate
12. dejection
13. subscript
14. include
15. corpuscle
16. dictaphone
17. fragile
18. ingress
19. appurtenance
20. deficient

14A
8. benign
4. capacity
9. cessation
15. deduct
19. deficit
14. detention
10. discipline
17. dissident
5. ejaculate
16. entertain
13. fragment
20. jurisdiction
1. malefactor
3. manicure
18. occlusion
7. prefect
12. progression
6. section
11. superscript
2. voluble

14B
bene
cap
cede
duc
fac
tain
cap
sed
jac
tain
fract
jud/dict
mal/fac
manu/cur
claus
fac
grad
sec
scribe
volu

14C
1. deduct
2. entertain
3. manicure
4. voluble
5. benign
6. jurisdiction
7. deficit
8. prefect
9. superscript
10. capacity
11. ejaculate
12. detention
13. cessation
14. progression
15. occlusion
16. section
17. malefactor
18. discipline
19. fragment
20. dissident

14D
1. occlusion
2. discipline
3. section
4. cessation
5. superscript
6. ejaculate
7. malefactor
8. capacity
9. progression
10. manicure
11. benign
12. entertain
13. dissident
14. deficit
15. voluble
16. jurisdiction
17. detention
18. prefect
19. deduct
20. fragment

15A

15. abscess
4. apperceive
10. aqueduct
13. assess
2. bonus
20. centrifugal
5. circumjacent
16. corporation
1. efface
6. fraction
18. imperceptible
14. impertinent
3. malediction
19. manacle
7. munificence
17. preclude
9. regress
12. retinue
11. succeed
8. transcribe

15B

cede
cap
duc
sed
bene
fug
jac
corp
fac
fract
cap
tain
mal/dict
manu
fac
claus
grad
tain
cede
scribe

15C

1. preclude
2. aqueduct
3. retinue
4. efface
5. bonus
6. abscess
7. manacle
8. munificence
9. succeed
10. impertinent
11. centrifugal
12. regress
13. imperceptible
14. circumjacent
15. fraction
16. assess
17. apperceive
18. corporation
19. transcribe
20. malediction

15D

1. malediction
2. retinue
3. efface
4. munificence
5. regress
6. corporation
7. transcribe
8. manacle
9. assess
10. apperceive
11. abscess
12. aqueduct
13. succeed
14. circumjacent
15. imperceptible
16. impertinent
17. bonus
18. preclude
19. fraction
20. centrifugal

16A

5. accede
10. assize
20. boon
1. capable
6. conduct
12. conjecture
4. corpus
18. efficacious
14. fracture
7. inception
13. maintain
19. malconduct
2. manciple
16. orifice
3. predict
17. recluse
11. retrograde
15. secede
8. sustain
9. transcript

16B

cede
sed
bene
cap
duc
jac
corp
fac
fract
cap
manu/tain
mal/duc
manu/cap
fac
dict
claus
grad
cede
tain
scribe

16C

1. boon
2. predict
3. inception
4. corpus
5. fracture
6. accede
7. orifice
8. capable
9. malconduct
10. efficacious
11. retrograde
12. sustain
13. transcript
14. manciple
15. maintain
16. assize
17. secede
18. conjecture
19. recluse
20. conduct

16D

1. capable
2. efficacious
3. maintain
4. retrograde
5. fracture
6. secede
7. predict
8. boon
9. manciple
10. conduct
11. transcript
12. inception
13. assize
14. recluse
15. conjecture
16. sustain
17. malconduct
18. accede
19. orifice
20. corpus

LATIN I ANSWERS

17A
19. abduct
14. abject
9. accept
17. ancestor
12. assiduous
18. corps
4. deception
16. dismal
13. efficient
7. infect
1. infraction
2. obtain
5. pertinent
20. retrocede
6. retrogress
3. scripture
10. seclusion
8. subterfuge
15. valediction
11. volume

17B
duc
jac
cap
cede
sed
corp
cap
mal
fac
fac
fract
tain
tain
cede
grad
scribe
claus
fug
dict
volu

17C
1. infect
2. scripture
3. accept
4. volume
5. infraction
6. pertinent
7. ancestor
8. deception
9. valediction
10. obtain
11. retrogress
12. subterfuge
13. abduct
14. dismal
15. seclusion
16. abject
17. retrocede
18. efficient
19. corps
20. assiduous

17D
1. dismal
2. scripture
3. ancestor
4. obtain
5. seclusion
6. volume
7. abject
8. valediction
9. pertinent
10. deception
11. accept
12. retrogress
13. efficient
14. subterfuge
15. abduct
16. infraction
17. corps
18. retrocede
19. assiduous
20. infect

18A
5. adduce
15. adjacent
9. anticipate
19. closure
1. corpse
13. facet
11. forceps
18. magnificence
20. maladjusted
2. pertain
16. procession
6. recede
8. refractory
12. refugee
4. retention
10. scribble
7. sedate
3. transgress
17. verdict
14. voluminous

18B
duc
jac
cap
claus
corp
fac
cap
fac
mal/jud
tain
cede
cede
fract
fug
tain
scribe
sed
grad
ver/dict
volu

18C
1. retention
2. transgress
3. refugee
4. anticipate
5. refractory
6. verdict
7. recede
8. forceps
9. procession
10. scribble
11. corpse
12. voluminous
13. adduce
14. maladjusted
15. facet
16. pertain
17. closure
18. sedate
19. adjacent
20. magnificence

18D
1. maladjusted
2. scribble
3. adduce
4. verdict
5. magnificence
6. recede
7. closure
8. retention
9. procession
10. voluminous
11. anticipate
12. transgress
13. facet
14. pertain
15. refugee
16. adjacent
17. forceps
18. sedate
19. refractory
20. corpse

LATIN II ANSWERS

1A	1B	1C	1D
6. accident	cad	1. component	1. controversy
13. amphora	fer	2. transmit	2. thermostat
11. aspect	spec	3. thermostat	3. reply
17. automobile	mob	4. accident	4. component
3. component	pon	5. devise	5. automobile
10. consecutive	sec	6. prostitute	6. retract
20. contort	tor	7. semaphore	7. prostitute
15. controversy	vers	8. amphora	8. semaphore
1. decuple	plex	9. contort	9. decuple
19. devise	vid	10. inadvertent	10. impending
8. dispel	pel	11. aspect	11. accident
5. impending	pend	12. retract	12. consecutive
12. inadvertent	vers	13. impending	13. metonymy
18. metonymy	nom	14. automobile	14. dispel
4. prostitute	sist	15. decuple	15. amphora
9. reply	plex	16. dispel	16. inadvertent
14. retract	tract	17. controversy	17. transmit
2. semaphore	fer	18. reply	18. aspect
16. thermostat	sist	19. consecutive	19. devise
7. transmit	mit	20. metonymy	20. contort

2A	2B	2C	2D
4. auspice	spec	1. distort	1. introvert
9. avert	vers	2. consequence	2. consequence
18. cadaver	cad	3. misnomer	3. surmise
11. circumference	fer	4. circumference	4. circumference
1. commotion	mob	5. subtract	5. sextuple
8. compose	pon	6. independent	6. auspice
13. compulsory	pel	7. auspice	7. transfer
3. consequence	sec	8. compulsory	8. distort
20. deploy	plex	9. surmise	9. commotion
14. distort	tor	10. sextuple	10. independent
2. envisage	vid	11. envisage	11. avert
16. independent	pend	2. commotion	12. misnomer
6. introvert	vers	13. transfer	13. compose
17. misnomer	nom	14. introvert	14. envisage
10. prostate	sist	15. deploy	15. systemic
19. sextuple	plex	16. cadaver	16. deploy
5. subtract	tract	17. prostate	17. cadaver
15. surmise	mis	18. avert	18. subtract
7. systemic	sist	19. systemic	19. compulsory
12. transfer	fer	20. compose	20. prostate

LATIN II ANSWERS

3A	3B	3C	3D
6. cadence	cad	1. extort	1. extrovert
20. catapult	pel	2. inverse	2. trace
10. circumspect	spec	3. catapult	3. submissive
15. compost	pos	4. submissive	4. envy
1. confer	fer	5. execute	5. penchant
9. demote	mob	6. cadence	6. confer
19. display	plex	7. triplex	7. inverse
14. envy	vid	8. compost	8. catapult
3. execute	sec	9. penchant	9. nomenclature
16. extort	tor	10. trace	10. compost
13. extrovert	vers	11. display	11. cadence
5. inverse	vers	12. suspect	12. display
17. nomenclature	nom	13. circumspect	13. superstition
11. penchant	pend	14. persist	14. extort
7. persist	sist	15. extrovert	15. circumspect
18. submissive	mis	16. demote	16. triplex
12. superstition	sist	17. nomenclature	17. demote
2. suspect	spec	18. envy	18. suspect
4. trace	tract	19. superstition	19. execute
8. triplex	plex	20. confer	20. persist

4A	4B	4C	4D
8. appeal	pel	1. diverticulum	1. duplex
15. cadenza	cad	2. extract	2. compound
1. compound	pon	3. nominal	3. obverse
20. conspicuous	spec	4. mobile	4. evidence
11. deference	fer	5. substitute	5. suspicious
2. diverticulum	vers	6. compound	6. cadenza
10. duplex	plex	7. conspicuous	7. tractable
17. evidence	vid	8. obstinate	8. mobile
5. extract	tract	9. triplicate	9. deference
13. extrinsic	sec	10. evidence	10. triplicate
6. mobile	mob	11. extrinsic	11. diverticulum
19. nominal	nom	12. appeal	12. obstinate
9. obstinate	sist	13. deference	13. conspicuous
12. obverse	vers	14. suspicious	14. appeal
3. pendulous	pend	15. remiss	15. substitute
18. remiss	mis	16. obverse	16. extract
14. substitute	sist	17. cadenza	17. remiss
4. suspicious	spec	18. tractable	18. nominal
7. tractable	tract	19. duplex	19. extrinsic
16. triplicate	plex	20. pendulous	20. pendulous

LATIN II ANSWERS

5A	5B	5C	5D
12. accomplice	plex	1. tart	1. improvise
1. armistice	sist	2. divert	2. tart
7. cascade	cad	3. pension	3. perversion
18. deposit	pon	4. despicable	4. nominate
10. despicable	spec	5. nominate	5. deposit
14. differentiate	fer	6. duplicate	6. promise
9. divert	vers	7. traction	7. accomplice
13. duplicate	plex	8. differentiate	8. obstacle
2. improvise	vid	9. armistice	9. cascade
4. intrinsic	sec	10. obstacle	10. divert
17. motivate	mob	11. substantiate	11. traction
20. nominate	nom	12. cascade	12. differentiate
16. obstacle	sist	13. motivate	13. intrinsic
3. pension	pend	14. improvise	14. despicable
15. perversion	vers	15. repulsive	15. pension
19. promise	mis	16. accomplice	16. repulsive
5. repulsive	pel	17. perversion	17. duplicate
11. substantiate	sist	18. intrinsic	18. armistice
8. tart	tor	19. deposit	19. motivate
6. traction	tract	20. promise	20. substantiate

6A	6B	6C	6D
5. applicant	plex	1. metastasis	1. retort
17. assist	sist	2. subsist	2. casualty
10. casualty	cad	3. retort	3. motive
13. despite	spec	4. dispose	4. tractile
20. dispose	pon	5. repel	5. ferry
3. diversify	vers	6. duplicity	6. pensive
15. duplicity	plex	7. premise	7. applicant
1. ferry	fer	8. diversify	8. metastasis
12. interview	vid	9. interview	9. repel
16. metastasis	sist	10. pensive	10. despite
19. motive	mob	11. despite	11. assist
8. nominative	nom	12. assist	12. subsist
14. obsequious	sec	13. retroversion	13. interview
9. pensive	pend	14. obsequious	14. dispose
18. premise	mis	15. casualty	15. nominative
7. repel	pel	16. tractile	16. duplicity
2. retort	tor	17. applicant	17. retroversion
11. retroversion	vers	18. nominative	18. premise
6. subsist	sist	19. ferry	19. diversify
4. tractile	tract	20. motive	20. obsequious

LATIN II ANSWERS

7A

7.	appliqué	
15.	circumstance	
2.	coincide	
9.	convert	
14.	employ	
3.	expose	
10.	fertile	
20.	inspect	
17.	interstice	
12.	invidious	
5.	mutiny	
18.	patronymic	
1.	penthouse	
19.	permission	
11.	persecute	
6.	repeal	
4.	revert	
16.	staunch	
13.	torment	
8.	trait	

7B

plex
sist
cad
vers
plex
pon
fer
spec
sist
vid
mob
nom
pend
mis
sec
pel
vers
sist
tor
tract

7C

1. interstice
2. expose
3. staunch
4. trait
5. patronymic
6. coincide
7. persecute
8. revert
9. permission
10. inspect
11. repeal
12. fertile
13. circumstance
14. mutiny
15. convert
16. appliqué
17. torment
18. invidious
19. penthouse
20. employ

7D

1. mutiny
2. employ
3. penthouse
4. torment
5. circumstance
6. permission
7. revert
8. appliqué
9. fertile
10. staunch
11. coincide
12. persecute
13. convert
14. inspect
15. trait
16. interstice
17. patronymic
18. repeal
19. expose
20. invidious

8A

7.	complex	
17.	converse	
12.	decadence	
15.	explicate	
1.	expound	
9.	institution	
20.	introspective	
3.	invisible	
13.	omission	
6.	perpendicular	
16.	promote	
10.	prosecute	
2.	pseudonym	
19.	pulsate	
5.	stature	
14.	subversive	
18.	suffer	
8.	torque	
4.	treatise	
11.	vociferous	

8B

plex
vers
cad
plex
pon
sist
spec
vid
mis
pend
mob
sec
nom
pel
sist
vers
fer
tor
tract
voc/fer

8C

1. decadence
2. pulsate
3. subversive
4. expound
5. prosecute
6. torque
7. institution
8. vociferous
9. complex
10. invisible
11. stature
12. omission
13. converse
14. promote
15. suffer
16. perpendicular
17. explicate
18. treatise
19. pseudonym
20. introspective

8D

1. expound
2. pseudonym
3. introspective
4. promote
5. subversive
6. explicate
7. pulsate
8. perpendicular
9. treatise
10. suffer
11. converse
12. torque
13. decadence
14. prosecute
15. complex
16. vociferous
17. invisible
18. omission
19. stature
20. institution

LATIN II ANSWERS

9A
8. abstract
13. deciduous
7. implicate
18. impose
12. instantaneous
1. missionary
20. perspective
2. preferable
16. preview
19. propulsion
6. pursue
9. recompense
4. recreant
15. remote
11. renown
3. specious
14. statistic
10. torsion
5. traverse
17. vocation

9B
tract
cad
plex
pon
sist
mis
spec
fer
vid
pel
sec
pend
cred
mob
nom
spec
sist
tor
vers
voc

9C
1. impose
2. torsion
3. missionary
4. recompense
5. implicate
6. renown
7. perspective
8. vocation
9. pursue
10. deciduous
11. specious
12. remote
13. preferable
14. statistic
15. abstract
16. propulsion
17. traverse
18. preview
19. recreant
20. instantaneous

9D
1. preview
2. recreant
3. deciduous
4. traverse
5. missionary
6. statistic
7. abstract
8. pursue
9. remote
10. perspective
11. torsion
12. implicate
13. vocation
14. impose
15. propulsion
16. preferable
17. recompense
18. renown
19. instantaneous
20. specious

10A
12. attract
5. impost
18. incidental
1. insistent
8. miscreant
20. missile
15. multiplicity
17. perspicacious
4. propel
7. propensity
9. providential
16. remove
11. sect
6. somniferous
19. spectacle
13. static
2. synonym
10. tort
14. universe
3. vocal

10B
tract
pon
cad
sist
cred
mis
plex
spec
pel
pend
vid
mob
sec
fer
spec
sist
nom
tor
vers
voc

10C
1. propel
2. spectacle
3. miscreant
4. universe
5. propensity
6. incidental
7. tort
8. static
9. providential
10. vocal
11. impost
12. multiplicity
13. insistent
14. somniferous
15. attract
16. perspicacious
17. sect
18. synonym
19. missile
20. remove

10D
1. spectacle
2. miscreant
3. propel
4. synonym
5. insistent
6. tort
7. incidental
8. vocal
9. impost
10. missile
11. sect
12. universe
13. attract
14. perspicacious
15. propensity
16. providential
17. remove
18. somniferous
19. static
20. multiplicity

LATIN II ANSWERS

11A	11B	11C	11D
10. averse	vers	1. manumit	1. revoke
17. contract	tract	2. tortilla	2. hemostasis
7. destine	sist	3. impostor	3. octuple
13. hemostasis	sist	4. stanza	4. tortilla
20. impostor	pon	5. occasion	5. prospect
15. impulsive	pel	6. averse	6. contract
2. incredible	cred	7. versatile	7. occasion
16. inference	fer	8. impulsive	8. provision
11. manumit	mis	9. stipend	9. averse
5. occasion	cad	10. octuple	10. toponym
1. octuple	plex	11. contract	11. versatile
18. prospect	spec	12. inference	12. incredible
8. provision	vid	13. sequel	13. sequel
4. revoke	voc	14. hemostasis	14. destine
12. sequel	sec	15. provision	15. stipend
3. stanza	sist	16. toponym	16. impostor
9. stipend	pend	17. prospect	17. manumit
14. toponym	nom	18. incredible	18. stanza
6. tortilla	tor	19. revoke	19. impulsive
19. versatile	vers	20. destine	20. inference

12A	12B	12C	12D
12. constant	sist	1. impound	1. heliostat
6. conversant	vers	2. torture	2. versus
17. detract	tract	3. intermission	3. intermission
20. discredit	cred	4. provocation	4. constant
1. heliostat	sist	5. detract	5. prospectus
9. impel	pel	6. stanchion	6. impound
4. impound	pon	7. constant	7. sequence
15. intermission	mis	8. versus	8. stanchion
11. metaphor	fer	9. prospectus	9. perplex
3. occident	cad	10. impel	10. revise
19. perplex	plex	11. trinomial	11. detract
10. prospectus	spec	12. metaphor	12. conversant
18. provocation	voc	13. sequence	13. trinomial
8. revise	vid	14. conversant	14. occident
2. sequence	sec	15. perplex	15. impel
13. stanchion	sist	16. heliostat	16. torture
14. suspend	pend	17. revise	17. metaphor
5. torture	tor	18. occident	18. provocation
16. trinomial	nom	19. suspend	19. discredit
7. versus	vers	20. discredit	20. suspend

LATIN II ANSWERS

13A	13B	13C	13D
3. agnomen	nom	1. expulsion	1. offertory
15. constituent	sist	2. recidivist	2. interpose
6. creed	cred	3. trousseau	3. stadium
19. distract	tract	4. gyrostatics	4. creed
11. emit	mis	5. supervise	5. supervise
1. expulsion	pel	6. plait	6. distract
10. gyrostatics	sist	7. emit	7. recidivist
16. interpose	pon	8. vertebra	8. trousseau
5. irrevocable	voc	9. propound	9. expulsion
17. offertory	fer	10. creed	10. gyrostatics
8. plait	plex	11. suspense	11. sequester
14. propound	pon	12. agnomen	12. agnomen
20. recidivist	cad	13. offertory	13. constituent
9. respect	spec	14. stadium	14. plait
4. sequester	sec	15. interpose	15. vertebra
7. stadium	sist	16. respect	16. irrevocable
18. supervise	vid	17. distract	17. propound
13. suspense	pend	18. sequester	18. emit
2. trousseau	tor	19. irrevocable	19. respect
12. vertebra	vers	20. constituent	20. suspense

14A	14B	14C	14D
20. accredit	cred	1. juxtaposition	1. plexus
16. anniversary	vers	2. accredit	2. vertex
10. anonymous	nom	3. dismiss	3. dismiss
7. append	pend	4. video	4. append
13. contrast	tract	5. entreat	5. invocation
5. dismiss	mis	6. rheostat	6. speculate
14. entreat	tract	7. paraphernalia	7. contrast
19. expel	pel	8. anniversary	8. anniversary
12. extant	sist	9. invocation	9. rheostat
6. invocation	voc	10. truss	10. respite
1. juxtaposition	pon	11. plexus	11. entreat
18. paraphernalia	fer	12. contrast	12. anonymous
11. plexus	plex	13. speculate	13. truss
9. provost	pon	14. expel	14. expel
17. respite	spec	15. provost	15. juxtaposition
3. rheostat	sist	16. anonymous	16. video
8. speculate	spec	17. respite	17. extant
15. truss	tor	18. vertex	18. accredit
4. vertex	vers	19. extant	19. paraphernalia
2. video	vid	20. append	20. provost

LATIN II ANSWERS

15A	15B	15C	15D
5. adverse	vers	1. demise	1. demise
17. aerostat	sist	2. retrospect	2. purpose
10. antonym	nom	3. vertical	3. adverse
20. clairvoyance	vid	4. credence	4. visage
1. compendium	pend	5. eponym	5. complicate
13. complicate	plex	6. pliable	6. specter
4. credence	cred	7. aerostat	7. aerostat
19. demise	mis	8. complicate	8. pliable
8. eponym	nom	9. specter	9. vertical
3. evoke	voc	10. periphery	10. antonym
2. opponent	pon	11. antonym	11. evoke
16. periphery	fer	12. purpose	12. retrospect
14. pliable	plex	13. evoke	13. opponent
12. purpose	pon	14. adverse	14. stabilize
9. restive	sist	15. visage	15. compendium
6. retrospect	spec	16. compendium	16. eponym
11. specter	spec	17. stabilize	17. periphery
7. stabilize	sist	18. restive	18. credence
15. vertical	vers	19. clairvoyance	19. restive
18. visage	vid	20. opponent	20. clairvoyance

16A	16B	16C	16D
12. adversity	vers	1. compromise	1. spectrum
6. apostasy	sist	2. equivocate	2. phosphorescent
17. cognomen	nom	3. adversity	3. repository
19. compensate	pend	4. plight	4. credential
2. complicity	plex	5. visible	5. positive
9. compromise	mis	6. complicity	6. apostasy
4. credential	cred	7. specialize	7. vertigo
15. device	vid	8. phosphorescent	8. cognomen
18. ecstatic	sist	9. spectrum	9. visible
11. equivocate	voc	10. cognomen	10. plight
7. phosphorescent	fer	11. repository	11. complicity
1. plight	plex	12. credential	12. device
8. portray	tract	13. positive	13. specialize
20. positive	pon	14. compensate	14. equivocate
16. repository	pon	15. restitution	15. adversity
3. restitution	sist	16. ecstatic	16. ecstatic
10. specialize	spec	17. vertigo	17. compensate
13. spectrum	spec	18. apostasy	18. portray
5. vertigo	vers	19. portray	19. compromise
14. visible	vid	20. device	20. restitution

LATIN II ANSWERS

17A

20. advertise
7. advise
5. belvedere
14. commit
11. convocation
2. credible
16. cryptonym
12. dependable
19. desist
4. distant
13. expend
1. homonym
9. posture
18. proffer
6. protract
10. quadruple
3. resist
15. specify
17. spite
8. vortex

17B

vers
vid
vid
mis
voc
cred
nom
pend
sist
sist
pend
nom
pon
fer
tract
plex
sist
spec
spec
vers

17C

1. expend
2. convocation
3. vortex
4. specify
5. advertise
6. homonym
7. distant
8. credible
9. protract
10. advise
11. proffer
12. resist
13. commit
14. spite
15. desist
16. cryptonym
17. quadruple
18. posture
19. belvedere
20. dependable

17D

1. distant
2. resist
3. vortex
4. expend
5. cryptonym
6. advertise
7. proffer
8. spite
9. credible
10. quadruple
11. commit
12. specify
13. dependable
14. convocation
15. homonym
16. belvedere
17. desist
18. protract
19. advise
20. posture

18A

6. admission
14. animadvert
8. avow
17. commissary
11. consistency
1. creditor
4. denomination
15. destitute
12. dispense
2. expense
20. ignominy
18. proponent
7. protractor
9. reconstitute
19. referee
3. replicate
13. specimen
16. supposition
10. transpose
5. vortical

18B

mis
vers
voc
mis
sist
cred
nom
sist
pend
pend
nom
pos
tract
sist
fer
plex
spec
pon
pos
vers

18C

1. reconstitute
2. destitute
3. ignominy
4. consistency
5. vortical
6. commissary
7. referee
8. dispense
9. admission
10. transpose
11. animadvert
12. replicate
13. creditor
14. supposition
15. proponent
16. expense
17. protractor
18. avow
19. denomination
20. specimen

18D

1. denomination
2. proponent
3. transpose
4. dispense
5. reconstitute
6. ignominy
7. admission
8. commissary
9. avow
10. supposition
11. expense
12. specimen
13. vortical
14. referee
15. destitute
16. creditor
17. protractor
18. consistency
19. replicate
20. animadvert

GREEK ANSWERS

1A	1B	1C	1D
17. altimeter	meter	1. engender	1. hexagon
9. anarchist	arch	2. theocracy	2. androgynous
5. androgynous	andr/gyn	3. hydrangea	3. pyrolysis
19. cyclonoscope	scop	4. mimeograph	4. zoology
11. diagram	gram	5. genealogy	5. mimeograph
14. engender	gen	6. altimeter	6. saxophone
1. genealogy	gen/log	7. hexagon	7. genealogy
4. geocentric	ge	8. isobar	8. orthogamy
20. hematology	log	9. cyclonoscope	9. anarchist
15. hexagon	gon	10. stethometer	10. topographer
8. hydrangea	hydr	11. pyrolysis	11. stethometer
7. isobar	iso	12. androgynous	12. isobar
2. mimeograph	gram	13. zoology	13. geocentric
16. orthogamy	gam	14. hematology	14. altimeter
3. pyrolysis	pyr	15. topographer	15. theocracy
18. saxophone	phon	16. diagram	16. cyclonoscope
13. stethometer	meter	17. saxophone	17. hydrangea
10. theocracy	crat	18. geocentric	18. hematology
12. topographer	gram	19. orthogamy	19. diagram
6. zoology	log	20. anarchist	20. engender

2A	2B	2C	2D
5. anachronism	chron	1. antipyretic	1. gentleman
17. androgen	andr/gen	2. eulogy	2. megaphone
13. antipyretic	pyr	3. millimeter	3. stereometry
8. bigamist	gam	4. graphology	4. eulogy
20. dictaphone	phon	5. micrograph	5. antipyretic
2. episcopal	scop	6. bigamist	6. program
11. eulogy	log	7. primogenitor	7. isotope
6. gentleman	gen	8. anachronism	8. androgen
3. graphology	gram/log	9. hydrant	9. perigee
16. gynarchy	gyn/arch	10. stereometry	10. episcopal
19. hydrant	hydr	11. trilogy	11. anachronism
9. isotope	iso	12. perigee	12. hydrant
18. megaphone	phon	13. episcopal	13. trilogy
1. micrograph	gram	14. program	14. bigamist
7. millimeter	meter	15. gentleman	15. millimeter
14. perigee	ge	16. dictaphone	16. gynarchy
10. primogenitor	gen	17. megaphone	17. dictaphone
15. program	gram	18. gynarchy	18. primogenitor
12. stereometry	meter	19. androgen	19. micrograph
4. trilogy	log	20. isotope	20. graphology

GREEK ANSWERS

3A

8. antiphony — phon
15. archangel — arch
6. cryptogram — gram
13. cytology — log
19. epilogue — log
1. gender — gen
18. geode — ge
7. gynophobia — gyn
11. hydraulic — hydr
16. isopyre — iso/pyr
2. lithograph — gram
14. micrometer — meter
5. philander — andr
20. polygraph — gram
9. primogeniture — gen
3. prologue — log
12. psychogenic — gen
10. symmetry — meter
17. technocracy — crat
4. travelogue — log

3B

phon
arch
gram
log
log
gen
ge
gyn
hydr
iso/pyr
gram
meter
andr
gram
gen
log
gen
meter
crat
log

3C

1. polygraph
2. isopyre
3. archangel
4. geode
5. antiphony
6. lithograph
7. philander
8. cytology
9. symmetry
10. cryptogram
11. primogeniture
12. gynophobia
13. technocracy
14. hydraulic
15. epilogue
16. micrometer
17. travelogue
18. psychogenic
19. gender
20. prologue

3D

1. hydraulic
2. travelogue
3. symmetry
4. philander
5. cytology
6. psychogenic
7. geode
8. primogeniture
9. antiphony
10. polygraph
11. prologue
12. gender
13. archangel
14. isopyre
15. gynophobia
16. epilogue
17. technocracy
18. micrometer
19. lithograph
20. cryptogram

4A

19. aphonic — phon
4. chronogram — chron/gram
11. digamy — gam
7. ecologist — log
12. genesis — gen
1. geographer — ge/gram
9. goniometer — gon/meter
10. gyroscope — scop
15. hydrodynamics — hydr
2. indigenous — gen
8. isotropic — iso
17. lexicography — gram
6. meteorology — log
18. monograph — gram
3. philanthropy — andr
20. polyphonic — phon
14. progenitor — gen
13. pyrosis — pyr
5. topology — log
16. zoometry — meter

4B

phon
chron/gram
gam
log
gen
ge/gram
gon/meter
scop
hydr
gen
iso
gram
log
gram
andr
phon
gen
pyr
log
meter

4C

1. pyrosis
2. zoometry
3. polyphonic
4. lexicography
5. gyroscope
6. chronogram
7. indigenous
8. ecologist
9. aphonic
10. meteorology
11. philanthropy
12. geographer
13. hydrodynamics
14. isotropic
15. goniometer
16. topology
17. digamy
18. genesis
19. monograph
20. progenitor

4D

1. zoometry
2. pyrosis
3. lexicography
4. gyroscope
5. indigenous
6. philanthropy
7. topology
8. geographer
9. progenitor
10. digamy
11. chronogram
12. monograph
13. polyphonic
14. aphonic
15. isotropic
16. hydrodynamics
17. genesis
18. ecologist
19. goniometer
20. meteorology

GREEK ANSWERS

5A	5B
19. acrography	gram
4. apologue	log
6. archduke	arch
10. cacaphony	phon
7. doxology	log
15. gene	gen
3. geodetic	ge
11. helioscope	scop
20. hydroelectric	hydr
13. isochromatic	iso
5. kilometer	meter
16. monogram	gram
2. morphology	log
17. nitrogen	gen
9. philogynist	gyn
18. plutocracy	crat
1. polyandry	andr
14. progeny	gen
8. psychograph	gram
12. thermometer	meter

5C	5D
1. geodetic	1. morphology
2. archduke	2. cacaphony
3. kilometer	3. thermometer
4. polyandry	4. philogynist
5. philogynist	5. psychograph
6. morphology	6. kilometer
7. apologue	7. acrography
8. isochromatic	8. nitrogen
9. psychograph	9. doxology
10. doxology	10. polyandry
11. nitrogen	11. helioscope
12. thermometer	12. plutocracy
13. acrography	13. apologue
14. gene	14. hydroelectric
15. progeny	15. geodetic
16. helioscope	16. monogram
17. cacaphony	17. archduke
18. monogram	18. gene
19. plutocracy	19. progeny
20. hydroelectric	20. isochromatic

6A	6B
9. anagram	gram
13. antiphon	phon
5. autogamy	gam
18. chronoscope	chron/scop
1 congenital	gen
11. degenerate	gen
16. dialogue	log
3. generalize	gen
14. geologist	ge/log
7. hexameter	meter
15. homograph	gram
4. hydrolysis	hydr
20. isogenous	iso/gen
17. orthogonal	gon
2. pedometer	meter
10. psychologist	log
19. pyrophobia	pyr
6. seismograph	gram
12. spirometer	meter
8. therianthropic	andr

6C	6D
1. orthogonal	1. pyrophobia
2. therianthropic	2. spirometer
3. generalize	3. geologist
4. pedometer	4. degenerate
5. homograph	5. isogenous
6. autogamy	6. dialogue
7. pyrophobia	7. pedometer
8. anagram	8. antiphon
9. dialogue	9. hydrolysis
10. chronoscope	10. orthogonal
11. spirometer	11. chronoscope
12. antiphon	12. seismograph
13. seismograph	13. anagram
14. hexameter	14. psychologist
15. degenerate	15. hexameter
16. hydrolysis	16. generalize
17. psychologist	17. therianthropic
18. congenital	18. autogamy
19. geologist	19. homograph
20. isogenous	20. congenital

7A	7B	7C	7D
7. archenemy	arch	1. logogram	1. petrology
10. autobiography	gram	2. phonetic	2. pyrometer
1. biogenesis	gen	3. stenographer	3. hydroponics
12. generally	gen	4. horoscope	4. lycanthrope
15. geomancy	ge	5. lycanthrope	5. generally
2. holograph	gram	6. somatology	6. isodynamic
17. horoscope	scop	7. archenemy	7. phonetic
11. hydroponics	hydr	8. telephone	8. stenographer
20. isodynamic	iso	9. meter	9. ochlocracy
3. logogram	log/gram	10. generally	10. holograph
14. lycanthrope	andr	11. autobiography	11. photogenic
16. meter	meter	12. photogenic	12. archenemy
5. ochlocracy	crat	13. geomancy	13. geomancy
18. petrology	log	14. isodynamic	14. telephone
4. phonetic	phon	15. biogenesis	15. somatology
9. photogenic	gen	16. holograph	16. autobiography
19. pyrometer	pyr/meter	17. hydroponics	17. meter
6. somatology	log	18. ochlocracy	18. horoscope
13. stenographer	gram	19. pyrometer	19. logogram
8. telephone	phon	20. petrology	20. biogenesis

8A	8B	8C	8D
4. apogamy	gam	1. polygenesis	1. pyre
13. autograph	gram	2. hexagram	2. microphone
18. chronology	chron/log	3. soteriology	3. necrology
7. dermatogen	gen	4. necrology	4. hexagram
9. generate	gen	5. kaleidoscope	5. hydrotropism
11. geometric	ge/meter	6. apogamy	6. autograph
15. gynecology	gyn/log	7. hydrotropism	7. kaleidoscope
1. heliometer	meter	8. dermatogen	8. geometric
16. hexagram	gram	9. pentagon	9. heliometer
12. hydrotropism	hydr	10. misanthrope	10. chronology
5. kaleidoscope	scop	11. gynecology	11. polygenesis
20. logarithm	log	12. heliometer	12. apogamy
2. microphone	phon	13. geometric	13. dermatogen
17. misanthrope	andr	14. pyre	14. stereography
10. necrology	log	15. chronology	15. generate
19. pentagon	gon	16. generate	16. misanthrope
8. polygenesis	gen	17. autograph	17. logarithm
6. pyre	pyr	18. microphone	18. soteriology
14. soteriology	log	19. stereography	19. pentagon
3. stereography	gram	20. logarithm	20. gynecology

9A
13. androphobia
4. archimage
20. autogenesis
15. chromatology
19. generation
11. genre
1. geophagy
14. heliograph
5. hydrous
17. isocracy
8. logic
16. metric
2. microscope
9. monophonic
7. polygamist
12. pyrography
3. spectrology
6. spherometer
18. syllogism
10. telegram

9B
andr
arch
gen
log
gen
gen
ge
gram
hydr
iso/crat
log
meter
scop
phon
gam
pyr/gram
log
meter
log
gram

9C
1. geophagy
2. autogenesis
3. logic
4. spectrology
5. polygamist
6. microscope
7. archimage
8. isocracy
9. syllogism
10. generation
11. monophonic
12. telegram
13. androphobia
14. genre
15. spherometer
16. heliograph
17. chromatology
18. metric
19. pyrography
20. hydrous

9D
1. syllogism
2. chromatology
3. genre
4. isocracy
5. geophagy
6. polygamist
7. autogenesis
8. logic
9. telegram
10. microscope
11. generation
12. pyrography
13. archimage
14. spectrology
15. hydrous
16. spherometer
17. androphobia
18. monophonic
19. heliograph
20. metric

10A
17. acrogen
19. anthropocentric
9. bibliography
6. biology
13. chronometer
7. cosmology
15. endogamy
1. epigeous
12. ergometer
14. generator
4. heterography
18. hydrogen
2. isometric
16. nomology
10. phoneme
8. polygon
20. psychometry
3. pyrite
11. stethoscope
5. telegraph

10B
gen
andr
gram
log
chron/meter
log
gam
ge
meter
gen
gram
hydr/gen
iso/meter
log
phon
gon
meter
pyr
scop
gram

10C
1. ergometer
2. isometric
3. chronometer
4. pyrite
5. acrogen
6. heterography
7. polygon
8. bibliography
9. nomology
10. endogamy
11. phoneme
12. biology
13. telegraph
14. psychometry
15. anthropocentric
16. generator
17. stethoscope
18. cosmology
19. hydrogen
20. epigeous

10D
1. nomology
2. telegraph
3. epigeous
4. phoneme
5. heterography
6. bibliography
7. psychometry
8. acrogen
9. endogamy
10. biology
11. stethoscope
12. anthropocentric
13. pyrite
14. generator
15. cosmology
16. hydrogen
17. polygon
18. chronometer
19. ergometer
20. isometric

11A		11B	11C	11D
11.	anthropoid	andr	1. phonoscope	1. monologue
7.	architect	arch	2. technology	2. tomography
18.	asymmetrical	meter	3. pornography	3. geophysics
1.	autocratic	crat	4. tomography	4. technology
12.	biographer	gram	5. genteel	5. ideology
19.	chronicle	chron	6. autocratic	6. biographer
9.	dehydrate	hydr	7. ideology	7. isomer
16.	generic	gen	8. monologue	8. hydrography
4.	genteel	gen	9. photometry	9. chronicle
13.	geophysics	ge	10. dehydrate	10. architect
17.	homogeneous	gen	11. anthropoid	11. asymmetrical
14.	hydrography	hydr/gram	12. homogeneous	12. pornography
6.	ideology	log	13. asymmetrical	13. photometry
20.	isomer	iso	14. biographer	14. homogeneous
8.	monologue	log	15. architect	15. genteel
3.	phonoscope	phon/scop	16. hydrography	16. anthropoid
5.	photometry	meter	17. geophysics	17. generic
15.	pornography	gram	18. generic	18. phonoscope
2.	technology	log	19. isomer	19. dehydrate
10.	tomography	gram	20. chronicle	20. autocratic

12A		12B	12C	12D
18.	analogy	log	1. chronological	1. phonotype
13.	anthropogenesis	andr/gen	2. misogynist	2. gentile
15.	cacography	gram	3. pyromancy	3. teleology
9.	chronological	chron/log	4. exogamy	4. parapsychology
10.	epigraphy	gram	5. gentile	5. metronome
2.	euphonic	phon	6. metronome	6. analogy
11.	exogamy	gam	7. parapsychology	7. hydrology
6.	generous	gen	8. analogy	8. chronological
8.	gentile	gen	9. periscope	9. periscope
3.	hydrology	hydr/log	10. morphogenesis	10. nomography
17.	metronome	meter	11. epigraphy	11. exogamy
1.	misogynist	gyn	12. trigonometry	12. generous
4.	morphogenesis	gen	13. anthropogenesis	13. euphonic
20.	nomography	gram	14. phonotype	14. pyromancy
5.	parapsychology	log	15. hydrology	15. cacography
14.	periscope	scop	16. teleology	16. epigraphy
12.	phonotype	phon	17. generous	17. anthropogenesis
19.	pyromancy	pyr	18. euphonic	18. misogynist
16.	teleology	log	19. nomography	19. trigonometry
7.	trigonometry	gon/meter	20. cacography	20. morphogenesis

13A	13B	13C	13D
15. analogue	log	1. hydrometer	1. phonics
20. anthropologist	andr/log	2. gentle	2. stereophonic
10. aristocrat	crat	3. pyrogenic	3. pyrogenic
19. barometer	meter	4. analogue	4. tetrology
13. calligraphy	gram	5. isomorphic	5. graphics
5. exogenous	gen	6. stereophonic	6. barometer
14. gentle	gen	7. graphics	7. monogenism
12. geothermic	ge	8. phonics	8. orthoscopic
6. graphics	gram	9. barometer	9. photograph
2. hexarchy	arch	10. monogenism	10. gentle
3. hydrometer	hydr/meter	11. photograph	11. analogue
18. isomorphic	iso	12. oceanography	12. hydrometer
17. monogenism	gen	13. exogenous	13. aristocrat
11. oceanography	gram	14. tetrology	14. calligraphy
9. orthoscopic	scop	15. geothermic	15. anthropologist
1. phonics	phon	16. aristocrat	16. isomorphic
8. photograph	gram	17. calligraphy	17. hexarchy
16. pyrogenic	pyr/gen	18. orthoscopic	18. geothermic
7. stereophonic	phon	19. anthropologist	19. oceanography
4. tetrology	log	20. hexarchy	20. exogenous

14A	14B	14C	14D
13. analogous	log	1. pictograph	1. diagonal
4. anhydrous	hydr	2. atmometer	2. anthropometry
20. anthropometry	andr/meter	3. crony	3. genetics
15. atmometer	meter	4. gamete	4. philology
19. cardiogram	gram	5. diagonal	5. matriarch
11. crony	chron	6. matriarch	6. horology
1. diagonal	gon	7. anthropometry	7. anhydrous
14. epigraph	gram	8. genetics	8. gamete
5. exogen	gen	9. polygyny	9. pictograph
17. gamete	gam	10. horology	10. cardiogram
8. genetics	gen	11. cardiogram	11. hydroscope
16. homogenize	gen	12. orthography	12. polygyny
2. horology	log	13. anhydrous	13. analogous
9. hydroscope	hydr/scop	14. philology	14. crony
7. matriarch	arch	15. exogen	15. phonolite
12. orthography	gram	16. phonolite	16. epigraph
3. philology	log	17. analogous	17. atmometer
6. phonolite	phon	18. hydroscope	18. homogenize
18. pictograph	gram	19. epigraph	19. orthography
10. polygyny	gyn	20. homogenize	20. exogen

15A		15B	15C	15D
15.	anthropomorphism	andr	1. neurology	1. isonomy
20.	bureaucracy	crat	2. phonograph	2. genial
10.	centimeter	meter	3. hierarchy	3. theology
19.	genial	gen	4. illogical	4. pantograph
13.	genuine	gen	5. genial	5. telescope
5.	geotropism	ge	6. hydropathy	6. illogical
14.	graphite	gram	7. pantograph	7. anthropomorphism
12.	hierarchy	arch	8. telescope	8. neurology
6.	hydropathy	hydr	9. isonomy	9. genuine
2.	ideograph	gram	10. geotropism	10. phonograph
3.	illogical	log	11. perimeter	11. hierarchy
18.	ingenue	gen	12. anthropomorphism	12. perimeter
17.	isonomy	iso	13. genuine	13. bureaucracy
11.	neurology	log	14. theology	14. hydropathy
9.	pantograph	gram	15. pyromaniac	15. graphite
8.	perimeter	meter	16. bureaucracy	16. ingenue
16.	phonograph	phon/gram	17. ingenue	17. centimeter
1.	pyromaniac	pyr	18. graphite	18. geotropism
7.	telescope	scop	19. ideograph	19. pyromaniac
4.	theology	log	20. centimeter	20. ideograph

16A		16B	16C	16D
7.	anthropopathy	andr	1. hydrophobia	1. pentameter
3.	apology	log	2. patriarch	2. scope
11.	choreography	gram	3. scope	3. pyrostat
17.	chronic	chron	4. genus	4. theologian
15.	cyclometer	meter	5. ingenuous	5. heterogamy
13.	genital	gen	6. pyrostat	6. chronic
2.	genus	gen	7. anthropopathy	7. monogynous
10.	grammar	gram	8. theologian	8. patriarch
19.	heterogamy	gam	9. isogonal	9. phonology
5.	hydrophobia	hydr	10. chronic	10. genus
14.	ingenuous	gen	11. apology	11. anthropopathy
20.	isogonal	iso/gon	12. pentameter	12. ingenuous
1.	monogynous	gyn	13. cyclometer	13. choreography
6.	paragraph	gram	14. heterogamy	14. cyclometer
18.	patriarch	arch	15. choreography	15. apology
8.	pentameter	meter	16. genital	16. isogonal
4.	phonology	phon/log	17. grammar	17. hydrophobia
12.	pyrostat	pyr	18. monogynous	18. grammar
16.	scope	scop	19. phonology	19. paragraph
9.	theologian	log	20. paragraph	20. genital

17A	17B	17C	17D
12. anthropophagy	andr	1. hydrophone	1. ergograph
8. apogee	ge	2. monarchy	2. ingenuity
14. cyclograph	gram	3. democratic	3. anthropophagy
1. decimeter	meter	4. regenerate	4. logomachy
18. democratic	crat	5. anthropophagy	5. parallelogram
9. dermatology	log	6. isosceles	6. apogee
17. ergograph	gram	7. pathologist	7. pyrotechnics
2. genius	gen	8. cyclograph	8. isosceles
16. hydrophone	hydr/phon	9. optometry	9. symphony
5. ingenuity	gen	10. ergograph	10. cyclograph
13. isosceles	iso	11. parallelogram	11. optometry
20. logomachy	log	12. decimeter	12. pathologist
11. monarchy	arch	13. symphony	13. democratic
3. optometry	meter	14. pyrotechnics	14. regenerate
7. parallelogram	gram	15. apogee	15. decimeter
15. pathologist	log	16. ingenuity	16. hydrophone
10. pyrotechnics	pyr	17. skeptic	17. skeptic
6. regenerate	gen	18. dermatology	18. dermatology
4. skeptic	scop	19. logomachy	19. monarchy
19. symphony	phon	20. genius	20. genius

18A	18B	18C	18D
10. androcracy	andr/crat	1. demography	1. logogriph
15. apologetics	log	2. oligarchy	2. heterogeneous
19. astrology	log	3. pyrotoxin	3. pyrotoxin
7. demography	gram	4. heterogeneous	4. androcracy
11. epigram	gram	5. ingenious	5. monogamous
3. etymology	log	6. logogriph	6. spectroscope
18. genocide	gen	7. etymology	7. ingenious
1. heterogeneous	gen	8. androcracy	8. pentagram
20. hydroplane	hydr	9. pentagram	9. demography
12. ingenious	gen	10. monogamous	10. oligarchy
4. isotherm	iso	11. epigram	11. phonometer
2. logogriph	log	12. synchronize	12. parameter
16. monogamous	gam	13. apologetics	13. genocide
5. oligarchy	arch	14. phonometer	14. synchronize
9. parameter	meter	15. isotherm	15. hydroplane
6. pentagram	gram	16. spectroscope	16. astrology
8. phonometer	phon/meter	17. hydroplane	17. epigram
13. pyrotoxin	pyr	18. genocide	18. etymology
17. spectroscope	scop	19. parameter	19. apologetics
14. synchronize	chron	20. astrology	20. isotherm

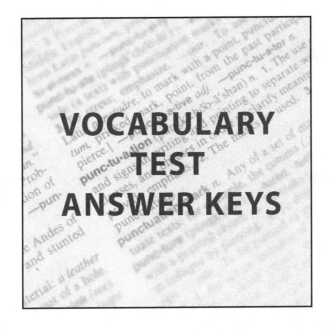

VOCABULARY
TEST
ANSWER KEYS

LATIN I TEST 1-9 ANSWERS

32 ABJURE	52 EMANCIPATE	63 PODIUM
59 ABSTINENCE	34 ENCLOSE	42 POSTSCRIPT
47 ADDICT	13 EXPEDITE	53 PRECEPT
24 AGGRESSION	10 FACADE	26 PRESCRIBE
79 ADJUDICATE	4 FACILITY	67 PRESIDE
7 ANIMATE	none FACSIMILE	45 PUSILLANIMOUS
37 ANIMOSITY	60 FACTION	76 RECEPTACLE
40 ANNIVERSARY	49 GRADIENT	80 RECEPTIVE
25 ARTIFICE	3 IMPEDE	70 RESIDUE
1 BENEDICTION	82 INCESSANT	43 SECTOR
19 BENEFACTOR	38 INDUCT	72-75 SECURE
83 BIENNIAL	64 INSCRIPTION	61 SEDENTARY
54 BISECT	22 INTERJECT	30 SEDUCE
65 CAPTION	15 INTERSECTION	none SICKLE
44 CENTENNIAL	74 JETTY	6 SUBSIDY
17 CONCLAVE	78 JOIST	21 SUFFICE
2 CONDUIT	57 MAGNANIMOUS	81 SUPERFICIAL
50 CONVOLUTED	8 MALADY	12 SUPERSEDE
39 CORPULENT	71 MALFEASANCE	62 SUSCEPTIBLE
18 DECEASE	23 MALIGN	20 TENANT
51 DECEIVE	5 MALIGNANT	16 TENEMENT
none DEGREE	31 MALNUTRITION	69 TRAJECTORY
41 DICTION	14 MILLENIUM	66 UNANIMOUS
68 DICTUM	35 NONDESCRIPT	29 VALVE
33 DISCLOSE	11 PERJURY	56 VIADUCT

LATIN I TEST 1-18 ANSWERS

22 ABDUCT

37 ABJECT

47 ABSCESS

78 ACCEDE

36 ADDUCE

70 ADJACENT

30 ADJUDICATE

97 ANIMOSITY

42 ANTECEDENT

81 APPERCEIVE

1 APPERTAIN

83 APPURTENANCE

74 ASSIDUOUS

64 BENEVOLENT

100 BENIGN

76 BOON

79 CAPACIOUS

12 CAPSTAN

25 CAPSULE

96 CENTENNIAL

90 CESSATION

62 CIRCUMJACENT

53 CLOSURE

15 CONCEDE

none CONCESSION

44 CONCLAVE

2 CONFECTION

49 CONJECTURE

68 CORPSE

85 CORPULENT

none CORPUS

40 CORPUSCLE

27 COUNTENANCE

none DECEPTION

72 DEDUCE

59 DEFICIT

39 DICTUM

3 DIGRESSION

28 DISMAL

94 DISSIDENT

4 EDICT

63 EFFACE

99 EFFICACIOUS

16 EGRESS

32 EMANCIPATE

7-60 ENCLOSURE

54 FACET

71 FORCEPS

21 FORECLOSE

89 IMPEDE

29 IMPERCEPTIBLE

92 IMPERTINENT

8 INCORPORATE

19 INDICT

73 INGRESS

51 INSIDIOUS

26 INTERDICT

45 JOIST

82 JUDICIOUS

33 MAGNIFICENCE

43 MALEDICTION

95 MALEFACTOR

6 MALFORMED

80 MANCIPLE

17 MANDATE

84 MILLENNIUM

48 MUNIFICENCE

none OCCLUSION

66 ORIFICE

23-38 PEDESTRIAN

9 PEDIGREE

89 PERTAIN

31 PODIUM

77 PRECLUDE

13 PROFICIENT

67 PUSILLANIMOUS

34 RECEDE

75 RECLUSE

69 REFRACTORY

88 REFUGEE

none RETINUE

50 RETROGRADE

35 SCRIBBLE

55 SEDATE

61 SEDENTARY

10 SINECURE

93 SUBSCRIPT

65 SUBTERFUGE

57 SUFFICE

98 TRANSCRIBE

5 TRANSECT

56 TRANSGRESS

18 TRIPOD

52 VALEDICTION

24 VENESECTION

14 VERACIOUS

20 VERIFY

58 VERISIMILITUDE

91 VOLUBLE

87 VOLUMINOUS

LATIN II TEST 1-9 ANSWERS

20-99 ABSTRACT	31 DEVISE	36 NOMINAL	76 REPULSIVE
30 AMPHORA	94 DIVERSIFY	21 OBSEQUIOUS	90 RETORT
6 APPLICANT	74 DIVERT	51 OBVERSE	50 RETRACT
44 ARMISTICE	70 DUPLEX	14 OMISSION	97 SEMAPHORE
none ASPECT	34 DUPLICITY	18 PATRONYMIC	3 SPECIOUS
26 AUSPICE	22 EMPLOY	96 PENCHANT	57 STATISTIC
24 CADAVER	85 ENVISAGE	43 PENDULOUS	none STATURE
47 CADENCE	15 EXPLICATE	78 PENSION	92 STAUNCH
none CADENZA	48 EXPOSE	80 PENSIVE	83 SUBSIST
39 CASCADE	98 EXTORT	82 PERSIST	61 SUBVERSIVE
89 CATAPULT	42 EXTRINSIC	4-65 PERSPECTIVE	29 SURMISE
49 COINCIDE	64 FERRY	56 PREFERABLE	35 SYSTEMIC
71 COMMOTION	52 FERTILE	33 PREMISE	73 TART
9-77 COMPLEX	28 IMPENDING	55 PREVIEW	69 TORMENT
32 COMPONENT	13 IMPLICATE	23 PROMOTE	10 TORQUE
84 COMPOST	17 IMPOSE	16 PROPULSION	none TORSION
79 COMPULSORY	100 INADVERTENT	67 PROSECUTE	72 TRACE
46 CONFER	19 INSTANTANEOUS	5 PSEUDONYM	25 TRACTABLE
87 CONTORT	68 INTERSTICE	95 PULSATE	40 TRACTILE
62 CONVERSE	75 INTRINSIC	12 PURSUE	86 TRAIT
93 CONVERT	91 INTROVERT	58 RECOMPENSE	11 TRAVERSE
59 DECADENCE	88 INVIDIOUS	7 RECREANT	63 TREATISE
54 DECIDUOUS	41 MISNOMER	45 REMISS	none TRIPLEX
37 DEFERENCE	2 MISSIONARY	66 REMOTE	8 VOCATION
81 DESPICABLE	53 MUTINY	1 RENOWN	60 VOCIFEROUS

LATIN II TEST 1-18 ANSWERS

14 ADMISSION

21 ADVERTISE

33 AEROSTAT

43 AGNOMEN

67 ANIMADVERT

37 ANNIVERSARY

87 ANONYMOUS

31 ANTONYM

27 APOSTACY

40 APPEND

75 AVOW

none BELVEDERE

51 CASCADE

86 CLAIRVOYANCE

30 COGNOMEN

19 COMMISSARY

82 COMPLICATE

78 COMPLICITY

16 CONSISTENCY

46 CONVERSANT

71 CONVOCATION

22 CREDIBLE

61 CREDITOR

24 CRYPTONYM

85 DEMISE

13 DENOMINATION

74 DESIST

8 DESTINE

18 DESTITUTE

49 DETRACT

29 DEVICE

66 DISPENSE

77 ECSTATIC

93 EMIT

42 ENTREAT

34 EVOKE

38 EXPEL

73 EXPEND

12 EXPENSE

100 EXTANT

none HOMONYM

70 IGNOMINY

54 IMPLICATE

11 IMPOSTER

96 IMPOUND

44 IRREVOCABLE

89 JUXTAPOSITION

58 MANUMIT

64 MISCREANT

52 OBSEQUIOUS

1 OBSTINATE

48 OCCIDENT

3 OMISSION

91 PARAPHERNALIA

35 PERIPHERY

98 PERPLEX

56 PERSPICACIOUS

none PLEXUS

84 PLIABLE

26 PLIGHT

25 POSTURE

69 PROPONENT

62 PROTRACTOR

60 PSEUDONYM

83 QUADRUPLE

94 RECIDIVIST

15 RECONSTITUTE

20 REFEREE

none REPLICATE

28 REPOSITORY

41 RESPITE

83 RESTIVE

47 REVISE

none RHEOSTAT

45 SEQUESTER

55 SOMNIFEROUS

17 SPECIMEN

5 SPECIOUS

50 SPECTER

76 SPECTRUM

65 SPITE

36 STABILIZE

97 STANCHION

2-53 STAUNCH

10 STIPEND

68 SUPPOSITION

59 TOPONYM

6-64 TORQUE

95 TROUSSEAU

39 TRUSS

7 UNIVERSE

9 VERSATILE

99 VERSUS

88 VERTEX

32 VERTICAL

79 VERTIGO

81 VISAGE

8 VOCIFEROUS

72 VORTEX

63 VORTICAL

GREEK TEST 1-9 ANSWERS

11 ALTIMETER

24 ANACHRONISM

71 ANAGRAM

74 ANARCHIST

15-58 ANDROGYNOUS

63 ANDROPHOBIA

36 ANTIPHONY

25 ANTIPYRETIC

98 APHONIC

35 APOGAMY

none APOLOGUE

79 ARCHANGEL

56 ARCHENEMY

93 ARCHIMAGE

89 AUTOBIOGRAPHY

85 AUTOGENESIS

57 AUTOGRAPH

70 BIGAMIST

91 BIOGENESIS

51 CACOPHONY

75 CHROMATOLOGY

23 CHRONOLOGY

8 CONGENITAL

34 CRYPTOGRAM

none CYTOLOGY

59 DEGENERATE

78 DIALOGUE

31 DICTAPHONE

2 DOXOLOGY

33 ECOLOGIST

18 ENGENDER

29 EPILOGUE

99 EPISCOPAL

47 EULOGY

20 GENEALOGY

42 GENERATION

72 GENESIS

14 GENRE

17 GEOCENTRIC

none GEOLOGIST

95 GEOMANCY

41 GEOPHAGY

65 GONIOMETER

27 GYNARCHY

80 GYNOPHOBIA

64 HELIOGRAPH

83 HELIOSCOPE

16 HEXAGON

68 HEXAMETER

90 HOLOGRAPH

96 HOMOGRAPH

55 HOROSCOPE

49 HYDRAULIC

69 HYDROELECTRIC

77 HYDROLYSIS

92 HYDROPONICS

39 HYDROUS

66 INDIGENOUS

48-13 ISOCRACY

45 ISODYNAMIC

none ISOTOPE

52 KILOMETER

1 LEXICOGRAPHY

73 LITHOGRAPH

none LOGARITHM

81 LOGIC

6 LYCANTHROPE

26 MEGAPHONE

12 METRIC

none MICROGRAPH

22 MICROPHONE

62 MICROSCOPE

7 MISANTHROPE

3 MONOGRAM

10 NECROLOGY

50 OCHLOCRACY

84 ORTHOGONAL

none PENTAGON

28 PHILANDER

53 PLUTOCRACY

none POLYGAMIST

97 POLYPHONIC

43 PRIMOGENITURE

4 PROGENY

100 PSYCHOGENIC

38 PYROGRAPHY

19 PYROLYSIS

5 PYROPHOBIA

21 SOTERIOLOGY

44 SPECTROLOGY

30 SPHEROMETER

none STEREOGRAPH

61 SYLLOGISM

82 SYMMETRY

32 TECHNOCRACY

94 TELEGRAM

9 THEOCRACY

87 TOPOLOGY

37 TRILOGY

none ZOOMETRY

80 ANALOGOUS	41 GENIUS	50 OPTOMETRY
74 ANARCHIST	56 GENOCIDE	38 ORTHOGRAPHY
57 ANDROCRACY	39 GENTEEL	45-90 PARAMETER
37 ANHYDROUS	78 GENTILE	33 PATHOLOGIST
36 ANTIPHONY	35 GEOTHERMIC	58 PATRIARCH
93 APOGEE	67 GEOTROPISM	20 PENTAGRAM
63 APOLOGETICS	94 GRAMMAR	68 PENTAMETER
99 ARISTOCRAT	12 GRAPHITE	64 PERIMETER
55 ASTROLOGY	65 HEMATOLOGY	none PERISCOPE
none ASYMMETRICAL	95 HEXARCHY	71 PHILOLOGY
22 BIBLIOGRAPHY	60 HIERARCHY	85 PHONIC
83 BIOGRAPHER	14 HOMOGENIZE	43 PHONOLITE
none BUREAUCRACY	none HYDROMETER	none PHONOMETER
89 CACOGRAPHY	96 HYDROPHOBIA	none PHOTOGENIC
15 CALLIGRAPHY	23 HYDROPLANE	53 PLUTOCRACY
88 CARDIOGRAM	31 ILLOGICAL	86 POLYGYNY
46 CENTIMETER	51 INDIGENOUS	4 PROGENY
61 CHRONIC	70 INGENUITY	27 PYROMANIAC
8 CONGENITAL	49 INGENUOUS	11 PYROSTAT
91 CRONY	87 ISOMETRIC	16 PYROTECHNICS
34 CRYPTOGRAM	48 ISONOMY	54 PYROTOXIN
79 DECIMETER	30 ISOSCELES	28 REGENERATE
69 DEMOGRAPHY	3 ISOTHERM	75 SKEPTIC
82 DERMATOLOGY	52 KILOMETER	21 SOTERIOLOGY
24 DIAGONAL	73 LOGOGRIPH	13 SPECTROSCOPE
2 DOXOLOGY	26 MEGAPHONE	47-66 SYMPHONY
5 EPIGRAM	81 METRONOME	40 SYNCHRONIZE
18-77 EPIGRAPH	7 MISANTHROPE	32 TECHNOCRACY
10 ETYMOLOGY	76 MONARCHY	44 TELEOLOGY
42 EUPHONIC	6 MONOGAMOUS	97 TETROLOGY
none GAMETE	98 MONOGENISM	9 THEOCRACY
72 GENESIS	none MONOGYNOUS	62 THEOLOGY
none GENIAL	19 NEUROLOGY	
100 GENITAL	1 OLIGARCHY	

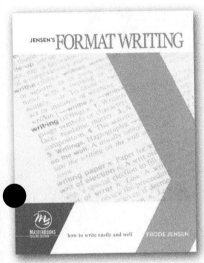

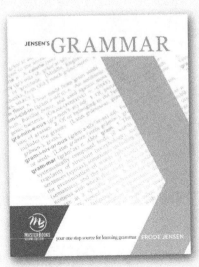
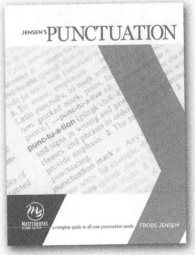